Acting Qs

Conversations with Working Actors

by

Bonnie Gillespie

and

Blake Robbins

Cricket Feet Publishing
Los Angeles

Thk You!
Blke
Rollins

For Michelle —
thank you for all
of the gimlet
nights!
Bonnie
Gillespie
6/05

Acting Qs: Conversations with Working Actors
© 2005 by Bonnie Gillespie and Blake Robbins
First Edition

Cricket Feet Publishing
P.O. Box 1417
Hollywood, CA 90028
phone/fax: 310.395.9540
http://cricketfeet.com
publisher@cricketfeet.com

SCB Distributors
http://scbdistributors.com

Unattributed quotations are by Bonnie Gillespie and Blake Robbins. Contributed quotations, sections, interview content, and photographs are used with permission of the copyright holder, as indicated herein.

Cover design by Karen Robbins.
Bonnie's headshot by Rod Goodman. Blake's headshot by Brigitte Jouxtel.
Printed in Canada.

LCCN 2005926439
ISBN 0-9723019-1-7

Cricket Feet Publishing titles may be purchased in bulk at special discounts for promotional or educational purposes. Inquiries for sales and distribution, textbook adoption, foreign language translation, rights and permissions, and future edition inquiries should be addressed as above.

Cricket Feet Publishing is a registered trademark.

What Others Are Saying about *Acting Qs*

This book is essential for anyone who wants to be an actor or for anyone who plans on working with actors. It is a fantastic reminder that acting is a grand and noble profession, filled with artists absolutely passionate about what they do.

—Liz Tuccillo, writer
Sex and the City,
He's Just Not That Into You

A great book for anyone considering a career in show business or for anyone curious about the lives in it.

—Sunil Nayar, producer/writer
CSI: Miami

This is a book I will pick up again and again when I need inspiration to keep up the good fight! These are *working* actors. They are still auditioning, marketing, and dealing with rejection. I am inspired by the way others deal with this part of our jobs!

—Judy Kerr, actor/coach/author
Acting Is Everything

Acting Qs: practical insight from people who make a living as actors.

—Sean Whitesell, producer/writer
Cold Case, Oz

Acting Qs spans so many different degrees of an actor's career. From beginner to novice to working actor, this is great stuff for every level!

—Jeannine Burkart, writer/producer
TV Guide Channel

This isn't an I-guess-I-should-start-sending-out-more-headshots acting book. This is an I'm-so-proud-to-be-an-actor book.

—Eitan Loewenstein,
actor

Acting Qs is an enlightening and heartfelt collection of interviews exploring the realities and challenges in the world of working actors.

—Denise Winsor, daughter of and
mother to industry professionals

Everyone *has* to buy this book. So many observations are very comforting or educational even for those in tiny markets making baby steps in this industry. My daughter, the performer, started reading Bonnie Dennison's chapter and was totally enthralled. Though we've never seen her, having never watched *Third Watch*, we are both fans now just from "meeting" her through *Acting Qs*.

—Lisa Winston, senior writer
USA Today, Sports Weekly

Reality checks that working and hope-to-be-working actors really need. The more stories I read, the more I realize that I'm in the right place and doing the right thing for me. Thank you for taking the time and doing so much work to get this out there for all of us to learn from!

—Julie O'Malley,
actor/voiceover artist

Acting Qs: the real reason actors act—not the *Entertainment Tonight* version.

—Laura Lock,
actor

Bonnie Gillespie has created a trifecta of must-have books for anyone in the industry. I continually recommend *Casting Qs* and *Self-Management for Actors* to my host peers and clients. Now I can add *Acting Qs* to that list. Joining Bonnie on this outing is Blake Robbins. Together they have created a book that inspires and reminds us why we chose the entertainment industry as a profession. From interviews with Joy Behar to Tom Everett Scott to my personal favorite, Angela Goethals, Bonnie and Blake have a winner on their hands!

—Kristyn Burtt,
host/coach

Once upon a time in every actor's life, a childlike inspiration pushed each of us to follow this dream path. Through the voices of our successful peers, *Acting Qs* remembers and recharges that burst of inspiration that put us here: that, "Me too! Me too!" clamor in our blood.

—Robin Gwynne,
actor

As an actor who always strives to learn more about this business, I want to see what the guys a level (or two) ahead of me are doing. Are they doing stuff that I'm doing? What's been or not been successful? How are they dealing with the new challenges? What can I do or avoid to help me at that level? These are the questions answered in *Acting Qs*.

—Bill Lippincott,
actor

Learning to be ready is half the battle. Once you understand that, the work becomes the driving force, not you. Working actors everywhere understand this concept and *Acting Qs* helps to bring this home through the inspirational sharing of firsthand experiences. Read the book and you are in the zone.

—Pamela Newlands,
actor/singer/songwriter

Acting Qs gets inside the hearts and minds of working actors. It is bursting with fascinating stories from craftspeople who have made the business work for them. A must-read for beginning actors, working actors who want to bring their careers to the next level, and anyone looking for inside perspective on acting.

—Madeline Molis,
writer

Acting Qs is replete with high-achieving performers' stories which are heartfelt and true-to-life, unveiling a wealth of practical how-to information necessary for creating an influential professional acting career.

—Joan Baker,
actor/voiceover artist/author
Secrets of Voiceover Success

It is sweet nourishment to actors to know that there are those who do celebrate and respect their toil, their idiosyncratic world, and their joy in exploring and expressing the vast and varied nature of the most troublesome of all critters: human beings. Thanks, Bonnie and Blake. This book is a must-have!

—Lyn Mason Green,
actor/co-author
Standing Naked in the Wings

Table of Contents

8–Acting Qs

Foreword

Before I started to write and produce television, I toiled in the theatre—yes, as a playwright, but also (to make proverbial ends meet) as a stage manager, casting director, house manager, publicity associate, and general factotum. As a result, I have seen actors from every angle: at auditions, pacing; in rehearsals, struggling; on stage, glowing; on camera, mesmerizing; in their dressing rooms, naked. Most of my closest friends are actors. For a time, I was even married to one.

Why do I admire these primordial creatures who thrive under artificial light? First, because of the Sisyphean task they perform on a daily basis, persistently pushing the artistic boulder up the mountain, despite the interference of network gorgons, studio trolls, casting harpies, and—gulp—producers like me. Second, because of the joyous and painful ongoing battles actors fight within themselves: the battle between vanity and vulnerability, between cynicism and hope, between insanity and—well—a solid night's sleep.

Thirty years ago, I worked with the artistic director of a regional theatre who told me, "You have to want to fuck *every* actor you cast." A daunting prospect even at a young age. Only later, after numerous fumbles, did I realize he meant that an actor has to elicit passion from you—and from the audience.

But passion isn't the only ingredient an actor needs. Laurence Olivier claimed that stamina was essential. Spencer Tracy—who, in my opinion, is the finest screen actor ever—possessed the elusive gift of honesty. From Father Flanagan to Doctor Jekyll, with or without Hepburn, there is not one false moment in a single frame of any of his films. His heart is always, always available to us, as we watch him flicker in the darkness.

Most importantly, the best actors I've worked with (Blythe Danner, Alfre Woodard, Kathy Bates, Kyra Sedgwick, Andre Braugher,

William Daniels, Lee Tergesen, Mark Ruffalo, the Winters brothers, oh hell, the list goes on and on) have been true collaborators, solving problems, jumping hurdles, not to make themselves look better but for the good of the production as a whole. In a selfish business, they are selfless. And magical. They're like ancient high priests, using long-kept secrets, creative conjuring, and ardent faith to turn my words into miracles.

I have often said that a bad actor ruins a scene I've written, a good actor does the scene exactly the way it should be done, and a great actor makes me go: "Wow, I'm a brilliant writer!"

Directors on TV shows which I've written sometimes ask me to do a walk-on, a one- or two-line wink to the folks back home in Buffalo. I always say no because I don't want to take a paying job away from a member of SAG. (Though, in the spirit of full disclosure, I did appear in the final shot of the final episode of *Oz* as the guy who turned off the lights. But you couldn't see my face, since I was wearing a HAZMAT mask. And I had no dialogue.)

However, every seven years—like those pesky locusts—I act on stage. I do this, not because I have any talent, but to remind myself how difficult the job is: learning lines, wearing makeup, revealing one's inner truths. And all in front of a bunch of strangers, who, despite Tennessee Williams, I've never depended on the kindness of. Each time, after I act in a play, I return to my desk, humbled, knowing that it's better for all concerned that I reveal my inner truths on a blank piece of paper at five-thirty in the morning, instead of on the boards.

So, I salute all the people in this book for having the courage to spill their guts. I've had the grand pleasure of working alongside three of them: Danny Pino, Jim Rebhorn, and Blake Robbins—a trio of more talented, intelligent, and engaging fellows you will not see. Their chapters are a delight and an inspiration to read. But, then again, all of the conversations that follow are. What could have devolved into pages and pages of petty whining is, instead, the celebration of a craft, chock-full of insight, enthusiasm, and panache. Not bad for $21.95.

I also want to salute those who will read this book, because the desire to act, whether on a high school stage or a sound stage, is a dangerous, remarkable, scary, exhilarating thing. I pray that the writers whose scripts you perform are as fortunate as I have been, finding such awe-inducing muses. No—why be so highfalutin? I've been lucky finding really cool kids to play with in the sandbox.

Tom Fontana
writer/producer
http://tomfontana.com

For actors:
the working,
the aspiring, and
the dreaming.

Introduction

Back in 1999, I (Blake Robbins) started hanging around a talented group of writers, directors, and actors. By "hanging around," I mean taking classes, going to their plays, participating in a weekly reading series, and eventually performing with the Naked Angels. My association with these people afforded me a wonderful opportunity to learn what it was like to be a working actor from people that knew.

In a class run by Jace Alexander and Tessa Blake, each week started with a company member or two talking about their experiences of the business. We heard from people like Ron Rifkin, Fisher Stevens, Michael Maestro, Rob Morrow, Ilana Levine, Marisa Tomei, Ned Eisenberg... the list goes on. As an actor, I found these conversations inspiring and informative.

Years later, it occurs to me that these conversations have been just as valuable to me as any acting class, career counseling, or industry meet and greet. For that matter, they've been just as valuable as anything I've done to improve my chances of "making it" as an actor. Why? Turns out, for me, that hearing other people's stories has helped me to discover my own path and my own place in the business.

The things I heard (and I'm sure certain things would resonate differently for each listener) shaped who I was to become as an actor and as a person. For example, who I am as a person will always be more important to me than who I am as an actor. That concept is not something I got from any particular conversation. It was a common theme with all the actors who came to the class to share with us.

These performers and their conversations were the initial inspiration for this book.

In July 2004, my good friend Subhash Mandal (whom I happened to have met in Jace and Tessa's class) invited me to a Hollywood Happy Hour event and introduced me to Bonnie Gillespie—who I later learned had written *Casting Qs: A Collection of Casting Director Interviews.*

Two months to the day after that first meeting, I approached Bonnie and Keith—her partner and publisher—at the Naked Angels' Tuesdays @9-LA weekly reading series and said, "Hey, I've got a great idea for a book."

* * *

When Blake first approached me (Bonnie Gillespie) about co-authoring this book, he suggested we schedule a meeting to discuss the concept. I didn't need to have a meeting. I could tell—from the first, enthusiastic sentence out of Blake's mouth—that this book was an outstanding idea and I would love to be a partner to the process of bringing these amazing actors together to share their stories. When we sat together and worked up a "wish list" of actors for this process, we both felt the electricity in the room. "Imagine how very different each of these actors' stories must be!" We knew there would be something exciting for everyone—aspiring actor or fan—who might pick up a copy of this book.

What I didn't know (and perhaps Blake knew for sure, due to his experience with the working actors who came to speak to his acting class years ago) is how deeply these actors' tales would touch me. After conducting a handful of interviews, I began to notice common themes. Working performers seem to have tapped into a sense of authenticity that most aspiring actors search for. They have learned how to detach from the daily rejection inherent in their job. They have found ways to continually create their own opportunities when things seem slow. And, most surprisingly to me, even working performers feel that they could be doing more, worry about what the industry thinks about them, and wonder "what if." It was in seeing these particular commonalities that I noticed working performers and aspiring performers really only have one major difference: where they choose to place their focus.

Working actors will always focus on their work, their "real" lives, and their authentic selves. Everything else seems to fall away. So, does this shift in focus come before someone is a working performer or is it only after someone is a working performer that his or her focus shifts? Yes, I am an academic at heart and I couldn't help but re-read these conversations with a research-oriented bent. Being left with these questions is further inspiring to me, as I work with actors every day. I am hungry to learn more—and am eager to partner up with Blake again for what will be a series of books filled with such conversations. This is fascinating, inspiring stuff!

* * *

Please consider, as you read these conversations, that they represent a snapshot in time for these performers. Shows get cancelled, contracts get terminated, agencies merge, people move across the country. While we have included an index of names in this book—so that you may cross-reference relevant people throughout many performers' careers—we strongly recommend that you use the most recent reference publications to track down agents or managers of interest. Also, note that performers here are sharing their personal experiences and no one has been paid to represent any company or service in good favor. The information provided herein does not represent, on the part of the participants or the publishing company, a recipe for success in the industry.

Since these pages contain—quite literally—conversations between the authors and the subjects, you will notice an occasional tangent, a question not quite syncing up with an answer, or a "chunk" presumably missing. Despite the fact that we spent hours with these performers in typical back-and-forth conversation, we chose to limit the representation of the authors' voices to the simple questions you see throughout the conversations. This is to maintain the focus on the performers' voices—and to do so beyond the typical blurb you may hear when one of these folks appears on a talk show to promote his or her latest gig.

After meeting with the performers included in this book, it is our heartfelt honor to have shared in this part of their collective journey. If you are a performer, it is our sincere hope that these conversations will help you along your career path. Let us hear from you. Contact information is on the inside-front page of this book and at CricketFeet.com.

Enjoy these actors, stand-up comics, and show-business personalities both here—in book form—and out there in the real world. These artists truly wish to make you laugh and cry, understand and think, and always come away moved and inspired.

Acknowledgments

Thank you Blake Robbins for initiating this project. I am blessed to know you and your wonderful wife, Karen Robbins, whose cover art matches perfectly the amazing content of these conversations. Huge amounts of love and respect—and a debt of gratitude like no other—go to Subhash Mandal, my secret-weapon matchmaker and casting-event arm candy.

As always, I owe thanks to the mentorship of Deborah Jacobson and Dan Poynter, as well as Judy Kerr. Your fingerprints are all over my success. Thank you. My family and friends, as always, I thank you for the unending love and support throughout this process and always.

Queens of the Style Manual—Courtney Denney, Robin Gwynne, and Jeannine Burkart—I bow to your brilliance. And to my proofer patrol—Julie O'Malley, Eric Halasz, Ali Sowels, Suesie Toole, Debra McCarthy, Lisa Winston, Hannah Knudsen, Cliff Jones, Katy Ruzicka, Laura Lock, Chip Woods, Denise Winsor, and Rose Auerbach—the drinks are on me!

Thank you so much to those who facilitated these conversations (a working actor's schedule is not always the easiest to negotiate): Shannon Walker, Carri McClure, Synthia Droke, Amy Dennison, Jane Edith Wilson, Eric Axen, and Bruce Smith. Also, thank you to the photographers whose lovely portraits of the actors round out these conversations.

Huge thanks to Tom Fontana for the beautiful foreword! And to those who help our promotional efforts—Bob Brody, Gary Marsh, Bill Tarling, Elizabeth Tindal, Madeline Molis, Lyn Mason Green, and Paul Molinaro—we truly appreciate the support! To Aaron Silverman and the gang at SCB, we love how you love us!

To all of the professors whose recommendations have landed my books on your college and university bookshelves, I credit you with expanding the world of an actor's academic training.

A very humble note of appreciation goes to the incredibly talented, courageous performers whose conversations appear within these pages. Your collective openness has inspired me as a writer, as a casting director, and as a person. I am so grateful to have become better acquainted with each of you through this process. I can only hope it has been as rewarding an experience for each of you.

Extra-special hugs and love to Art Weaver, the Harbin family, Aunt Heddy, Elizabeth Johnson-Stevens, my Gimlet Night ladies, the Hollywood Happy Hour gang, my ever-growing online support system, and most of all to Keith Johnson. You, my dear partner, keep me focused and balanced. Thank you for always pointing out the hummingbirds on our path.

Bonnie Gillespie

* * *

Thank you to the twenty-nine actors here for giving of themselves so freely, so generously.

Thank you to Bonnie for being the best and only person I could have done this with and for all of the talent you've brought to this work.

Thank you to Keith for who you are to Bonnie and for making this book possible.

Thank you to Subhash for the introduction and for being the definition of a friend.

Thank you to Karen for love and happiness. My marriage to you has brought me everything good in my life. And thank you for the beautiful cover art.

Thank you to my daughters Molly and Emily. You bring joy, laughter, and wonder into my life every day. You make every day a good day—tough to do in this business sometimes.

Thank you to my mom and dad, who taught me to love stories and storytellers, and, among the countless other things, taught me integrity.

Thank you to Larry. You have shown me courage and strength. I am so grateful for your amazing generosity.

Thank you to my brother Bo and sister Kira—amazing people—for your love, support, and friendship.

Thank you to Ron Van Lieu—the best acting teacher I have ever known—for your love of actors.

Thank you to the Naked Angels—individually and as a collective—for your artistry and passion. You have created a really cool sandbox for actors to play in.

And since I just borrowed his metaphor, thank you to Tom Fontana, a living model of what an artist should be. A rare commodity in this business, you think for yourself, you have loyalty, and you have generosity. To work with you is a gift for any actor. When I first thought this book might happen, I wanted you to write the foreword. Thank you for that.

Blake Robbins

The Conversations

Jill Andre

Jill Andre is a producer, director, and an actress. She was co-founder of the Pleiades Theatre Company, a nonprofit organization created to develop playwrights in LA. She was also co-founder of the American Renaissance Theatre in New York. Jill was able to travel around the world as a faculty member of the University of Pittsburgh's Semester at Sea, where she produced and directed workshops during the spring of 1993.

In LA, Jill directed Bodies Unbound, *which also played at the Edinburgh Festival. Some other productions she directed include* Collected Stories, Three Weeks After Paradise, Trust, Comings and Goings, *and* Last Summer at Bluefish Cove *(co-directed with Dorothy Lyman). In New York, some of her directorial work includes* Bus Stop, The Last Sortie, Navajo Memoirs, Easter Weekend, Nightgames, Chicago Impulse, *and* Baby Grand. *One of her most pleasurable experiences was directing* Bus Stop *at the William Inge Festival in Kansas in 2003.*

As an actress, Jill appeared on Broadway in such plays as Children of a Lesser God, The Trip Back Down, Sunrise at Campobello, *and* The Great White Hope, *as well as many Off-Broadway and regional productions. Some of her many television and film credits include* Twin Falls Idaho, And the Band Played On, Return of the Living Dead III, Ghosts of Mississippi, Lost in America, The Practice, NYPD Blue, 21 Jump Street, Picket Fences, *and several soaps.*

A very recent highlight was a role in a short film, The Moor—*story by Russell Banks, directed and adapted by Caerthan Banks—in which Jill played a woman in her eighties and, in flashback, in her fifties. It was a particularly satisfying experience, as roles like that don't come along often. More information is available at http://us.imdb.com/name/nm0028149.*

photo by Lisa Franchot

When did you know you wanted to become an actor?

I didn't. It sort of came upon me through growing up in a theatre family. My mom was an actress. My dad was a stage manager and a director and ran a little summer theatre in Cleveland. My uncle was actually one of the founders of the Cleveland Play House. I kind of grew up watching my mom go to auditions for plays and films. And I watched her work in little theatres in the Valley, as well as on and Off-Broadway.

What was your first paid gig?

I did my first movie when I was five months old. It was a fluke, of course. My mother was playing the nurse in a Bette Davis movie that I think was called *From This Dark Stairway*. I actually still have the funny contract with my twenty-five dollars pay. It was shot at Warner Bros. and we lived over on Hollywood Way at the time, having moved from New York.

So, your parents were enthusiastic about your career as a performer.

Absolutely. They were so ahead of their time. They felt so strongly that we should do whatever we really wanted to do. My mother gave us each our own names—not as a theatrical thing but as a sense of our own individuality, for us to really have that sense of ourselves. She always said that she didn't feel we should be beholden to or tied down to a family name that we had to live up to or down to or anything like that. So, my name was Jill Andre—that was what I was given at birth—and my sister had her own name and my brother had his own name. It was really amazing. That was way back! There were five names on the mailbox and of course there was some confusion at school about why we had different names. But I love that she did that.

They were ahead of their time! Consequently, when we were little and my parents would get a job in New York, we'd get in the car and go to New York. My dad was stage-managing the revival of *The Red Mill* on Broadway and I was in the sixth grade. We went that year then back again another summer for my parents to do summer stock. It was just after the High School of the Performing Arts had started. I had heard about it and I said I wanted to go and my mom said, "Well, let's think about it." Of course, she was just itching to get back to New York at that point in time. So, they sent me on early for the audition in October. Because I had come in from California, once I was accepted, the school admitted me right away. My family wasn't prepared to come to New York just yet, as they still had to sell our house in Santa Monica, so I lived with this wonderful couple—friends of my parents. Amazing, incredible people. Their apartment on Riverside Drive was like a museum. They knew all of these artsy, liberal, unusual people in the City. I got to live with them almost that whole first year I was at PA until the following year, when my family made the move to New York. I loved PA, but it still wasn't about acting. Acting was an okay thing. I enjoyed it. I struggled with it at times and I wondered if it was really what I wanted to do.

I was president of the senior class at PA and Arthur Mitchell was my vice president. Dom DeLuise had preceded me at school and my dad had hired him at his musical theatre in Cleveland. Herby Gardner was one of my closest buddies in school. He scribbled his early, nebbish drawings on our apartment walls. There were wonderful people that I got to know and that I still have in my life. That was the most important thing to me at that time. When I graduated high school, I went to City College for a while and then I took some courses at Columbia. Then I realized that I didn't want to go to college for more training. I had had wonderful training at Performing Arts and I'd had a lot of private classes, too. I decided I was just going to try and work in the theatre.

How did you get your first agent?

My mom had a wonderful agent, Barna Ostertag, who was a very famous agent at the time—wonderful agent. And I didn't have an agent for a while because you could make the rounds in those days. Often my mom and I would make the rounds together. Go to a producer's office, meet the person at the desk, and if there was something in production or casting soon I'd either get an interview or not. I remember touring some of the summer stock theatres with *The Happiest Millionaire* with Conrad Nagel. During that summer tour, my mother's agent came out to see me and decided to work with me, which was very cool. It was just amazing to work with Barna Ostertag. She was a woman of great integrity.

In fact, in '55, I think, I did winter stock in Erie, Pennsylvania; did my first Shakespeare as Rosalind in *As You Like It*. That was an interesting time. I was feeling my way as a professional in the business and becoming an independent adult, which is joyful and terrifying at the same time. I did another summer stock thing where I learned a major, major basic big lesson! We were doing one-week stock. That was really hard. We were doing *My Three Angels* and I was playing the young girl, the ingénue. I thought I knew my lines but I didn't. I'll never forget the horrific panic of standing off stage, gasping and sweating. Somehow, I remembered my first line and it was okay, but it was *the* lesson: "Do not ever, ever, EVER pretend that you know your lines when you don't."

What was your training like?

I had always had good training. I started out with some very good teachers, fortunately. Sid Lumet, actually, was one of my first teachers at Performing Arts. I don't really like to say "Method" or "a method" or "somebody else's method," but my training over the years has certainly been working internally—developing a character from an internal source—and then incorporating all of the outside elements, the physical elements. But beginning with clear intentions and developing emotions and then finding out how this person walks and does her hair, that's how I've always worked and how I've always taught all these years. Knowing the character's history and understanding the relationship to the entire play; these are basics for me.

I studied modern dance with Lester Horton in California when I was little and then I went back in New York and studied with May O'Donnell and Gertrude Shurr, who were both Martha Graham's people. I always loved the dance world. There is something about the physicality of it that excites me, even though I knew I'd never be a dancer. I just loved it! I know that it very much helped with discipline I had as an actor. For the longest time, I didn't know how to jump. I remember a class one time when Gertrude was teaching and she was putting us through our jumping paces and made the very clear picture of what it looked like when you jumped. She would say, "You jump and extend the rest of your body out from your shoulders and tighten your butt and legs and it's UP like a *V*!" I remember the day I *got* that and I remember her yelling, "Yea! Jill is jumping!" It was sheer joy. That part of it, the discipline, the sense of order, and the sense of learning something that you can't learn all at once—you have to do it step by step—that is the pleasurable part of acting for me. I feel integration is so important. It's layers upon layers of creative activity that you keep discovering and opening up and then meshing and blending with the role that you're working on.

What drew you to teaching?

It was a natural process. When I was in New York in the early '70s, I was looking for a theatre company to join—a group of people that I had some kind of commonality with and whose work I liked. I started going to all of the small theatres to see performances. If I liked the feel of the place and the people, I would go back afterwards and say hello. I went to see this Japanese Noh production of *Hamlet* at the Terry Schreiber Studio. I was very taken with it. I introduced myself to Terry and we had a long talk. He said, "You're just so right for the play I'm going to open my next season with." It was a John Bishop play called *The Trip Back Down*. I read it and said, "Yes! This is me. This character is so potent for me. I want to do this." We had the first read, opened successfully at Terry's Studio Theatre, and then of course it went on to Broadway. It was very exciting. I got to do it on Broadway after originating the role. I had understudied before and I wanted the experience of creating a role from scratch.

I'd occasionally sit in on Terry's classes just to see how he was doing it. Well, later that year, he had to go out of town to direct something and he asked me to take his class. I had often worked with actors as a coach and I had started directing at Hunter Playwrights. When Terry expanded the school, I kept teaching there until I moved to LA. Now, I mainly do private coaching. It's very gratifying, teaching. Very.

Where did your dance training take you?

One winter I was just busting to get a theatre job. I was making the rounds and I must've left my picture with a talent manager. I was in my bathtub in the kitchen of my cold-water flat in Hell's Kitchen. It was nearing Christmas. The phone rang and this gruff voice said, "Hello, Honey. Wanna go to the Dominican Republic?" I said, "Yeah! What do I have to do?" And I remembered one day having gone into an office to drop off my picture and hearing this gruff voice: "Hello!" I remembered that I was wearing my winter woolies and my hat and scarf, wrapped up to *here* and I hear, "How are your legs, Honey?" Of course, I had DANCER on my resumé, so that's what he was asking about. This was that guy calling, sending me out for this show—as a dancer!

This was a variety show going out for a World Trade Fair in the Dominican Republic and we were part of the entertainment. This show was produced by the son of one of the most famous burlesque producers, Harold Minsky. Fortunately, a girlfriend of mine was also hired as a dancer. This was 1955 and out of the country! This was when the Trujillos were in power in the Dominican Republic. There were acres and acres of this fair exhibit representing countries from all over the world in this huge, vast place. To be part of the entertainment was great! I learned a lot. I ended up being line captain at one point, which was a sheer fluke. There was so much I didn't know! How could I be voted line captain? Well it was my own naïveté. The gal who was line captain split. She was scared and there were too many things going on in this country. There were some pretty tough cookies who were these strippers from New York. I didn't know anything about that. I think my innocence actually saved me. It was a great trip! Somehow, we arrived safely back in New York a few months later. I decided it was a great way to see the world. I could get dancing jobs like that and travel! I really have gypsy in my blood. I love to go everywhere!

The next summer, I did stock in Wisconsin and our wonderful stage manager—a Southern gal named Bimmie McGee—had been to Rome and she talked about it all summer! She said, "Y'know, I might be able to start a theatre there." We all said, "Of course you could!" and, "When are we going?" The following January—this was in 1957—we sailed a big ocean liner to Italy. Bimmie got some family money, found a little theatre in Rome behind one of the big major opera houses, rented it, and we opened a season of two-week stock. We did *Picnic, Solid Gold Cadillac,* and a couple of other plays before we folded. Nobody knew we were there! There was no publicity. But, I stayed for a year in Europe—mostly in Rome, dubbing films and dancing in a revue that toured Sicily. We traveled to Greece, then to Paris—where I got another dancing gig—in the early live TV musical extravaganza days.

What do you wish someone had told you at the beginning of your career?

I think people give a lot of advice about how to study, who to study with, techniques and all that, which is all very important. But there's something about developing yourself as a human being, really understanding who you are, that is so basic to me. Having the freedom to be all of yourself is part of what I teach now. I wish someone had really taught me how to trust my instincts and value my imagination. It took me a long time to find that freedom. I still have to be patient with myself and stay fully in the present moment.

How do you prepare for a role?

A lot of different ways. Sometimes when I read the material, I know that I can connect to what's inside that person's emotional center; I sense their needs. Sometimes when I can't connect, I just have to keep reading it, and reading it, and reading it, and then some little aspect will reveal itself and will trigger a series of things. I might research that person's history and background or I might have a visual concept of the person or I will see something another character has said about mine that makes sense to me. Sometimes it starts with a feel for a certain physical look: how they wear their hair, what kind of shoes or clothing that is real for this character.

What is your favorite thing about being an actor?

That's changed. I think at this point in my life, it has to do with the community involved with the particular project, the people I choose to work with. That is so meaningful to me. On an internal level, I think it's about finding a sense of ease with the work process. That makes me feel really good and comfortable and I know I've dropped into the right place.

Who is *your* favorite actor?

Judi Dench. She's so forthright and she's so committed. And she has a wacky sense of humor I see peeking out behind everything she does. And she is a sexy, mature woman!

What made you choose Los Angeles?

The first time we came out to LA as an adult, I was on the road tour with *Sunrise at Campobello* with Ralph Bellamy playing Roosevelt. I was playing Anna, the daughter. The tour ended here, so my husband Dick Franchot and I stayed here and had our first child, Gabrielle, in 1960 and our second child, Pascal, in 1962. After we separated in 1967, I went back to New York again. I put down roots for the next fifteen years, doing a lot of theatre, on and Off-Broadway, did many commercials—which helped put my kids through college—and started directing and teaching. After a two-year run in *Children of a Lesser God*, it seemed time to head to California again. I'm so glad to be back. New York is great for going back to direct a play, visiting friends, going to the theatre—I love doing that. But this is home now. I have my dog and my big backyard, and New York is just a JetBlue away! It's the best of both worlds!

Joy Behar

Joy Behar, currently a co-host of ABC's Daytime Emmy Award-winning The View, *is among today's leading comic talents. Whether performing stand-up comedy or interviewing politicians and artists, she is a comedic original and a leading woman both on stage and screen. Armed with an MA in English Education from SUNY at Stony Brook, Joy originally began a career in teaching. She then set out to pursue comedy professionally and immediately received bookings from such famous New York clubs as Caroline's and Catch a Rising Star. Joy went on to win three MAC awards and a Cable ACE Award.*

On television, Joy starred in her own HBO special and was a regular on the series Baby Boom. *Other appearances include the voice of a hilariously neurotic patient on* Dr. Katz, *which won the Cable ACE Award,* The Tonight Show with Jay Leno, The Daily Show *with* Jon Stewart, Live with Regis and Kelly, *and* Late Show with David Letterman.

For three years, Joy hosted a popular call-in radio show on WABC, where she discussed politics with a deadly humorous bent. Her film appearances include Cookie *with Peter Falk,* This Is My Life *directed by Nora Ephron, and Woody Allen's* Manhattan Murder Mystery. *In theatre, she had a successful run in the Off-Broadway hit* The Food Chain, *where she earned rave reviews in the starring role. She was also in the critically-acclaimed play* The Vagina Monologues.

Joy is a recipient of the Safe Horizon Champion Award, the Gracie Allen Tribute Award from the Foundation of American Women in Radio and Television, and the New York City Public Advocate's Special Advocate Award for her outstanding friendship to the gay community. Joy is heavily involved with numerous philanthropic organizations and is a frequent contributor to several charitable foundations. More information is at http://wma.com/joy_behar.

photo courtesy ABC Photography Archive, ©2005

When did you know you wanted to become a performer?

I was basically programmed as a child to entertain the family. No TV set, so I was it. They basically rewarded all of my performances. Every time they'd ask me to sing and dance and do a Shirley Temple number, or whatever else I was doing at the time, a whole bunch of Italian relatives would clap and encourage me to do more. In fact, the story is that they prevented me from going to bed sometimes: "Oh, do another song!"

I went through my teen years and I was humiliated by the whole idea of performance. It seemed like I was just a trained seal and I shut down on it until I was around thirty. By that time, I had had a baby and was married and I started to say, "Well, what else am I going to do? I've done that." I went to college. I did everything I was supposed to do. I was a teacher, I lived in the suburbs, I did the whole thing and then I just took to my bed in a post-partum fog of, "What in the hell am I going to do now?"

I did not really throw myself into stand-up until I was a single parent who had been fired from *Good Morning America* and who had had a near-death experience. I had an ectopic pregnancy that ruptured. That put me in another head altogether—the fact that I could've been dead. I figured, I almost died in real life, how bad could it be to die on stage? Everything is relative. That is what it took for me to get on stage and go for it. I needed that much. And once I decided to do it because I had nothing left to lose—me and Janis Joplin, defining freedom—I went for it. I started to be successful almost immediately. I was really emotionally prepared for it at that point and I had no choice. I just kept pushing.

I believe that this business is not something you choose. It kind of chooses you. They say sometimes you choose your parents, which is a crazy thing to say. I don't really agree with that, but I do agree that the business chooses you in a way. It's like I had no other choice. And if you speak to a lot of people who are as into it as I am, you'll hear them say that they had other jobs, nothing worked, they couldn't gel, they couldn't stand their jobs, they hated the nine-to-five, they weren't good at anything else, they went to Law School and hated it. You will hear that over and over again and I think that sometimes it's a compulsion almost. And if there's this compulsion, but you're too scared to do it, you're in turmoil. That's Hell. You've either got to give it up or overcome it.

I've done everything that you could possibly do, at this point, in the industry. I've hit on every medium. I wrote a book, I did acting, I worked with Woody Allen in a movie, I've done television, I've done panelist—which I'm doing now—and, of course, stand-up comedy. I don't sing and dance, that's it. The most rewarding is the stand-up only because it's my production. I get to make it up, produce it, direct it, control it. Nobody tells me what to do. In that way, it's the most rewarding. But I also like the radio. I had a radio show for three years. I'm looking forward to another radio show at some point in the future.

What advice would you give to a performer starting out?

I think people should ask, "Is there anything else I can do that's easier?" This is not an easy field. I don't know at this point—after twenty some-odd years in the business—that I would do it if I knew the exact road it was going to take me down. It's not easy to do! It looks like it's more fun than it is, I think. It's a *lot* of work! It's a lot of work, a lot of stress, a lot of rejection, a lot of backslides.

It doesn't happen overnight. It takes five to ten years to be a decent stand-up. One year, I was doing six sets on a Saturday night, in a row. I would go from the Improv to Catch a Rising Star to the Green Street Café to Folk City to the Five Oaks to the Duplex. I'd just bounce around the City. At some point, you don't even remember: "Did I tell you that I was a teacher?" But that's how you do it. You've got to do it over and over again. Still, one of the misconceptions about stand-up is that I'd have a great set—I'd kill—and I would think, "Okay, now I'll have a career." Wrong. You have to do it again and again and again. You have to see it like sex. It doesn't have any diminishing returns.

What was your first paid gig?

I got seven hundred fifty dollars to do a doctor's night. They were all doctors. Previous to that, I had done "safer" venues where I wasn't getting paid, like gay cabarets. The gay audience is just so hip and so fun and they love to laugh and have a good time and they love a woman comedian. So I was always very comfortable there. If I got on at Catch a Rising Star or one of the comedy clubs, it was harder, but I wasn't getting paid. I might have gotten cab fare. Then one day I got a call from a friend of mine who's a doctor's wife. She said, "They want to hire you to perform for this event." You don't know what the hell you're doing, in the beginning, in terms of different kinds of jobs. It was seven hundred fifty dollars and my rent was only two-seventy so seven-fifty at that point was three months of rent, almost, just for doing what I'd been doing for free. But when you're getting paid for it, you feel extra pressure. And doctors are not really the best audience. They're only interested in hearing about themselves. So after I finished schmoozing with them *about* them and I started to talk about me, I lost them. It was the first time that I had brought my now "practically husband" (I've been with him for twenty-three years). He said, "You were funny. They were bad." I figured, "I'll never let go of this guy!"

What do you wish someone had told you at the beginning of your career?

Nobody told me shit. I guess it would be this: You can either make the audience laugh or you can scare them. If *you* are scared, they will be scared. So you have to project confidence and that's the one thing you don't have in the beginning. You fake it. You bite the bullet and you just do it again. My very first set that I ever did was a character I did at the Improv. It was killer. I was vomiting beforehand. It killed. And it was in front of a full house at ten o'clock at night at the Improv. It really did well. You can imagine how shocking that is to somebody, the first time they're up on stage like that. It scared me so much it took me about six more months to get up there again. The next time I got up, I didn't get the ten o'clock spot. I got the 2am spot: two drunks. I died like a dog. Same material. I thought it was me. No one said to me, "Listen, Joy, it's because of the time. It's because of the audience. It has to do with the room. Of course you're going to die!" And then you get scared because you're not getting the laughs. It snowballs into recklessness.

You should know that, in the beginning. It takes a while. There's the emotional part, there's the work, there's the ego part, the confidence, all of it. And that takes time. I suggest that everybody has a therapist when they're in this industry—or in any industry—because people get in the business and when they're not hot, they're not invited to the parties anymore. You can't pay attention to fame. You can't. It will be gone the next week and then what have you got?

What is your favorite thing about being a performer?

I like the work. I like the idea that I have a creative thing that I do, that's mine, that I can do it until I fall into the grave. I like that I can make people laugh. This may sound schmaltzy but when I was on the radio, I got letters from people saying, "I was literally suicidal. I was about to slit my wrists and then I heard you on the radio." It's stuff like that. And you can feel it sometimes with your audience. They're so happy to hear someone speak the truth and make it funny and elevate their existence a little bit with humor. It's a great thing. That's the altruistic part of me. The other part of me is, "I'm getting a laugh! I dig it!" I mean, I'm not a social worker. It's like a latent function of your own narcissism in a way, your own ego, to release people's endorphins.

What is your least favorite thing about being a performer?

I'm not crazy about flying around. I don't like that part too much. I'm trying to think: What don't I like about the business? I'm always complaining, you'd think I'd come up with something! I complain on a regular basis about little things that go wrong within the course of the day: "This didn't work." "That one irritated me." "Well, if she thinks I'm going there, she's wrong." But the overall level of satisfaction is very high. I like the control that I have. I can control my career to a large extent. But I'm not greedy. If you're greedy, you lose control. You always have to maintain control over yourself because it will wipe you away like a tsunami if you don't. Don't be too mercenary and make decisions only based on money. That's a big mistake. Then you get used to living too high and then you can't pull it back when the next job doesn't come in.

How did you get hired to be a panelist on *The View*?

I was asked to do an event for Milton Berle. I said, "I grew up with Miltie. Sure, I'll do it." I went to the Waldorf Astoria and we had a dinner. Everybody was there: Barbara Walters was there, Regis

Philbin was there, Milton was there with his then-considered young wife. He was eighty-nine, she was fifty, so she was considered jailbait to him. So, I got up and I said to Steve, my boyfriend, "This is going to be brutal. I don't know who these people are." I got up and I did a story about old guys with young women. It's nice, as a comedian, to have an arsenal of material because I could look at the group and say, "Here's Miltie, who's old, with a young wife, relatively. Let's go for that. It's relevant." Of course, he's a comic, so he loves it! I did really, really well.

I got off stage and Steve said to me, "Everybody was laughing, but Barbara Walters was *not* laughing." I said, "Listen, when am I going to work with Barbara Walters? She's a newswoman. Who cares?" The next day I ran into Regis Philbin, who I knew. He said to me, "You were really funny last night. And Barbara Walters said to me, 'Who is that woman?'" A few months later, I got the call that she was interested in me for the show. So, you show up to do your thing and you never know what's going to happen.

How do you choose the material you work on?

I write it! There's a Chinese saying about the longest journey starting with one step. The same thing with stand-up material: The longest set starts with one joke. And then you have two jokes and then three and then four and then five. You start with like five minutes because open mics, wherever they have them, that's all they want you up there for. I would recommend that people do five minutes of jokes that are related in some way. Then you have what comedians call a "hunk" of material. Then you add another hunk and another hunk. And then it just keeps building.

I would be in a conversation and I would be funny in the conversation or at a party and, once I made a conscious decision to do this for a living, I started to notice when people would laugh at something I said and then I would write it down. I even try to do that now. I'm always taking notes. You never know where you're going to come out with it. Write it down and keep your notes, even if they're all over the house—we're not the most organized group! You keep them and then when the pressure is on and the gun is to your head, you pull them all together. I'll even write something on stage, as I'm going. I'm a big proponent of adding to what I already have. I think Phyllis Diller said this: "The act is an hour and it becomes a piece of living sculpture. You put in, you take out, you add, subtract, all the time." It keeps taking a different form as you keep doing it. Then you can go off the act, if you want, which I do all the time.

When you don't have a lot of material and they want you to do a half-hour and you only have fifteen minutes, you learn to work the crowd. You schmooze toward the material you do have. Let's say you have some jokes on marriage. Now you talk to people in the audience: "You married?" "Yes." "How long you married?" And then they'll say something stupid to you and you'll get a laugh off of them! You keep delving and delving and you have a little relationship with the people you're talking with—you remember their names—knowing, that in a couple of minutes, you're going to hit them with a good line and you've sucked up time there.

Was your family supportive?

Of course. If you don't have support, it's a very lonely road. You need somebody in your life who's going to not only be supportive but also will tell you the truth—someone who cares enough about you to tell you the truth. My husband—I was married before—he also was very supportive. I don't pick rejecting men. I don't need that at home! People get *paid* to do that. Some people, I've observed, thrive on the rejection because they've had a rejecting family. Now they're in the business and the rejection doesn't mean anything to them.

How do you handle rejection?

Shrink therapy. I've been in therapy for a long time. I also handle it by doing stand-up. Anyone who wants to do stand-up needs to know one thing: Everyone who's funny at a party thinks that they can do it. It's the double-edged sword of the industry because it is the hardest thing to do and yet it is the thing that gives you your oxygen. The same can be said for both acting and stand-up, really. I find even now—when I'm on *The View* and I get frustrated with the job and I feel straight-jacketed because I'm on television and I can't say everything I want—that when I get on stage and just let it go, I feel ten times better practically for the whole week. At the same time, I'm always reluctant to get on stage because it is so hard to do. It's a paradox. The thing with stand-up is, you're dealing with immediate rejection and immediate acceptance. You get hooked on it. It's very, very addictive, that laughing. Most comedians will tell you they were hooked on that when they were young. It's like drugs.

How did you get your first manager?

Catch a Rising Star was a club that I finally got into—you had to really bust your ass to get in there, at the time—and the guy who ran the club became my manager. He would see me perform all the time. And once the guy who runs the club is your manager, you get better spots. They would have showcases and the agents would come in. Showcasing is the best way to get an agent when you're a stand-up. You get on stage and people patrol the clubs and then they'll see you.

Actors think that they can be comedians first because they'll be seen that way. They sometimes do get picked up and become sitcom actors but they were never comedians in the first place, in my opinion. Any way you can be seen is fine. If you're funny, good. But you're not going to have a career as a stand-up comedian if you only do it for five minutes and get picked up for a sitcom.

What made you choose New York?

New York is easy. I'm five minutes from where I work. I don't like LA. I can't take that schlepping around constantly. I lived in LA for six months while I was in a TV series called *Baby Boom* with Kate Jackson. I lived in West Hollywood at the bottom of Laurel Canyon in what looked like an old-age home to me. People walked around with walkers! It's not my cup of tea. I'm a ghetto girl. I'm a definite type for a sitcom. I always was. But I wasn't interested in living in LA. I've always managed to have a career that's not as big maybe as it could've been because I insisted on staying in New York.

How did your stand-up comedy lead to series work?

I didn't really ever pursue acting. I think they may have seen me doing stand-up. That was a time when a lot of stand-up comedians were being picked up by sitcoms. There was a run on that for a while. They were getting development deals. There was a guy who was working for Warner Bros. who saw me in some kind of a TV thing and he got me a development deal with Warner Bros. It's really haphazard in certain ways. People see you. In the beginning, it's just: Get them to see you. But you don't want them to see you before you're really ready. If you're seen immediately, you don't have time to develop. You need to be bad and you need to survive that. There's good news and bad news to being seen immediately. You need to be emotionally ready for success. It's better to be successful when you're older, but the business is very ageist. I think that a lot of meltdowns that go on are because people are not ready to be successful. They have no idea what it means to be successful. They have a fantasy that that's going to make them happy. Success doesn't make you happy; it just makes you successful.

Daniel Bess

Daniel Bess was born and raised in Honolulu. In high school, he worked with Mark Medoff in his production of Stephanie Hero *as well as working with the Honolulu Theatre for Youth. At seventeen, he moved to New York and trained in the Conservatory at Purchase College. Upon finishing his training, he began working on the New York stage. His debut was in a production directed by Michael Mayer at the Vineyard Theatre. He also worked with Michael Greif at New York Stage & Film and other productions before moving to LA to pursue a film career.*

Daniel's television debut was on Fox's 24 *as the character of Rick in the first season. He has also guest-starred in other television shows such as* Firefly, JAG, Grey's Anatomy, *and* ER. *He is now playing a recurring role on* Veronica Mars *and just shot the pilot episode of* What About Brian? *for ABC. Daniel has produced and starred in a film called* Waterfall *that was shot in the mountains and beaches of Oahu and is currently in post-production. His official film debut is in* Constellation *and he is now working on producing his yet-to-be-titled road film with his partners at WcJeWop Productions. He is also a Country-Blues-Hawaiian-Rock singer/songwriter. More information is available at http://us.imdb.com/name/nm1101442.*

photo courtesy Daniel Bess

When did you know you wanted to become an actor?

Honestly, it was a pretty simple thing. I did my first play in like seventh grade at junior high. I had always played music as a kid. So, I did a play—and it was the funnest thing I'd ever done—and then I did another play. I basically started realizing that this is what I was best at and what I enjoyed more than anything. I'd seen that there were people on TV so I knew that you could make a living at this. It was very simple.

I did plays and played music all through high school—I had my own rock band—and there was a really good performing arts program. One year, I went away to Italy—which was the best year of my life, socially—because living in Hawaii as a White boy is a little tough every now and then. Well, when I got back, they had turned the performing arts program into a performing arts high school—the first ever in Hawaii, Mid-Pacific School of the Arts—and the director of it got his Master's in Directing at California Institute of the Arts. This was Andy Mennick—such a pure artist. He was a real Zapatista-type teacher. He became my mentor. If it wasn't for him, I wouldn't have known about SUNY Purchase, where I ended up. Purchase was kind of a mystery to me, but I came to LA and had auditions for Purchase, Boston, DePaul, and Cal Arts and got into all of them. When I visited Purchase, it was kind of the most "no-bullshit actor guy" kind of program I'd seen. They took it all very seriously. It's not a very pretty campus, but in New York, theatre is the biggest draw.

Of course, you can't make a living as a theatre actor. You can't have a career. There's maybe twenty musical theatre stars that make a living doing it, but that's it. Basically, I love film. And even the best of TV, in its nature, is kept so heightened, hour by hour. It has to go a little away from reality for that. So, for me, it's film and theatre. But until you get a name, you can't just take the summer off and go do *Hamlet* in New York. Once I realized that, I moved straight out to LA. I did about two-and-a-half years of theatre in New York before I moved to LA. My first play was *True History and Real Adventures* at the Vineyard Theatre with Michael Mayer directing. Kathleen Chalfant was in it. It was just an amazing experience. Then I did this other play—*The Hologram Theory* at the Blue Light—and it was very different from the first one. In one play I was a drunken Welsh tortured kid and in the next I was a gay androgynous kind of kid. If I could get paid eight hundred bucks a week to do that for the rest of my life, I'd be the happiest guy on the planet Earth. But it dries up. I did a play with Michael Greif at New York Stage & Film and after that it was literally a year-and-a-half of nothing.

I almost left Purchase a few times, like almost every actor does with conservatory. Conservatories really kind of destroy you. For every few teachers there that really try to bring out the best in you, there's a few that just try to break you and mold you into what they want you to be. What saved me was guest directors. Our senior year, we did the William Saroyan play *The Time of Your Life*. I got to play Joe. We worked with an amazing director named Amy Saltz, who was the head of teaching directing at Mason Gross. It changed my life. It made me realize what I was capable of. I was so kind of keeping myself from getting smacked that I would never raise my head up.

After that, I kind of said, "Fuck you," to the rest of the school and I got three great parts. The agents in New York started coming up during those plays, so I really got to show my best. I actually got signed by J. Michael Bloom right before graduation. As soon as I graduated, the whole company broke up. It was the funniest thing, but in a way it was freeing. I had this manager from 3Arts who picked me up right away. After I booked my Michael Mayer play, they took me to Innovative. I started booking. Being a White, young, leading man is the most castable combination you can get. I was very lucky.

What do you consider your first break?

For me, spiritually, doing the first play with Michael Mayer was the break. It was the greatest directorial experience I've ever had. He comes from such a place of love but he challenges you. As long as you're giving one hundred-fifty percent and challenging yourself every time you come in there, he'll take you to the next level. Unless you're fucking up and not working as hard as you can, he will never, ever berate you in any way. He'll just ask more of you. It's like how, in acting class, every now and then you'll just see that breakthrough where somebody starts bawling and they finally get that one moment. What we all strive for, as artists, is what's going on at times like that. That's what doing that play was like.

After that, there was a long process of depression: no work, struggle, everything else. I would've never quit, though. I knew that in my heart there was no way to leave this life. I would've done whatever it took: leave a girlfriend, live on the streets, go back to Hawaii to get my shit together, whatever it would take, but I wouldn't quit. It wasn't just the lack of work. It was personal stuff that I had to do to come to the place that I am now, as a person, where I can do the best work possible. It doesn't matter how great—how talented—you are if you still have shit in your personal life that's negative, you've got to come to terms with it. If you don't like yourself, no matter what you do, your work isn't going to *work*. What got me through that—and what gets me through that still—is class and being willing to ask for help.

I had finally broken out of this relationship that wasn't good for me but I was dirt poor. I mean, literally, my grandfather died but I couldn't afford to get to the funeral, I got hit by a car, I got held up at gunpoint, and then broke up with my girlfriend all within like a month. And then I booked a guest-star on one pilot—it was just a guest-star *for* the pilot—and I regrouped, hung out, and then two months later I was told they wanted me for ten episodes. That turned out to be *24*. Then they needed me for twenty episodes, which was pretty much the whole first season. That gave me enough cash to get started in LA and gave me a foothold in LA in terms of television.

I had no fucking clue what I was doing because I had never been in front of a camera on a real set where somebody brings a tape measure up to you. I had only made my own films—that turned out like crap—in high school. We had a public access comedy show that my brother and I did, but nothing like having to cry because my good friend just got his head blown off and—two seconds before, "Action!"—there's a tape measure a quarter-inch from my eye. It's a whole different way of working. You've got to train to do it, and I was just running on gut instinct. During *24*, I started taking class with this Meisner-based, New York-style teacher named Chris Fields. He taught me a way of working—especially preparation—that works when I have to go inside a casting director's room or in front of the camera on a set. It always works for me.

How did you handle the instant notoriety from *24*?

I was painfully shy—and not just with the girls—I just couldn't really do the, "Hey, let's hang out," thing after a day of shooting. There's such a false hype of everything at that point. I went to class, I talked to my friends, I spent my time with Jack Daniels at home from time to time, but I never really did the party thing. It was cool to get a nice little touch of it, hanging out with Kiefer Sutherland and going to premiere parties, but it was weird, too. At these parties, a couple of kids from some other shows were getting a lot of attention and it was just really gross. These hardcore newspeople were there, getting all taken in by the celebrity bullshit and getting off on their own star power. What would be a turn on, for me, would be to get to a place in my career where I could work with Martin Scorsese. None of that other stuff.

Who are *your* favorite actors?

I really like what Chris Fields calls "Lunchpail Actors." They come to work, do their work, go to class—it's all about the work. It's the Robert Duvall-type thing. You never hear about any diva moments from him. He always gives a great performance. He makes these quirky, indie films, and he never—for one moment—is all about pyrotechnics in his character acting. Jeff Bridges is the same way too. No matter what they do, you're just enjoying the film with these guys playing the characters. There's nothing fantastical about it. You're just in it. Daniel Day-Lewis is probably my all-time favorite. You can't help but notice how pyrotechnical he is, but it's always an explosion that's built from the ground up with him. Also, I would add Robert De Niro, Meryl Streep, Viola Davis, Kathy Bates, Morgan Freeman, Jimmy Stewart, Javier Bardem, and Steve McQueen. They all resonate with me because I've never seen a single moment from any of those actors that I didn't believe. They all can do character work and slip into parts without showing anything. They just *are*. You don't see them acting because you already believe them from the moment they start. You just go on the journey with them. They have a certain humanity and blue-collar ethos about them in the way they approach their work. You don't care about their personal lives. You care about their work. Oh, also, Will Ferrell. He is the funniest actor I have ever seen and isn't some crazed, coked-out celebrity. He's a real actor and a normal human being who just happens to be absurdly funny.

What is your favorite thing about being an actor?

I'm not really into any one religion, per se, but there is an idea that comes from Zen and from Buddhism of Satori or Nirvana—that moment where you truly stop all thinking. The best moments on stage are that moment. I don't think I've found that yet, on film. Actually, in *Constellation*, I did have that moment. I did! I had two lines, but I had to be basically breaking down in every scene. I definitely had that in the play I did with Angela Goethals and Michael Mayer. You may only ever get it in one scene or one part of a scene, but it's beautiful.

What is your least favorite thing about being an actor?

Ah, just the business. Just the whole notion of it as a business. They don't call theatre "the business" like that. If you're going to be an artist, you have to have a certain awareness of the business. What's a good thing for me—since I don't tend to focus on it—is that my manager started saying, "Dan, your feedback's been great. You're doing great auditions. You know how to do it all. We're going to go to Armani Exchange and spend eight hundred dollars." Honestly, I swear to God, I've been to test for a couple of things! I go in there wearing a nice fucking suit and this is such an image town that it makes a difference. It's working! She was right. She knows how to play the game because she's a producer. She knows all the bullshit you've got to do and how you've got to look and the car you've got to drive on set with. It makes a fucking difference! I'm starting to realize that I'll play the game until I've got a name and then I'll do whatever I want, go live in Italy, whatever.

How do you handle rejection?

More than anything, I take stuff into my own hands. I produced a film. I got my brother to write it, chose all the actors, got the director, and put it all together. The thing is, I need to pump another forty grand into post-production. We shot on a 24P camera, which looks great, and it's all shot in the mountains and waterfalls of Hawaii. It's kind of like a *Stand by Me* story. Anyway, doing your own thing helps with rejection because you're not looking to be called in on anything—you're too busy on your own thing. It's like you have to spiritually kiss ass to get work but you start getting work when you stop kissing ass.

Also, I always stay in class. I work on my music—an alt-Country-Hawaiian kind of thing: Lucinda Williams meets Ry Cooder—and I have some great people behind me on this CD I'm doing. I stick with the best people I know in the world: my friends. Falling in love doesn't hurt. And every few months of enough rejection, I go out with Blake and get pissed drunk and eat a whole pizza and then wake up sore the next day and get on with it. What can you do? At least, as an actor, you can make a living so much better than a musician or a dancer can. Everything I've learned and been through since being out of school has made me more confident as an actor. My friends, continual study in class, and the knowledge that nobody knows a thing in this town until it's spelled out for them keeps me going. Despite the constant rejection—and Lord knows I've had less than many—and the fact that I would never want my children to do this for a living, I still could do nothing else.

Do you prefer theatre to film and television work?

It's hard to say. I've done some readings for the Mark Taper Forum, but as hard as I've tried, I haven't been able to get "in" with the LA theatre world like I was with New York. The good thing about LA is that there is a plethora of theatre here—although most of it is crap—and there are some really great playwrights doing some amazing stuff here. On camera, the thrill is visual. In theatre, the thrill is audial. What I'm starting to really appreciate about film is the ability to be real. You don't have to make your voice louder. I have the instrument to do that, to really bring it down. You don't have to do more than what needs to be done, on-camera. It takes having full confidence in your training to know that it's going to show. You just know when you've got it, when you're centered in the work. And being centered as a human will also inform your work.

Honestly, I've changed more in the last six months than I had in the fifteen years before. A lot of things finally came together. I did

Constellation down South and almost all of my scenes are opposite Gabrielle Union. The older version of my character is David Clennon, who won an Emmy for *thirtysomething*. He's probably the kindest man on the planet Earth. He is one of the most wonderful humans I've ever worked with. He literally memorizes the crew list before showing up. He knows everybody by name. Anyway, I worked on this for three weeks. I came in with no money—I was really deep in debt from making my own film—and I hadn't been hired to work in the two-and-a-half years since *24*. Relationship-wise, I was just hopping from whatever to whatever. For some reason, with that director there was such a deep sense of importance to the film. That film's producer has now become my manager. The cast was just incredible. Whether or not the film is a success, it changed my life for the better.

Alonzo Bodden

Even before appearing on NBC's Last Comic Standing, *Alonzo Bodden knew there was nothing that would ever make him give up comedy. "That's the drug," he says. "When they laugh, it's like I'm a jazz musician and they hear it and they get it. It's power to take the crowd wherever I want them to go. I love it when they laugh, especially when they relate through laughter. It's a beautiful thing. It also means I'm going to get paid, which is nice."*

A graduate of Aviation High School, for nine years he earned a paycheck as a jet mechanic for Lockheed and McDonnell-Douglas. While comics around the country were making audiences laugh at airline jokes, Alonzo was working on the top secret Stealth Bomber. It was during a stint as a trainer that Alonzo discovered his ability to entertain a group of people.

Alonzo has ventured off the stage to have fun with his many roles on television and in film. He was the security guard, bouncer, crook, and/or a cop in Bringing Down the House, Angel, *and* Grounded for Life, *to name a few.*

Alonzo describes his material as "cynically good-natured in an angry suburban Negro kind of way." While he strongly believes that all young comics should study Bill Cosby, he freely admits that his mom is the funniest person he knows. When his family and friends attend his shows, he loves and appreciates it.

One of the great things about Alonzo's career is that he can make you laugh and fix your Learjet. One day Alonzo hopes to have his own Learjet. More information is at http://alonzobodden.com.

photo courtesy Alonzo Bodden

When did you know you wanted to become a performer?

I used to be an airplane mechanic. That was my first career. Then I started training—teaching mechanics—in '89. I could see the end of it coming by 1993 and it just kind of struck me. I was always funny, but it wasn't until I started teaching that I knew I could just be in front of a group and be funny all the time. Some background: I'm clean and sober. And my main meeting place was a place called Studio 12. The joke was that the stars went to Betty Ford and the crew went to Studio 12. Really, that's what it was. It was like a recovery home for the unions, the tradespeople. That was my first exposure to people in the entertainment business. I didn't know what I could do in the business but I really liked it. The reason I talk about that is because the support of those people just saying, "You can do it. Go for it," was everything.

I could always make people laugh. I wasn't the class clown type. I was the type that sat in the back and made the person next to me laugh really loud and when I kept a straight face, they would get in trouble. That was more my style of humor. Still is. I always could make people laugh but it wasn't until training that I knew I could do it in front of people. It's a whole different thing. The difference between a comic and a funny guy—and I don't know who said this, originally—is that a funny guy can make his friends laugh. A comic has to make a hundred strangers laugh on cue. That's what I learned when I was a teacher: that I could make people laugh. I call it the gift. I don't know what it is or where it comes from, but I have it.

When I got my layoff notice from McDonnell-Douglas, I was dating someone and she gave me an ad for a comedy class. The reason I wanted to go to the class was I didn't want to be the only person on stage for the first time. I knew about open mics and stuff, but I didn't want to be the only one doing it for the first time that night. If I went to a class, at the graduation, everyone's doing it for the first time. The graduation performance was really cool. We were at the theatre and there were a lot of people there—all friends and supporters—and my second joke, everyone laughed. It threw me! Because we had never gone over in class what to do when a group of people laughed. I'm kind of standing there like, "Oh, shit. What do I do now?" I did my set and it was really great for a first set ever. They definitely laughed. I got off stage and a friend of mine said, "Well, it looks like you finally found out what you're meant to be doing." That was the exact feeling I had. I always had that feeling about it—I *still* have that feeling about it. I have to do stand-up. I love doing stand-up.

From there, I got into doing open mics. I would get up anywhere. I'd talk to people who were working and say, "What do I do?" and they'd say, "You gotta do open mics." So, I started doing them. I started doing comedy when I was thirty. I couldn't do that starving artist lifestyle. I'd already had a good job and a career. I was used to living a certain way. I wasn't going to live in a one-bedroom with six roommates. A friend of mine who was a location and transportation guy back when I was with McDonnell-Douglas gave me a call and asked me if I could drive a truck. He said, "I need a truck driver for this new show called *Mighty Morphin' Power Rangers*." I was like, "Okay." I showed up and I drove for him a few days and it was cool.

Then I didn't hear from them for a few months. About four or five months later, I get a call from *Mighty Morphin' Power Rangers* asking if I'm interested in being a transportation captain. I said, "Hang on a minute. Let me do something. I'll call you right back." I called my buddy and asked, "What's a transportation captain?" Literally, that's how it happened. He said, "Don't worry. You can figure it out. You'll learn it as you do it. Take the job."

So I took the job. They were just great. When we started doing the show—I was there pretty much from the beginning—everyone thought the show was the most corny, bad thing, but it took off! It was a real blessing. The producer liked me, the people on the crew liked me. I forget how they saw me do comedy; they came to an open mic I did or something. By now, I'd been doing it almost a year. They liked it and they said, "Look, pursue your career. Your job will always be here. If you've got to leave town or whatever, you go." It was such a great job because I only worked when we were on location—like two or three days a week—and I could make enough money to pay my bills. The other great thing is I was learning what everyone does in the business. I learned, "Oh, so that's what a gaffer is. That's what an electric is." And I learned how shows were made, setting it up and the whole bit. Meanwhile, my comedy career was slowly blossoming.

What was your first paid gig?

A few people had hired me to open for them or do little one-nighters around here where you make twenty bucks, fifty bucks, whatever. People were getting to know that I was funny. I did the open mic at the Laugh Factory and Jamie Masada said, "I'm looking for a doorman. Work as a doorman and I'll give you spots when people don't show up." I started doing that and one night Frasier Smith saw me. In the '80s, he was one of the top DJs in LA. He had a midnight comedy show on 97.1, back when it was a rock station. So, he hired me to warm up his crowd for his midnight show every week. That was great, because every week I had to do a new five minutes. It pushed me to write and write and write and write. I tend to be topical, so my material is always changing. Also, I'd get to do the show once a month, which would be a twenty-minute spot. Somewhere in my first or second year of doing that, something great happened. I knew Tommy Davidson—I had met him—and I asked him for tickets to a show he was doing. He said, "Do you want to open it?" I was like, "Hell, yeah!" It was so funny, Tommy got paid five grand and I got paid a hundred bucks—and I wasn't allowed in the green room. That's really the difference between being the headliner and the opener. Opening for Tommy was a great break because his manager, a guy named Rick Rogers, saw me and took me on. That was my first real representation. Rick had me start opening for Tommy in other clubs. That's how other clubs would see me for the first time. That was great for my career.

I was asked to do *The Apollo Comedy Hour*. That was frightening. At this point, I had maybe two years of experience. The whole thing about the Apollo is: Don't get booed off! That's your only concern. It was my first time working in New York, which is where I grew up. I got there and I went to the Boston Comedy Club because some LA comics had told me to check it out; it's in the Village. The comics there were like, "Oh, you're doing the Apollo? We can get you up in this room, that room, the other room, just to run your set." This is back when *Def Comedy Jam* was really big. I'm not a Def Jam comic. It's not where I come from. I don't knock it, but it's not my style. I went to this club called Manhattan Proper. It was in Queens, about two miles from where I grew up. I didn't tell anybody I was going to be there. I just went. That crowd—second or third joke—started booing me and ran me right out of the room. That was my first time getting booed like that. I had bombed before. I would have jokes not work. But that was the first time it was that kind of reaction.

I got to the Apollo and it's much smaller than it looks on TV. They had us downstairs in a bullpen. They would have a music act and then a comic, but they wouldn't tell you who was next. I either followed or went right before Biggie Smalls. I went out there and my first joke was: "I grew up in New York. I moved to LA. Damn, if I was a rapper, I'd have to shoot myself." They loved it! My set just went. People ask me if I get nervous and I generally don't get nervous—even back then I didn't get too nervous—but whenever I'm doing something new, it's always about getting the first laugh. That's when I can relax.

How did you begin crossing over into acting?

Rick was sending me out on auditions. It was really funny because I had no idea what to do. I didn't know about the sign-in sheet, nothing. I was just an idiot. I can only think now how horribly bad I must've been at that point. The difference between comedy and acting is a comic can always work. An actor, if he wants to practice, he has to pay to go to class. Comics can always work for free. We can always find stage time somewhere. It may be the back of a coffee shop, but we still get to get up and do it. I think that's the big difference. Rick also got me hip-pocketed at APA, which is a big agency. They had me showcase for the Montreal Comedy Festival, which is the biggest comedy festival in the world. There's over a hundred comics there doing all different shows: New Faces Show, Urban Comedy Show, Jewish Comedy Show, Best of the Fest, Nasty Show, Alternative Show—it's a phenomenal festival. I've done it a few times now and I love it. I went in, they picked me for the New Faces Showcase. This was in '97, my fourth year of comedy. This was the big show to be in. I figured, "Now I have to go up there and get a deal!" I can't ever waste time enjoying it; I've always got work to do!

This was one of my best moments in comedy. I was doing New Faces and I said, "I don't like hockey." The whole crowd starts going, "Boo! Boo! Boo!" I just looked at them and said, "Shut up!" And then I continued, "I don't like hockey because the only thing black is the puck. Now, golf on the other hand...." So, the crowd roars. After the show, I walk outside and I'm attacked: "I'm from NBC." "I'm from ABC." "I'm from this studio." "I'm from that studio." This was back when they still made deals at the festivals. It was funny because, for me, it was just a set! I probably had the best set of the group, but I was just thinking, "This is what I do." The guys from APA said, "Listen, we've got to go over to the Gala and hang with Denis Leary." The Gala is one of the biggest shows they have and Denis Leary was one of their clients. I was like, "What? Guys! This is when I need you, fellas. I don't know how to talk to these people. I'm not supposed to talk to these people. That's *your* job." William Morris was just bird-dogging me after that. I could not turn around without bumping into a William Morris agent. It was the funniest thing.

Rick, my manager—who was up there with me—called me when we got home and said, "You're about to make a ton of fuckin' money." We went in and signed with William Morris, I got a deal with a company called Greenblatt-Janollari, I left *Mighty Morphin' Power Rangers*—that was when I crossed over to full-time comic. My deal with Greenblatt-Janollari was my learning deal. I didn't know I was supposed to come in with my idea for a show. I just thought, "Okay, I'm funny. You guys, do your thing." I met with a bunch of different writers. We shopped a show to NBC, everybody got their hands on it and it died—but they did let me keep the money. Rick, the whole time, was talking about the deal getting renewed, but it expired. I was kind of languishing but I was still working the clubs.

After I did my New Faces, a guy named Willie Mercer—one of the producers of the festival—came by and said, "I'm going to have you back in two years to do a Gala." Sure enough, he did call me a year and a half later and said, "You're going to do your gala this summer." I went back to Montreal in '99. Rick Rogers left the business, so I didn't have a manager for a while. I got hooked up with Willie Mercer, the guy who had booked me for Montreal. I knew he was a manager and I knew he was a man of his word. In this business, it's almost shocking when someone actually does something they say they will do. By the way, once the deal expired, I wasn't the hot guy at William Morris anymore.

Note to comics: Don't make fun of your agent when they have a big ego. There was a room called Dublin's on Sunset. This was 2000 maybe '01. This friend of mine, Ahmed Ahmed, had booked me. He would do comedy anywhere—pool halls, bowling alleys, bars. We did it once in the back of a Cuban restaurant. He started doing comedy at Dublin's and said, "Come on down." It was basically like an open mic workout room. It wasn't new comics but it was comics who work, working out new material. Dublin's was really organic and really great. It was me, Dane Cook, and a guy named Darren Carter. We were kind of the anchors. A lot of other comics would come. People liked seeing us different than they saw us at the Laugh Factory or the Improv and we liked having a crowd. They fed each other: The crowds got bigger and that made bigger-name comics hear about it and want to do it. It just grew and grew. Then it became this show. My thing was, I would always go in there, sit on a stool, and just talk and see what would come out. That's how I'd get new material.

I'd been rippin' on the Clippers one week. The guy who wrote *Juwanna Mann* was in the crowd and he came to me and said, "I'm doing this movie about the WNBA and I think some of your Clippers stuff might be interesting to use." I was like, "Okay, whatever." I guess he did research, found out who I was, and contacted William Morris because the next week, William Morris had people down there. Now, I had told them about this room. I had said, "You guys have really got to see what I'm doing at Dublin's," because it was different than my stage stuff. At Dublin's, I was usually really dirty, really raw, and people weren't used to seeing that from me. So, they came down and I said, "Yeah, my agent's here. My agent asked what I've been doing. That's like my mother asking me how old I am. You should know!" There's roaring laughter. I said, "I'm not going to mention the name of the agency, but they're on William Morris Boulevard and they've been hawkin' me for a hundred dollars for a year. I don't know, but I'm thinking, if there's a street named after you in Beverly Hills, maybe my hundred ain't puttin' you over the top." Well, the next morning, Debbie—who was Willie Mercer's partner—called and said, "You know, there have only been two days your name has been on every desk at William Morris: when they found you in Montreal and when they dropped you this morning." At the end of the day, I went to Debbie and I said, "Was it funny?" She said, "Fucking hilarious." I'm like, "Okay. Then it's fine."

How did you get your SAG card?

It was really funny. I had gotten my SAG card in a role because a friend of mine was a director. He said, "I need an undercover cop for this thing. I'll set it up where you'll say a few lines so you'll be eligible for your card." I did that and then I actually got a recurring role on *The Visitor* on the second-to-last episode. That started my acting career as a man in uniform. I've been an Air Force Lieutenant, security guard, prison guard, bouncer. All of it.

One great thing William Morris did was turn me on to an acting coach named Janet Alhanti. Janet is phenomenal. Janet isn't one of those artsy types. She's nuts-and-bolts: This is what you do. And if you try any of that artsy stuff, Janet will say, "What's that? What are you doing?" I love Janet. Janet was the first person with whom I began to understand acting and what acting is. That's when I started going into auditions basically having an idea, knowing what I was doing. She taught me how to break down sides and make choices. She explained what making a choice means—you decide: "This is how I'm going to deliver this," and you do it. You don't flounder or anything. That's when I started the grind. I was on the road doing my club thing, I was doing auditions, I was doing Janet's class.

When did you feel like a "real" comic?

When I did New Faces in '97. That's when I felt like, "Okay, now I'm a comic." The comics who were working the Laugh Factory and managers and people who had seen me as "doorman," they were congratulating me. When you get it from your peers, when you get it from Dom Irrera or from Barry Katz, that's real. They're talking to me like I'm one of them. It's weird! But that's what really felt good—beyond the money, the networks, the agency—it's being accepted by your peers. Now I'm one of them.

There are a lot of LA comics that do LA open mics and that's all they do. I was on the road. I was working shitty one-nighters in Montana, Idaho, Washington. I did a couple of circles around

Texas—you drive to Texas and circle the state. I did New Mexico. But that's how you get good. I tell new comics that: "You don't get good staying in LA." You certainly aren't going to get good Saturday night at the Improv. You get good doing comedy in places it should never be done: Wednesday night at a biker bar in Montana. Your ass *will* be funny. That's how you get good.

There were a couple of years that were really lean. I was really lucky that, when I got that big development deal, I had a friend who was an accountant bookkeeper. She handled the money. She made the money last a couple of years. She also got me to buy a house. In '01, when I was broke, I was able to take a second on the townhouse and live. I was really lucky in that respect.

How did you get your second development deal?

I went to the Aspen Comedy Festival and there I bumped into Judi Brown who used to book comedy for HBO. Judi and I knew each other. Judi was someone who had always been honest. Rick had tried to get me into Aspen and Judi said, "Nah. HBO thinks he's a festival guy." It used to be, you could do Montreal or Aspen, but only big names got to do both. Judi said, "Well, I'm traveling and I'm asking, 'Who should be at Aspen?' and your name keeps poppin' up so we're going to showcase you." I showcased and that was really fun. Aspen is completely different than Montreal. I don't think it works the same. I think it's more of a "casting and executives who like to ski and we may drop by a show" thing at Aspen.

Well, another comic named Jeremy Hotz, who is a phenomenal comic originally from Canada, is a very neurotic, Woody Allen-ish kind of guy. We're friends. I've known him for a few years. We were having lunch and an agent who happened to represent Jeremy at the time said he couldn't believe Jeremy and I were friends because we're so opposite. I'm laid back, Jeremy is very on-edge. He said, "That's a show. You two are a show." We came back to LA, we worked on it, we pitched it. We went to Castle Rock and they were like, "Eh, we kind of see it. We don't really get it. Work on the pitch and come back." The second time we went, Jeremy had just bought a car and I helped him do the deal. We were literally walking into the office arguing with each other. Glen Padnick from Castle Rock was sitting behind his desk cracking up, just dying laughing. We were like, "Okay, we're ready to pitch," and he said, "No. No need. I got it." So, Castle Rock took on the project. What had changed since I was in Montreal and got a deal and this Aspen deal, is that now studios don't pay when they take on a project. They don't pay you until they sell it. So, there was no big fat check. Castle Rock took it out to Fox; they didn't buy the idea. Then the idea just kind of died on the vine. The thing I love about Hollywood is that they never say, "No." They just stop talking to you. You never know—me and Jeremy could become superstars and then they've got our show, ready to go, since they didn't ever really say no.

How did you get involved with *Last Comic Standing*?

Judi Brown was working for *Star Search*. I did *Star Search* in '02 or '03. It was pretty cool for me. I had done another show in 2001 called *Next Big Star* with Ed McMahon for PAX. I won that one. It was kind of a low-budget cable version of *Star Search*. I won a car. It was right on time, but it costs a lot of money to win a car. You gotta pay taxes on the car, you gotta pay registration on the car, and you have to pay income tax on the price of the car—a lot of people don't know the car is considered *income* at retail value. It would've cost me about eight or nine thousand dollars to win that car, so I sold it back to the dealer, bought a cheaper car, and pocketed some cash. When I was asked to do *Star Search*, I had done it before, in terms of doing ninety-second sets. I knew how to put together a ninety-second set.

When they did the first season of *Last Comic Standing*, I went in for the initial two-minute interview, routine, whatever you want to call it. They said I'd have to drop everything in my career to do this show. I had gotten a role in a movie called *The Girl Next Door*. I said, "Forget this. I'm not giving up a part in a movie for this unknown reality show." I passed on it. It went that summer. It was sort of a hit. That fall, the guys who had been on the show were making a ton of money live. That's when everyone's interest piqued: "Whoa, this is great exposure!"

When it came up again in January of '04, they asked me if I wanted to come in. I had a great two-minute set and then I did the Improv that night—the three-minutes—and then I made it to the New York round. In New York, we had to do five minutes. That was the first good experience on the show for me. I did a routine about Bed, Bath & Beyond. Colin Quinn questioned me: "Black comic? Bed, Bath & Beyond?" And I hit him with the line, "Look, Colin, Black people wouldn't get it because we don't buy *sheets*." And the crowd just cracked up. It was the first time on the show I was able to do a, "Look, I'm good at this. You want to mess with me? I'm going to mess right back with you." I made it to Vegas and then I made it to get in the house.

The house was a great experience. It was really weird because none of us knew what to expect. Most of the time, the house was boring because there was no TV, no telephones, no Internet, they even stopped us from buying the newspaper. No outside influence for twenty-eight days. We used to joke about the gunline: "You could walk down the driveway to a point, and then if you cross that gunline, you're gonna get shot!" The bathroom situation was miserable: Five guys shared one bathroom. It worked out for me, because I just got in the habit of waking up early and getting in there first.

It was mostly good times. As each person left the house, it got quieter. Jay Mohr would tell us, "Don't strategize, don't team up, no alliances. Pick the person you know you can beat. That's the strategy." I stuck to that. And I wouldn't tell people who I was going to vote for. There was definitely tension whenever somebody would be leaving. The day of the votes, there would be tension. If you didn't have to perform in a challenge, there would be a big exhale of relief. Through the experience, I never got challenged. The only time I got challenged was in a "challenge off." The way it worked was, we'd go in a booth and say, "I know I'm funnier than *blank*." Whoever got the most votes, they'd have to perform and they'd have to pick one of the people who voted against them. In the house, I think I was respected. People had seen me in clubs and knew what I could do. That was a good experience, even though I didn't win.

We were immediately asked to do the third. I think my advantage was that I'm a writer—I'm always writing new stuff, always coming up with new stuff—and a lot of people couldn't reload that fast. We had two weeks between seasons. They didn't have new material to do that fast. It was grueling because we would be doing live shows Thursday to Sunday, fly back Monday, do rehearsals, shoot the show on Tuesday, maybe be off on Wednesday but more likely be flying to another city. It was a grueling six or eight weeks. But I had a good run! We were all exhausted but we were all making great money. Jay Mohr told us about this, but I don't think any of us believed it until it started happening. You're literally making in a week what you used to be lucky to make in a month. It was crazy!

I went from being a twelve-hundred to two-thousand dollar a week club act to bringing in three, five, ten-thousand dollars a week, depending on the club. And then on top of that, there was payment from the TV show and residuals from the repeats of the summer show. So, money was just flowin' in. And my season—season two—was winning all of that fifty-thousand dollar bonus money every week that we got to divide. In the third season, they did tell us that the final prize was two-hundred-fifty-thousand dollars. We did the deal, we put up with all the stresses, it came down to the final four. I knew I had a set that was going to kill. We performed, I killed, and the next day they called us and said, "The series has been cancelled. There'll be no final episode." I laughed. This is the business. This is Hollywood. Suits have no souls. They don't care about people. They just do what they do. This is network suits I'm talking about. Our show's producers were generally pretty cool. But, hell, I won the show. I was like, "I still get the money, right?" One of the nice things about winning all this money is I now have a "Jay Leno Starter Set" of four bikes. But it still annoys me when people say to me that I should've won. "I did win! You just don't know it." It's not a big thing, but an annoyance. I missed out on getting to do all of the interviews after the big finale aired, since it never aired.

All the stuff, the money, the toys, cars, motorcycles, whatever; it's all a by-product of the work. It's still all about the work to me. I feel as a result of this exposure and winning this show, now people expect more. I can't coast! I've got to come up with new stuff that's better than what you've been seeing. I'm still shootin' for Chris Rock and Dave Chappelle. Those are the top two guys and that's where I want to be. Believe me, it's comical how much money I make now and to compare it to what I was making. I'm happy, I'm comfortable, I'm taken care of. I have great people working with me: agent and business manager who handle all that stuff. I'm lucky to have those people around me that I trust and who are good and who I believe have my best interest at heart and have a good track record.

What impact has performing had on your personal life?

I think that great comics really love the comedy more than anything. I think we comics all have this thing inside us that we really want to be loved. Compromises to the personal life are part of the deal. There are definitely sacrifices in the area of personal life. But, my personal life happens to be fantastic in that my family is close. My sixteen-year-old niece refers to me as her "famous uncle." Making her laugh kills me. She has this deep laugh for a little girl. Whenever I make her laugh, I feel great. My little nephew—he's not little, he's twelve—is really cool. He had this thing where I had to send him something to prove to the kids at school that I was his uncle. I sent my backstage passes and stuff so he got schoolyard cred. I have friends that I've known from before I got into comedy and a lot of them enjoy this more than me. To me, it's work. To them, it's: "I know that guy! He's my boy! We grew up together!" In that respect, it's fun.

The dating, relationship thing—I don't know how that works. I've never been any good at it. I'm still not good at it. I don't know what's going to happen there. Groupies are out there, but I'm not that kind of guy. I'm not twenty-five anymore. It is fun—and I'm not saying I'd turn it down, ladies reading the book—but they almost have to hit me on the side of the head with a club because I'm just not looking for that kind of vibe. There are times it is more fun to have dinner with someone on the road than to sleep with them. Conversation and company are really fun.

The acting, I hope to do more of it. Right now, I'm so busy touring live that I can't audition. This is because of my contract with NBC. I'm very limited to what I can do, TV-wise. So my agent and manager and I agree that we may as well use this time to build up my live shows and bookings. If NBC calls, of course I'll go in for them. And once that contract ends, I'll be more open. I don't have the confidence in my acting that I do in my comedy, but then I don't do it as much. It could come with time and getting some work and things like that. I think what *Last Comic Standing* did was show all these people that I'm funny. I'm always cast as the cop or the security guard or "big guy in bar." Now, they say, "Hey, if we let him talk, he's really funny." Maybe I'll get a chance to show that. I never know what my overall goal is with my career. I look at what's next. I think my next goal is another part in a movie—hopefully bigger—and television, I don't know. I don't know if they're going to let me do what I want to do on television. Maybe cable or something like that. I think there's more ahead. I think this is a start, not a finish.

I've done honest work. A lot of people in this business have never done honest work. Consequently, they think that *this* is hard work. They don't understand that there are places where they don't feed you lunch every day, there isn't a table of food waiting for you, and they don't send a car to your house to pick you up. There are people who literally go home tired every day! Overall, I have to say that I love what I do. That's the biggest gift. I get to make a living—and now it's a really good living—and I love what I do. A lot of people don't get that. I understand the beauty of the family thing: the wife and kids and stuff. I don't know if I'll get that or not. Maybe I will. Maybe I won't. But I got this.

Bob Clendenin

Bob Clendenin immigrated to Australia with his parents in the early '70s but returned to the United States to attend Cornell University where he barely earned a BSc in Engineering in 1986. Knowing the world would be safer if he were not designing bridges, Bob went on to Penn State where he received an MFA in Acting. After several years in regional theatre, he came to LA in 1992.

The fish didn't bite immediately and Bob survived with one job teaching an SAT-prep class and another job that involved wearing a hairnet. This went on far too long, but after a series of demeaning auditions for horrible projects, Bob booked a demeaning role in a horrible project and his career was off and running. Since then, he has done over seventy television guest appearances and a dozen studio films. He has done numerous commercials (most memorably a Carfax ad where he was teaching a dog to drive) and has had recurring roles on The Practice; Caroline in the City; Ally McBeal; Popular; That '70s Show; Felicity; Good Morning, Miami; Scrubs; *and* Rodney.

Bob is very proud to have been a co-founder of Circle X Theatre Company. He continues to serve on their Board of Directors. He lives in Burbank with his wife, son, and a pug named Helmut. More information and his complete television and film credits are available at http://us.imdb.com/name/nm0003928.

photo by Erin Fiedler
http://erinfiedler.com

When did you know you wanted to become an actor?

Probably not 'til college. I went to Cornell in the Engineering department because I've always been very analytical. That informs my acting, and sometimes not in a good way. I was loading up on math and science to become an engineer, but something wasn't grabbing me. I fell into just auditioning for a local, almost campus version of, community theatre. But the people were so cool and I really, really enjoyed what I started to learn in the process. There was something about an artistic pursuit that was so antithetical to what I'd been doing as an engineer, that I started to really dig it. So, I auditioned for a couple of plays that were actually legitimate campus productions at the Theatre Cornell and there was a guy there named David Feldshuh who had just taken the artistic directorship of the theatre. He's Tovah Feldshuh's brother and he wrote *Miss Evers' Boys*. He's a phenomenal guy. He's a trauma surgeon and a Pulitzer Prize-nominated playwright. When you're nineteen and you see somebody like that—well, it really lit a fire under me. He directed *A Midsummer Night's Dream* and cast me as one of the mechanicals and it was one of the most glorious experiences.

Plus, the actors knew how to party too. The engineers did not. I tested them both, and the engineers were losing badly. So, I stayed in the Engineering program—I graduated with a Bachelor of Science—but I was getting more and more involved in theatre and spending more and more time at the Theatre department. It was sort of out of deference to my father, who was spending a lot of money on tuition, and to have something that looked like a career when I left college that I stayed in the program. But I never ended up working as an engineer.

I went immediately into a grad program in acting at Penn State. I had no real actor training because my options were so limited in undergrad, in terms of electives, so I was pretty raw when I got there. It was a really good program for me, and it offered an assistantship, so I didn't have to look to my parents to fund what could be a lark. It was a three-year program. I loved it. I think I learned a great deal and left it being a pretty competent stage actor. I did a little regional theatre for about two years, got my Equity card in a god-awful children's show, and then realized that I didn't have it in me to be a gypsy and do the regional theatre thing. As appealing as it was and as much as I liked being in a show, to be scrambling to find a show to enter after this one closes and know you're moving from Kansas City to Milwaukee—that just wasn't appealing to me.

What made you choose Los Angeles?

I knew I had to go to either New York or LA. I didn't really have connections in either place, but I knew that I had no chance at musical theatre because I do no singing and my dancing's not pretty either. I thought, given that, why not go to LA? I knew that musical theatre was a real focus of people that were going to New York. This would've been '90, '91 and there were still a lot of real heavy musicals there. I also had never felt particularly comfortable in New York. There's something claustrophobic about it that some people really love and I don't. I'm tense there. But you see it in LA and you see it in New York: people who are not content living where they're living, regardless of how their careers are going. And that sort of discomfort is going to inform how you pursue your career, how you are in an audition room, how you are on a set. We've all met the really miserable actors who can't understand why they're not getting cast, but I know after talking with them for three minutes that they're bringing an energy into the room that just sucks the life out of people. Living where you don't want to live will contribute to that. So, I chose LA. I had one friend from undergrad that was here and had an apartment so I was able to crash with him a little bit 'til I got on my feet and found a place.

Also, I took a really hard look at what I thought my strengths were, as an actor. I don't think I would've had much longevity in regional theatre. When I compared myself to other actors in my graduate program who I felt were just kick-ass actors, I didn't think I had a shadow of what they had, in terms of approaching a stage role and crafting a character. I felt my strength lay in the fact that I've got a really weird look that's very, very identifiable and I've got pretty good comic timing. A lot of people—in the program and outside—had encouraged me with, "Hey, y'know, you might want to consider TV or film. That might be a better medium for you." I don't have a particularly strong voice, from a stage actor's perspective. I've got a good *character* voice, for TV and film, but it's very different from what you hear when you hear somebody who's been doing the Guthrie for twenty years, where it's like the room vibrates. So, there was a little bit of self-searching there.

What was your first paid gig?

I think it was probably Utah Shakespearean Festival. I'd been paid for regional theatre, doing summer stock stuff while I was still in school, but this was right after I left and there was a company feeling about being at a festival like that. You've got thirty actors who are all right at the end of their programs or fresh out, staying in an apartment complex, rehearsing three shows during the course of the day until you get 'em all up, and there's a feeling that: "Oh, this is a job." You get a paycheck every two weeks. That was the first time I think it dawned on me that maybe this was a career I was starting.

Was your family supportive?

My father passed away about ten years ago and it was when I had just made the move to LA. So, he had no knowledge of what was going to happen for me, TV and film-wise. Even up until that point, my parents had been really supportive and I think really excited. They had come to school and seen some productions. When they realized that I wasn't bad, that I was okay at it, and that other people thought I was okay at it, they couldn't have been more proud. They were still cautious in the sense of not wanting me to be fifty years old and asking if they could front me a couple hundred for rent. But they were never heavy-handed. I just knew they were concerned, and they would've bailed me out if I had been in a jam. And I knew that.

What do you consider your first break?

I don't think I've ever had a *big* break because to me a big break is when you become known as: "The guy from the Budweiser ad." Even with all the TV and film I've done, I don't think that people go, "Oh, that's the guy from..." whatever. Some people know me from *That '70s Show*, some people saw me in *Dude, Where's My Car?* But I don't get, "You're the guy from *that*." I never felt, in those terms, that I've had a big break that launched other jobs.

That said, my first job here got me Taft-Hartleyed and ostensibly helped me get a better agent. I'd done a mass agent mailing when I got here—I wasn't in the union, I didn't have an agent. The only one that nibbled was this agency in Oceanside, California, which is about halfway between here and San Diego. This agent's gig was, she would represent some LA actors as local hires for the San Diego market. Back then, there were a bunch of Stu Segall things like *Silk Stalkings* and the show *Renegade*, which was just starting. She would send her actors from LA down to San Diego, pretending they were local hires, so the producers didn't need to pay per diems or travel or lodging or whatever. She called me pretty quickly after signing me and said, "Would you drive down for this audition for the pilot for *Renegade*?" I did. I got in the car, drove two-and-a-half hours. I was a prison warden that said, "Inmate 456, get up." And he said something smart and I said, "Shut up, Hog. Back in your cell." So, two lines, right? I drove two-and-a-half hours just for the casting director and I did, "Shut up, Hog." He said, "Ooh, that was good! Can you come back tomorrow?" So, I said, "Sure!" I was kind of excited because this was all so new to me. I don't think I'd even auditioned before for TV. So, I drove home, drove back the next day, and this time the room had four people in it. "Shut up, Hog." "Ah, that's great!" I drove home, got the call: "They'd like to hire you. They're willing to Taft-Hartley you into the union. You just need to show up in San Diego, get yourself a hotel, and stay for the one day of shooting." And that was it. I don't think that was a gig that would actually count as something that was going to open doors. It was a crappy show on Channel 13, but that started the ball rolling. I was now a union actor. I kind of had representation. I didn't want to be doing the San Diego thing all the time, but beggars can't be choosers. I stayed with that agent for another year maybe and then moved on to better representation and more jobs.

What are your thoughts about agency mailings?

I tried to be smart about my mailings. All the books I had read said, "Take a little bit of the 'mass' out of the 'mass mailing' thing. Be selective. Don't send to everybody at once. Don't send to William Morris, ICM, or UTA." I got the agency book and pulled out who the more boutique-y agents were, who looked for character people who weren't necessarily gorgeous, that kind of thing. I did a little research and narrowed it down to maybe somewhere between thirty and fifty people. Did all the things right: cover letter, picture, my resumé with all the regional stuff. And I think on my first mailing, nothing bit. It's frustrating when that happens. Making some kind of personal connection will help. If you can get somebody to see the

99-seat show you're doing, your letter is then, "Thank you for coming to..." whatever. Anything that separates you from the pack.

Of course, now people have become so desperate to separate themselves from the pack that you've got people doing arts and crafts on their envelopes. They tack those mailings up on the wall so they can have a laugh in the office. Now, there is an actor I know who did have a gimmick work. He had become so disgusted with the industry that he literally had his boxes packed. He said, "I'm going to take one last shot." He got a friend of his to do his headshot and shoot the back of his head. Blew it up. All it was was hair and ears. Sent it out and I think he got three responses: "This guy is crazy enough to do that, I'm just curious to meet him." Whether any of those panned out into anything, I don't know.

What do you wish someone had told you at the beginning of your career?

There's a lot that I wish I knew before I got out here, in terms of the difference: how different this world was than what I'd been trained for, as a stage actor. We had a really crappy Acting for the Camera class. I would laugh now at some of the misinformation that was given to us. There's nothing that I didn't learn on my own in about two years, but it would've been nice to have a little bit more of a heads up about some of the differences. Everyone was just so quick to tell me how bad the statistics are. So, I knew that. I don't know that there was much else I needed—or particularly wanted—to know.

I could've saved myself some heartache by knowing that you have to let things go. What we learn, as regional theatre actors, is that we're blank slates. We take on these characters, we do this research, we start to develop these characters. Producers in LA are terrified of actors. They don't understand the process of acting and they don't want to be reminded that they're looking at an actor. What they want is to see the real deal. That gives them comfort that, if they hire you, you're not going to be a headache. If you go in there and do your, "I need to take a moment so I can do my warm-up and focus," they're running for the hills! They think, "What if we're on a set and we've got five minutes before we go into Golden Time or a meal penalty and this guy needs to do his warm-up? I need to know that you can produce, on the spot, the same way every time, and then that's one thing that I can check off my list of potential headaches." They don't want to see actors because they don't understand actors. This is one of the things that resonates: View it from the other side. Know that the most important thing to them is that they've got a checklist of a hundred things that they need to accomplish. Don't be the one that's going to be a problem. Once you start thinking of it in those terms, it can start to inform how you enter the audition room, what you present to the people when you walk in, and how you can help them achieve that goal.

When you're a regional theatre performer, you get the role and you work with the director for three to six weeks, making choices: Try it this way, try it that way. But on-camera is absolutely result-oriented. When you go into the audition room, what you're showing them is what you're going to do on set in two weeks. That's part of the thing that leads me to say that it's not ultimately rewarding—or can be a little less rewarding—because that process part is taken out. If you get the role, you show up and do what you did at the audition. At a guest-star level, when you're not a name, there's not room for you to do a whole lot of experimenting. They want to see, in the audition, what you're going to do on the day of the shoot.

What is your favorite thing about being an actor?

Right now, my favorite thing is the lifestyle it affords. I make a lot more money than I deserve and I don't have to work very hard to get it. I wish I could find a nicer way to say it. I spend all my time with my son and it's great. The work itself *can* be rewarding. You end up learning what your bag of tricks is and what you do really well as an actor and what's going to get you jobs. In terms of being artistically fulfilled, there's not quite as much room for that when you're doing what you do well and you're turning that out consistently because that's what they're paying for. I never get bored, but it's with the couple of plays that I've done that I get really exhilarated. That's when you're creating something, you're failing, you're getting back up, and you're succeeding. I don't do as much theatre as I'd like, but it's enough to sort of keep me fresh. My favorite thing about acting overall is the lifestyle. It's a great lifestyle.

I've never stopped realizing how fortunate I am to be in the position that I am and pursuing what I love. To be pursuing this business actively, we are all truly blessed. Diva behavior, I don't grasp. Maybe that comes from those years, starting out, of getting up and working at a factory at 6am every day. No divas there and no divas now, for me.

What is your least favorite thing about being an actor?

Now that I have a family, it's the uncertainty of it—that all of that can be pulled out tomorrow and I may not work for eight months. It's starting to wear on me because I'm now looking at—five, ten years from now—do I really want to be the fifty-year-old guest-star who's working a week in January and two weeks in February and got tuition coming up. Now those questions are what I'm really thinking about.

What would you do if you weren't acting?

I would go to a college and teach kind of what you are doing in your books, Bonnie. I think what I can bring to a university is real, working experience of the film and television world. And I'd love to do it. I don't think I would miss this particularly. We'd have summers off and I could try and shoot a film each summer. I've talked to actors who, if they were not allowed to act, would collapse. I'm not that. I can stop acting. I like carpentry; I love playing with my son. There are a lot of things I can do to feel rewarded. If this were taken away, I would survive just fine. Right now, it's really hard to imagine looking a gift horse in the mouth to leave, because it's going very well.

But, as an actor going into an audition, I can't tell you how much the world changed when I stopped caring too much. I'd been booking enough that I knew, if I didn't get *this* job, I was probably going to get another one in a couple of weeks. It's very arrogant and it didn't always happen that way, but I started to have a real sense of comfort that it was out of my hands. I think there's something that happens to you as an actor—there's a confident energy you give off—that is positive and appealing to them. If you can take it or leave it, there's something that's appealing and professional about that.

I think a lot of actors don't realize what a career-killer desperation is and how easily it reads. You think, "I'll go in and tell 'em I just want to do it and I'll do it for free! I just want to be involved!" That will *kill* it. They will never, ever hire you. I can't tell you how much things change when you make decisions about what you'll no longer do. Five years ago, my manager and I made a decision that we weren't going to take any more co-stars. Just won't do it. And when you start saying no, suddenly it doesn't shut doors. It opens them! They're like, "Oh, he won't do that? Nobody says no to us! Does he have something else going on instead? Let's get him!"

If you're not evolved as a human being—or at least getting close—it shows in your work. That's when desperation starts to creep in, anger and resentment creeps in, cynicism creeps in. If you've got a good network of friends and activities are keeping you busy, you have a happy home life, and you can take or leave this job, you'll find that your booking rate goes through the roof compared to what it was. But there is a fine line between not needing it and having contempt for it. You see a lot of bitter actors here. They've been at it too long or they're angry that they're there—at an audition at this point—in the first place. That's very different than someone who comes in engaged, interested in the project, but projecting an energy of: "And if you don't need me, good luck with it." That's what you want to bring in, if you can.

Do you ever feel like giving up?

No. I do, however, think about my timeline for LA. My wife Erin and I talk about this. What I've come up with is that in a few years, Willem is going to be ready for school. If I don't have a series by that point, then we're going to pull the plug. I think it's pretty cut-and-dried. A series would change everything because it would start to provide at least a little stability. I think it's attainable. I come close every year. But if it doesn't happen, it doesn't happen and we can call it and start figuring out where we're moving in 2008. I'll be in my early forties and it'll all time out well for Willem and school and everything.

How do you choose the material you work on?

I'll do almost anything if the money's right. I just did a show called *Rodney*, a sitcom. It's not a particularly good show. I won't turn down something that's going to pay me top-of-show just because it's bad material. I don't have that luxury yet. I will turn down some commercial stuff—the guy with diarrhea that's making a funny face—it's just not worth it. It's not that I have a problem being "the guy that's got diarrhea," it's just that you've got to have a clever hook to it. There's got to be something that's interesting for me as an actor—or that I think is going to be funny or moving in the final product—to make that worthwhile. If you're going to make me do really demeaning stuff, there's got to be a great creative payoff, even in commercials. I'll still work for free if it's material or a director that I really like.

How do you prepare for a role?

I think a lot of the prep work is done prior to the audition. I try not to get too strung out about anything. If I did it right the first time, I trust that it's going to be there. I try to be as relaxed and centered and content as possible. I guess there was a role in *Philly* and one in *Ally McBeal* where I had to break down on the stand. The crying can be a little bit more anxiety-producing, the night before: "Is everything going to come together?" You have these horrible actor nightmares where they have to shut down for four hours because you can't do what you're supposed to do. But I'm not one of those actors that has to be in an emotional place for something to happen. And that's good and bad. In some ways, it contributes to why I wouldn't consider myself an incredible actor like some of the people I've worked with on stage. I don't go to the place that they go to. But, that also preserves my sanity a lot more. Some actors I know are so messed up. It's a trade-off. You can be such a basket case after a lifetime of going there, emotionally, all the time.

When I go to an audition, I really try to stay focused on why I'm there. A lot of people get carried away with chitchat or networking: "Am I going to say something clever when I go in the audition room?" and having the shtick ready. I've always stayed away from that. I've found it's best if you're prepared, go in, do your job, and say thanks on the way out. They're really not looking to make new friends. People think, maybe, "Oh, if I can charm them or tell a funny story, that'll win them over." They have friends! They want somebody who's going to do the job right!

What do you do when nothing is happening in your career?

I do whatever it takes to get out of my actor-head. I try not to care, which can kind of be hard if the wolf's at the door a little bit. One of the surest things I think that really works when things are really bad is to book a trip somewhere. I'm now four out of six, where I've booked a trip and gotten a job that shoots while I'm supposed to be in Hawaii or something. It's vexing. But maybe it comes down to not wanting it. You go on the audition, but you know it shoots while you're out of town, so you don't want it. You phone it in. And then they're like, "Wow! He brought a really interesting new energy to it."

Who are *your* favorite actors?

The first one that comes to my mind is Christopher Walken. I find he makes some of the most interesting choices. I find him absolutely compelling. For the same reason: Sean Penn. I like Kevin Spacey a lot. John Malkovich is another one, although he can get big sometimes. I did a movie with Dustin Hoffman called *Moonlight Mile* and I just had a couple of scenes with him, but I've always adored him as an actor. What impressed me the most was that he is a genuinely warm and together human being. He liked talking to people on set and finding out what they were about. It was so comfortable working with him. And when you work with somebody at that level and have a "moment" in your work, that's pretty cool.

Matthew Del Negro

Matthew Del Negro has been a professional actor in television, film, theatre, and commercials for a decade. Most notably, he appeared as cousin Brian Cammarata, Tony's financial advisor, on HBO's smash hit The Sopranos. *Aside from the award-winning cast of* The Sopranos, *he has worked with such esteemed veterans as Ethan Hawke, Uma Thurman, Darren Starr, Joe Mantegna, and Chad Lowe among others. In the recent past, he has been seen on stage Off-Broadway opposite Tom Everett Scott and in several national network commercials including the award-winning Miller Lite "bartender" spot.*

Recent television guest spots include The West Wing, Law & Order, Joan of Arcadia, Navy NCIS, Whoopi, MTV's *Damage Control,* Tempting Adam *for* Oxygen, All My Children, *and recurring roles on* The Guiding Light *and* As the World Turns. *Last season, he booked the CBS pilot* Cooking Lessons *directed and produced by legendary filmmaker Ivan Reitman. He recently wrapped shooting on the independent films* Why George *and* The Development *and was an invited actor at the prestigious O'Neill Playwright's Conference. More information is available at http://matthewdelnegro.com.*

photo by Peter Hurley
http://peterhurley.com

When did you know you wanted to become an actor?

It really was at the end of college. My dramatic incident was that I was in Italy for the summer between my sophomore and junior years of college. I was studying over there and my girlfriend at the time was studying over there as well. She basically dumped me while we were in Italy. I started doing a lot of writing. I was trying to figure out what I wanted to do with my life. The summer before, my friend and I had driven cross-country and the whole way, I was thinking, "What do I want to do? What do I want to do? I want to do something that I love." My father is a lawyer, my mom is a teacher, and I've always kind of thought that I would do one of those things. I liked the idea of both of those careers. I always figured I'd become a lawyer and then I realized eventually that I'd just rather play a lawyer on TV.

Was your family supportive?

Oh, yeah. I've got to give a shout-out to my parents! I went to Boston College—expensive school—and then I said I was going to be an actor. It was huge, but they couldn't have been more supportive. The whole time, I think they knew that I wasn't going to screw around if I said I was going to do this. They were very supportive. My dad has been to way too many of the little shows I've done. I know a lot of people's parents who aren't supportive of this life choice. I don't *think* I take it for granted, but I'm sure I do. I feel bad saying, "Don't come to so many performances. I need to grow." I've had to have that conversation with them.

How did you get started as an actor?

I had never done anything in high school or anything beyond the senior class picking me to play a game show host in some senior act. I had always played sports and never had anything to do with the theatre. When I was in Italy, dumped, starting to do some writing in my journal, all of a sudden a lot of stuff came out. I started to think, "Maybe I want to write. Maybe I want to do something artistic or creative." I took a real one-eighty. I had been playing lacrosse at Boston College and, when I was out of my element in Europe, I really thought, "Do I really want to be playing lacrosse anymore?" That was part of my identity at school. It was great and I had a great time doing it, but I started thinking that maybe I wanted to do something else.

When I first got to BC, I was a Psych major because I figured I liked psychology, just learning about people. But when I started taking psych classes, I realized it was just kind of putting labels on things that I felt like I already knew. That wasn't so appealing to me. By default, somehow, I wound up an English major. So, that worked with being in Italy and feeling like I wanted to write. In that journal, I was questioning what I wanted to do and one of the things I listed as a possibility was ACTOR. That was the first trace of it. So, I got back to school and started playing lacrosse again, but was still mulling over whether I wanted to do it or not. Finally, after a lot of thought and a lot of angst, I went to my coach and said, "I think I'm done." It was a big deal. Now it doesn't seem like such a big deal, but it was a huge deal at the time.

That winter, my roommate and I decided we were going to go out for the play. He had never done theatre either. We both auditioned. He ended up getting one of the leads. I didn't even get a callback. A month later, I auditioned for a play and I ended up getting the lead in it, but it was literally a play that was done in a lecture hall for two nights. It was *Hello Out There* by William Saroyan. I played a guy who wakes up in jail and has allegedly raped this woman. I had to say, "Hello out there," about four hundred times. It was a great experience and I loved it. I said, "This is what I'm going to do!"

I started taking acting classes at BC, started taking film classes—I ended up getting a Film Studies minor—and I knew nothing about film. I had seen *Raiders of the Lost Ark* like twenty times—because that's the movie we got when we got our VCR when I was a kid—but I was so behind on any kind of film history. I had a reality check my senior year on Christmas break. I said to my cousin, "What am I doing? I say I'm going to be an actor. I did one play." He gave me great advice. He said, "How old are you?" I said, "I'm twenty-one." He said, "Okay, so if you do this for three years and you get nowhere, then you're twenty-four and you go get a real, nine-to-five job." I was like, "All right. If I do this for three years and I really put my mind to it, I know I'm not going to get *nowhere*." That was the best advice. What that did was give me the right to go ahead. Once I was doing it, there was no way I was going to stop at three years if nothing had happened.

How did you get your first agent?

I stayed at home in Pound Ridge, saved up some money, started taking commercial classes in the City twice a week, taking the train in and out. And eventually I moved into the City. I got into a scene study class which my cousin, Artie Tobia, was in—this is the same cousin that advised me to give it three years. That class, that spring, we ended up doing a showcase of scenes and monologues for industry people in a black box theatre. I had no "in" into this business except for an actor named Pat Collins. He did a youth group in my hometown in high school. He's a great guy and he was kind of my mentor. He said, "I'll introduce you to my commercial agent, but not yet. You gotta do stuff first." He eventually introduced me to his agent at SEM&M and I felt good. They liked me and started sending me out for commercials. My current commercial agent I actually got because I ran into a guy that I went to high school with, randomly, and he was like, "Oh, I know a girl who's an assistant at Paradigm. Does that help?" I was like, "Yeah!" So I sent my stuff in to her, they called me in for a meeting, and the meeting went well. I was freelancing with Paradigm and SEM&M. I went on tons of commercial auditions. I would guess that I went on somewhere in the vicinity of two hundred auditions before I booked a commercial. Then, once I got one, I went bang-bang-bang and got like three in a week or two weeks.

When you're freelancing, you have to make it clear, "Oh, Paradigm called me for that already," or if Paradigm called me for a Miller Lite, I'd have to say, "Oh, SEM&M already cleared me for that, so go through them for that." I really liked both of them and eventually I had to make a decision on *one* and I decided Paradigm "got me" more. I'm still with Paradigm commercially. I've always tried to get with them across-the-board. They've got a great legit department. The closest it got was, they looked at my reel, they all loved it, but this one person didn't like it, so they've never wanted to run with me, on legit.

What was your first paid gig?

That was *way* down the road. My first paid gig would've been a commercial for Bugles Corn Snacks. I had no SAG card, but I had been on tons of auditions and they had always said, "If you get the commercial, you'll get your SAG card." So I did it, and that's how I got my SAG card. It was a commercial with Mark Martin, NASCAR driver, and I was dressed up in the whole getup. I was supposed to be in his pit crew and I hand off this snack and it was like slow-motion. C'mon, a monkey could've done it! Right after that, I got CVS Pharmacy, which was a nice commercial where I was doing all the talking as a young father, going to get diapers. It was shot up in Boston. It was so nice to all of a sudden be flown up to Boston, put up in a nice hotel, all that. Then I had a Head & Shoulders.

I was doing black box theatre all throughout that. I was doing theatre at the Terry Schreiber Studio, which is where I studied. I did a great play there, *Loose Ends*. I love that play. I got to meet Michael Weller in the rehearsal process. That was great. I've done a lot of terrible stuff too, of course. I did a few student films and a couple of them, they actually finished the films and I had clips for my reel.

My first paid network TV job was *The $treet* with Tom Everett Scott. At the time, I was with a smaller agency and I would never get the whole script. I would never know what I was going in for. And I went into see Jen McNamara and Cami Hickman, thinking I was going in for an independent film, since I only had this one scene. I had no nerves. It was a party scene. I did the audition and the agent called and said, "Oh, you got *The $treet*." I was like, "Oh, cool," with no idea what it was. They said, "It's a TV show. You're going to have a read-thru in Jersey City. Meet the van on the Upper West Side, Fifty-sixth and Broadway." And I said, "Okay." I see two vans, I get in a van, there's a couple of other actors in the van, I don't recognize any of them, but everybody seems to know what's going on. Not me. All of a sudden, I see—crossing the street—Adam Goldberg and I'm like, "I know that dude." I see Tom and I'm like, "I know him, too." They're getting in the other van and now I'm trying to play it cool. Everybody in the van is from LA and they're all talking and I have no fucking clue what is going on. We go to some conference room and Darren Star is there. I don't really know who Darren Star is except that, at the time, my agent had told me he did *Beverly Hills, 90210*, which I have to say I'd never watched. So, we do a table read and I still don't really know what we're doing. They say it's a pilot. I don't know if I really knew exactly what a pilot was. But it was a cool job.

That was my first TV gig and that was way into my career, really. I
had been doing this for a while. That was after three years of being
in the City.

What do you consider your first break?

I don't think there is *the* break. I think there's *a* break. The
movie *The North End* was a huge break for me. I got it through *Back
Stage*. It was nonunion when I went in for it. I was essentially playing
the alter-ego of the director—Frank Ciota—and his brother Joseph
was the writer. I was kind of playing them. We hit it off. It was a
love triangle between my character, my roommate, and a girl. It was
done in the North End of Boston and they couldn't find anybody to
play my roommate. One of my friends, Mark Hartmann, who was
in that first scene study class with me, told me he had gone in for it.
He told me he had a good audition but that he hadn't heard. I called
the director and said, "Look, my friend Mark came in for you." He
was like, "Yeah, yeah, yeah. We remember him. Yeah. He was good."
I said, "You should cast him. I know him already, we're going to have
the relationship." And they needed a guy who was going to be big
enough to be a beefy football player. I was playing an ex-quarterback
who was now a documentary filmmaker and he was playing like an
ex-lineman who was an investment banker now. They cast him. So,
we got to go up to Boston together and we had a blast. We drove
up there.

Frank had been a PA on *Casino* and had gotten the script
to Frank Vincent who was in *Raging Bull* and *Goodfellas* and all of
Scorsese's movies. He got him the script and he ended up signing
on to be the don of North End, who takes me under his wing. He got
his friend Tony Darrow, who was in all the Woody Allen movies, to
sign on. Now the movie became a SAG Low Budget film. We did the
movie, I was the lead in it, it was great. We shot two weeks of it, they
put a trailer together to raise money, then we went up and shot the
rest of it for a month. It was a great experience. It went to all of these
festivals, so Mark and I drove up to Montreal for the Montreal Film
Festival. We went to the Boston Film Festival. It ended up playing in a

Boston theatre in Revere and it was on for seven weeks and sold out. It was great. We kind of got exposure. They had us signing posters for this line of people. I was just laughing because I was thinking, "Little do they know, they could come into Turtle Bay tomorrow and make me pour 'em a pint of Guinness." It was just very funny. I realized the bullshit of all that celebrity stuff.

What are your thoughts about agency mailings?

I did a mailing to like two hundred people in the beginning. I was very lucky. I had good shots. I had heard about doing mailings from being in a class. In a class, you're in with people who are all in the same boat as you. I actually teach a class now and I always tell people: "Get into class! You guys get so much information from each other. You gotta eat, sleep, and drink this stuff." So, I did a mailing after I went through a big process choosing a photographer. I had wasted money on my first headshots in Boston, thinking I didn't have work to do to find out what good headshots look like. So, this time I had great headshots and out of two hundred pictures going out, I got like seven responses, which is really good—and I didn't have very much on my resumé.

How do you choose the material you work on?

I don't turn down a lot of work. I'm not really in the position to be turning down a lot of work. But there are some things that I'm like, "No." There's a sense of empowerment in realizing, "I don't have to do this. I can choose what I do. It's my career." I've turned down things like offers to do something at the Long Wharf in order to come out to LA for pilot season. I struggled with it, but I wanted to make a little headway in the TV world. I'm glad that I did. I ended up getting a pilot.

What was it like going to LA for pilot season?

The first year, my wife and I sublet our apartment to somebody—we were only renting in New York at the time—and we sublet an apartment in West LA. We probably overstayed a little bit. We spent a lot of money. It was a tough year. I didn't book anything. I thought I was close to a lot of stuff. I was coming off *The Sopranos*, my agents and manager wanted me to be out here, I had tons of auditions, tons of meetings. I just didn't book anything. It was tough. The second year, I came out here and stayed with a friend of mine from BC. He's a "suit" in the industry. He's my friend, but he just so happens to be in the business. He has been nice enough to let me stay at his place in the extra bedroom. I stayed with him my third pilot season too. Now, I'm toying with the idea of moving out here.

What made you choose New York?

The two major things for me that were dilemmas in this career have been: "Do I go to grad school?" and "Do I go to LA?" I chose not to go to grad school because I started getting jobs and I was learning and in class anyway. I'm jealous of people who've been able to go to conservatory and kind of be in a bubble for three years, just really delving into plays. On the other hand, there's something to be said for going out there and scrapping. That's the path that I chose.

The LA thing, I always have my little catchphrase: "I'm going to make a name for myself in New York and if something brings me to LA, I'll go." That's kind of happening. I'm not a name, but I feel like in New York, I did some things. The biggest thing that I did that was high exposure was *The Sopranos*. It was a nice enough gig that people recognized it and after that, my agent said, "You've got to go out to LA." Meanwhile, I own a piece of a place in the Village called New Gate Bar and Grill that I have to plug. It's a great bar atmosphere with pub food and an outdoor deck at 535 LaGuardia, just north of Bleecker.

What was it like going to producers on *The Sopranos*?

I had been to Georgianne Walken for tiny roles about four other times on *The Sopranos* and I never got anything. But I knew this was my role. I knew I was going to book it. Before I went to producers, she brought me in to work with me on it. She really pulled for me. She was awesome. I went in for producers, I felt good, and then I heard back that I was the number one choice but that they needed to see a couple more people they hadn't seen yet. As soon as they said that, I started thinking, "I'm never going to get this!" I had to go *back* in to producers again. I looked on the sign-in sheet and the two other guys there were with like William Morris and some other big agency. I thought, "They're bringing in the big guns now." I remember sitting there before going in, really stressed. David Chase came by, smacked me on the shoulder, and was like, "Cheer up!" I went in, I felt good in the audition, I left it on the floor, and thought, "I did my stuff. It's either going to happen or it's not."

I left, went into a deli, had an egg sandwich, was reading the paper, my phone wasn't working inside, so I came out and had a voicemail. I was going to get my wife Deirdre a Christmas gift and I got the voicemail as I was walking down the street: "Hey, Matt. It's Georgianne Walken. Just want to thank you for coming in and to let you know..." and I was like, "Fuck!" She had such a down voice. And then she said, "You got the part, kiddo! Congratulations!" I was dancing on the street! I went into Barneys to get a perfume for Deirdre. There was like a little one and a big one and I said, "Y'know, I'll take the big one! I'm doing *The Sopranos*!" I had to go that afternoon for a table read on the episode, so all of a sudden, I'm sitting there with the entire cast, reading, and it was really frickin' cool. I got Georgianne flowers, brought 'em by the office. And it was a great job. They treated me like one of the group. They were very, very respectful. And it was a break, for sure. I'm in for much different projects now than I was before then.

Do you ever feel like giving up?

I don't think I've ever seriously thought about giving up. I remember the first time I ever had any real concern. It was my twenty-eighth birthday. I have a lot of friends—and my brother and his friends—that are all in the finance world and they all do very well. I'm "the actor guy" out of the group. Most of my friends that I hang out with are not actors, although I do have my actor friends. I was bartending at Turtle Bay and things just weren't clicking. People care about the things they can tell their friends about. I did some really good plays that a handful of people saw. But people don't care about that. I would have friends come in while I was bartending and say, "Dude, this is my friend who's on the Head & Shoulders commercial." I'm pouring my buddies a beer and going, "What am I doing? I'm twenty-eight years old. Am I really making any headway or am I just kidding myself?" That was the first time I checked that, but it never really lasted.

Now, during the commercial strike, I got certified to be a real estate salesperson in a five-day crash course. I've never used it, but that was a strike-related choice. I'm always open to other ideas about how I can be a businessman about this career. I realize that, if you don't think that way, there's the danger that you'll get cynical about this business. If you can do things that bring in income that can kind of keep you afloat and a little more steady while doing this crazy up and down thing, you keep your positive attitude. You don't get bitter. Having friends outside the business also helps with that. It's a crazy business and it's a shitty business, but if you get back to why you got into it in the first place, you can keep from growing bitter. If you're not enjoying it anymore, don't do it. There's hundreds of things you could do that are probably easier, so really enjoy it if you're going to do it.

What impact has acting had on your personal life?

I think the biggest challenge is financial. It's just so up and down that you really have got to figure a way to make everything happen financially. It's a career that never stops. You're never really on vacation from being an actor, I don't think. Romantic scenes are definitely a challenge because this is what we do, in this job. My wife Deirdre is not in the business, so it's tough. We both just have to be open about what's going on. That's the best way to deal with it, I think. When I did *The Sopranos*, I had a scene where I had to do a shot of tequila and lick salt off of a stripper's breast. I told Deirdre all about it and I warned her. We were engaged at this point. We watched the show together. It got to that scene and she said, "Oh. That's it? Oh. That wasn't that bad at all." I'm thinking I'm totally in the clear. She was working—in ad sales at the time—in an office and guys in the office were talking about it the next day. They were all saying, "How could you let him do that? Do you know how many takes he probably had to do?" She told me this and I said, "Are you kidding me? These guys screwed me!" So, I told her that we did it in one take and actually it was my tongue double.

What advice would you give to an actor starting out?

Do your thing. Prepare. Have faith—whatever you want to call it. It's going to happen or it's not going to happen. You really can't control it, so don't bother trying. Embrace the chaos and try to enjoy it.

Bonnie Dennison

Bonnie Dennison, age sixteen, was born and raised in New York City. She attends private school there full-time. In school, Bonnie studies both French and Spanish and loves to play volleyball; her team enjoyed an undefeated season this year. Bonnie also studies dance and yoga and attributes her love of sports and movement to her older sister Sally, who attends college in Pennsylvania.

Bonnie first became interested in acting at age nine when the PBS show Reading Rainbow *visited her fourth-grade class to select children to review books for their young viewers. She thoroughly enjoyed everything about the experience and knew she wanted to do more.*

Although Bonnie began acting as a lark, it quickly became a passion and she began studying acting on weekends, both privately and in group classes. She soon booked Sidney Lumet's 100 Centre Street, The Education of Max Bickford, Law & Order, *and* Law & Order: SVU. *Since there aren't many New York-based shows, when the call came for a recurring role as Emily Yokas on NBC's* Third Watch, *it seemed too good to be true (and Bonnie felt she had blown the audition. Bonnie has since learned that reading the reactions of casting directors isn't her strongest talent). She joined the cast and has been with the show for three years. Most recently, Bonnie performed Off-Broadway in a T. Schreiber Studio production of* Hurlyburly.

Although there is no question that Third Watch *is the biggest thing that has happened in her career, Bonnie will always recall being on* Saturday Night Live *(even though her lines with Jimmy Fallon were cut ten minutes before show time) as the most exciting. More is available at http://us.imdb.com/name/nm1216253.*

photo by Dave Cross
http://davecrossphotography.com

When did you know you wanted to become an actor?

I was actually eight and the PBS show *Reading Rainbow* came to my school. I auditioned for that because my principal just thought I was a chatty kid and that I'd like to do something like that. She was right. I just remember in the audition—I just kept talking, I wouldn't stop talking. Even other people's questions—I'd answer them. I got that and it was so thrilling, going to the hair and makeup room and getting to make the lines sound fun and stuff.

I begged my mom to get me a manager for months, I was just nagging her. She had a friend who had a manager so I ended up meeting with the manager. That's how it started. But, I guess maybe in second grade I was in a play. Our class teacher wrote a play about the environment called *Recycle It, Renew It*. I was Elizabeth Gimme, the horrible, selfish woman who wore fur and tortoiseshell clips and was just very lavish. I had a great monologue. That was fun, actually. I remember that as my very, very first gig.

What do you consider your first break?

It would probably have to be *100 Centre Street*. That was the first legit thing I booked. It was a cable show—that's since been cancelled—on A&E by Sidney Lumet. Before that, whenever I auditioned for anything legit, or even commercial, it was almost like there was no chance I was going to get it. It was like a one out of a thousand chance. But as soon as you get that one credit, it kind of makes things possible.

100 Centre Street had me in quite a demanding scene, actually. They wanted me to cry and it was for no apparent reason that I could see, from an acting standpoint. The character just burst out into tears. That was beyond what I could do, at that point. Sidney Lumet called me over and said, "Do you think you're going to be able to cry for this?" I said, "I don't know." So, they ended up putting Tiger Balm around my eyes. I wasn't expecting it. They said, "This will tingle a *bit*." Uh, yeah. The tears aren't really from the Tiger Balm—they're from the *pain* of the Tiger Balm! That was definitely stressful. Now, if I'm given time, I can get the tears going. And I've since discovered the Essence of Menthol. Much better! Much less pain, much more effective, no red, unsightly marks.

How did you get your SAG card?

My SAG card came from a stint on *Saturday Night Live*, actually. I was an extra and I had a line, but then they cut it last-minute. It was still a lot of fun.

How do you handle being a working actor while in school?

I'm not homeschooled. I'm in regular school. For a while there, I was contemplating maybe the Professional Children's School. But my school has been great about it. I just tell them I'm going to keep up my grades and they say, "Okay, fine. Miss as much school as you need to." As long as I'm keeping up my grades, they don't seem to have a problem with it. Right now, it's exam time, and I'm working tomorrow. I've got math and history exams Friday and I just got news that I have a play audition tomorrow, after I'm working. So, it's a lot of emailing teachers and buying them cookies at Christmas for being so helpful. It's just so strange because there will be two weeks where I will be attending school every day, have nothing to do on weekends, be bored out of my mind, and then all of a sudden things will speed up. It's never interspersed nicely and calmly.

In my school, I'm the only actor. I'm the one exception, for them, for this scheduling thing. But being the only actor in school provides a certain amount of stress. Today, all the girls want to be actors or they want to be in the limelight somehow. There's a lot of jealousy. And then there are a lot of people who will come up to me and all they'll talk about is acting because they are interested in getting into the business. It's hard in that respect. But I have a handful of close friends that I know aren't really interested in that aspect of my life. The hardest part is just getting catty comments now and then and having to understand that it's not anything to do with what they really feel about me.

Is your family supportive?

My mom is wonderful. She does everything. She is my personal manager and partner in crime when it comes to this. My manager has a lot of other clients, so she can't devote all her time to me. Mom can. That's the thing about being a child actor: You have to have a supportive guardian with you. I remember there was a time when I wasn't really booking and after every single audition, Mom would say, "Y'know, this has been fun and you've had a lot of really interesting experiences. Whenever you want to quit, it's fine." I would just say, "No. I want to keep at it." It's a lark, really. We're in New York, we're right here, there's so many people that commute from Pennsylvania for a little voiceover audition. We never understood that. At that stage, when you're going on so many auditions with very little to show for it, it can get pretty discouraging.

How do you handle rejection?

On TV, it's portrayed as though you go on the audition and they tell you right there and then if you've booked it or if you haven't. It's not so much like that. You go on the audition, and if you don't hear about it for a month, you assume you haven't gotten it. So, it's kind of like a distilled rejection. It's quite the opposite of direct rejection. It's not as horrible as they make it out to seem. I can never tell what casting directors think of me. It's hard, of course—especially when you do get attached to a role or you get particularly excited about something—but it's the whole mentality of, "There will be more," that helps. You really have to believe in fate to be in this business. You have to believe that some of these jobs weren't meant to be; you weren't supposed to have a role for whatever reason. Like maybe you were meant to do something else and you wouldn't be available for that if you were doing the other job. I can't say that I've never had a jealous thought towards someone that's gotten a role that I wanted. Of course, jealousy arises, but you just have to keep perspective because it happens so often that you wouldn't be able to stay in the business if you walked around jealous and angry all the time.

How will you choose between New York and Los Angeles?

While I'm in New York, I would love to do stage work. I did my first theatre last spring, actually: a production of *Hurlyburly*. That was so much fun. I enjoyed that a lot. I would love to continue that as long as I am in New York, since this is the center of stage. I've never been out to LA. I've done pilot season from New York, putting stuff on tape, but that's not quite the same as going out, of course. I would love to go out to LA, once *Third Watch* is over. I wouldn't know how much I'd want to head in the direction of television. I think I'd be leaning more towards film or theatre. Television is fun, but I feel like I've tried it and I want to try everything else.

I recently did a commercial for Differin acne gel. I like commercials with a lot of copy—a lot of script—to do. It's fun for me. Surprisingly, it takes a lot of energy, but commercials are fun.

Obviously, it's not acting, per se, but it exercises creativity. It's more intense than people think it would be, at a commercial shoot. It's a lot of takes packed into one day and you have to do every line ten different ways. It's fun to see this commercial on TV because it's probably the most widely-distributed that I've done. For a while at school, everyone was coming up to me saying, "Oh, I saw you on TV! You're in this acne commercial!" It's hard because everyone thinks they're the only one who has seen it. So, coming up with things to say is tough: "Oh, did you? Great." And being known as "the zit girl" gets old after a while. There is a downside to it being a very, very public ad. At least, if someone misses an episode of *Third Watch* where I didn't like the way my hair looked, they probably won't see it again.

How do you handle being recognized?

The first time I was recognized, I was on the Second Avenue bus and a person right across from me was staring at me and said, "Oh, aren't you the girl from *Third Watch*?" I said, "Oh, yeah! I am." That was the first time, so it was really fun. And then the person next to him said, "You are? Oh, I love you. I love the actress who plays your mom!" And then the person next to her chimed in and soon it was like the whole bus was telling me about their love for the show. It was kind of intense. I got off at my stop and it was kind of dizzy-making. It's still fun, but I don't get it. I don't understand why people are giving me funny looks. That's mostly what I get: people who can't place me. We live right near a police academy and the show is quite popular among law enforcement. It's always funny, walking past there. Heads turn. Actually, the building complex I live in has a lot of kids who watch the show. One time these little public school boys were playing basketball and I walked past the court and heard, "Emily! Emily!" They all ran up to the gate. It was a little scary but it's fun.

What is dating like when you're on a network show?

It's not very productive. The thing is, I don't spend a lot of time in school. So, there are social drawbacks. I can't really devote as much time to dating as some of my peers would. But acting has kind of helped me in that way; I don't obsess that much about school and about social stuff, because I kind of have perspective that there is a life outside of high school. It's really easy to get absorbed in that. I see it in my friends a lot: being obsessed with one guy and getting kind of boy-crazy. It can't really happen to me because I don't spend that much time at school and I just realize, "Yeah, but I have an audition tomorrow," so there's a different perspective. High school can be very consuming.

What do you do when you're not acting?

I'm always on the volleyball team, which I somehow manage and I never know quite how, but I make it through every season. I do yoga. I had to give up a lot of my extracurricular activities, but I like to read. I like all of the subjects in school pretty much. I got a lot of that in before things really picked up in the business. I took dance class for a bunch of years and I took singing class before I got too busy to do anything beyond that. I feel like I explored different areas. It's kind of ridiculous to say, at the age of sixteen, that I've kind of found my calling, but I found something that I really enjoy and I feel like I've looked into other areas as well.

How do you prepare for a role?

I'm not sure what method I use—maybe you can tell me—but what I do depends on what kind of role it is. If it's for a Disney-esque movie, then I'll usually read through it and try and make the lines as interesting as I can. I usually focus on how I'm reading the lines and maybe the superficial emotion of the scene, because I just know from experience that I'm not going to take time to form a character for that sort of thing. That's not really what they're looking for. But if it is a more meaty role like in a play or an independent film, I usually start by looking at the basics. I start writing down differences between the character and me, physically and emotionally. Then I look at what kind of food they would eat: junk food or healthy food. What kind of music would they listen to? I do this just to get a basic view of the character. Then from there, I write down facts about them: what their parents are like, what they're like in school, what kind of boys they like, stuff like that. A lot of it is written, at first. And then, from there, it's mostly intuition. I learned that from my terrific acting coach. He has a teen acting class and I've taken private classes with him too. His name is Peter Miner. I take his teen class at the T. Schreiber Studio. It's a great acting fix every Saturday.

What is your favorite thing about being an actor?

The acting. It's the actual performing. I think that's what I really like about the theatre. It's none of the technical stuff. You don't have to pause for lighting. There's no cutting because the camera went wrong or you forgot your line. You're out there and it's pure performance and you're purely in the character. That's when I feel like you can really allow it to be intuition. You can't think. You have to just be there. And just the rush of totally forgetting who you are—that's why I keep doing it.

What is your least favorite thing about being an actor?

Probably the stupid Disney-esque movies that I have to audition for. Those take the fun out of it a lot of the times. It's the auditions I'm not inspired by. And I don't book those. I don't know if I could if I wanted to. It's hard and I know I have to put forth a decent performance just because I'm meeting a certain casting director who might be doing something of substance later. So, I know I can't totally slack off and do nothing, but it's hard for me to get going enough to make these horribly-written lines sound like something I care about. It's really difficult for me. With those roles, I kind of like to always go back to reality. I look at the lines and look at the scene and say, "Well, they're saying that this is really happening. What if this were really happening to me?" As far-fetched as some of them might be—they're saying that my dad is turning into a dog or something—I just try to put it back into reality, but I'm really not good at that stuff. Still, that's when I leave it up to intuition. And that's when some of the best stuff happens, when you relax and say, "Y'know what? You've been at this for many years. You can probably pull it off." That's what I do once I get into the audition and I'm usually happy with the way I read it once I'm actually in there.

Who is *your* favorite actor?

Right now, I really like Mark Wahlberg. I just saw him in *I Heart Huckabees* and *Boogie Nights*. I really like him.

How do you choose the material you work on?

I get three kinds of movie scripts. I get the Disney-esque movies, I get movies where I'm supposed to be naked, and I get movies where I'm held hostage. I get onslaughts of those kinds. Of course, I won't do nude scenes. It's so easy to get pigeonholed. Once I'm over eighteen, if the nudity adds to the scene, maybe I'll do it. It's not so much content that I'm worried about. *Hurlyburly* for example—that's a very racy play—and the character is quite provocative. But it's a really good play. It's multi-layered. It has substance. And it's an interesting character that's fun to play. It's not superficial. So, to me, a racy play that's got a lot of cursing and a lot of implied sexual situations is better than a Disney-esque movie that's wholesome. And it's more fun to do! And my whole family is in agreement about that. It's something that we've decided. Adult content is okay. I essentially grew up with adults because that's what the business is comprised of. In a lot of ways, I find myself most comfortable in discussions with adults.

What are some of the ways you stay on the industry radar?

I'm very reluctant to book out. The first year that I started acting, that summer—like all the summers past—we went up to the country house and stayed out there the whole summer through. I booked out that summer and when I came back in the fall, it was just like starting back over again. I had to re-meet all the casting directors and no one felt like they really knew me. It was only two months, but it made everything disappear somehow. In New York, at least, a lot of the casting directors like to go out to their country houses on the weekend too, so on weekends things kind of slow down. I still get a lot of time out there, it's just a lot of commuting now. We don't get to stay out there the whole time. Of course, there are some sacrifices, but it's better to not have to reestablish all of those relationships every fall. I send postcards if I'm going to have a big scene or if I book something new. If I haven't seen an agent for a while, I'll make an appointment just to say hi. I try to keep up with stuff like that.

What advice would you give to an actor starting out?

It's not going to happen overnight. Don't expect that, as much as it seems to be what the case is when people talk about how they made it. There's always work put into it. Also, if you are not able to pursue it for some reason—because you don't have supportive guardians or something like that—just train. Be in school plays. Go to classes. Read about it. Watch good movies. Go see plays. Inform yourself as much as possible, because then once you actually do pursue it, you'll be ready and rarin' to go.

Samantha Droke

A native Texan, Samantha Droke was born on November 8th, 1987, in Deleon. She is the daughter of Lyndon and Synthia Droke. Samantha possessed a love of performing from a very young age. She started out singing and modeling and then, after meeting with manager Kristy Martin, her interests began to move to acting. She truly believed that she was destined for the silver screen. Samantha began modeling and acting in plays and commercials locally. She was discovered by agent Nicole Conner at the tender age of fifteen.

Within two weeks, she landed her first independent feature film Truce *directed by Matthew Marconi, co-starring alongside Buck Taylor (who played Newly in* Gunsmoke*) and Oscar-nominated actor George Kennedy from* Cool Hand Luke*. After wrapping* Truce*, she had then truly caught the bug. Her family packed their bags and moved to LA. This year, at seventeen, Samantha has begun to hit her stride. She landed a national commercial for Cingular Wireless and recently booked a guest-star role on the Hallmark Channel's* Jane Doe: The Wrong Face *(directed by Mark Griffiths) and a starring role in the feature film* Don't Be Scared *(directed and produced by Percy Miller and Lil' Romeo).*

Samantha also performs at the LA Connection Comedy Improv Club. Not only beautiful and intelligent, Samantha has the kind of drive and determination rarely seen in actors her age. More is available at http://us.imdb.com/name/nm1534182.

photo by Synthia Droke

When did you know you wanted to become an actor?

When I first started acting, I was really, really young. My dad has been in bands since he was fifteen. So, I kind of started singing and performing—and I like taking pictures. So, my mom signed me up for some modeling thing. When I went to do modeling, they got me into acting. I was like, "I'll try that out. That's fine." When I went to audition, they gave me a commercial and I loved it. It was really fun. That's how I got into acting. I was ten. From then on, I started taking acting and modeling classes. I kind of moved away from the modeling and really loved acting. I'm from a really small town, Gustine, Texas. It's about two hours from Dallas. My mom would drive me to Dallas every weekend—two hours, back and forth—for classes.

A lady that my mom had met at the classes had stayed in contact with her over the years. She told her about this lady in San Antonio that her daughter was with—she was a manager or agent. I went and saw this lady—her name's Kristy Martin—and interviewed with her. She loved me. She told me that she had this showcase that she does here in LA called "LA 101." It's a showcase where she has maybe ten agents out here come and see her clients—who travel to LA—perform for them. She brought us out here to see these top agencies. We worked with her in Dallas for about three weeks and she worked with us on scenes and monologues. When we came out here, we would perform a commercial and a monologue for the agents. If they liked us, they would bring us in and interview us. I had about three agents interested in me out of the ten. I was fifteen when I did this.

I went with the agent I was real comfortable with and that liked me. While I was here for the showcase—I was here for a week—she sent me out on four things in two days. The day before I was supposed to go back to Texas, she had a producer of an independent film in her office. I came into the office that day and she brought me in to talk to the producer. The next day, they set up a meeting for me to come and audition for him and the director. The scene was a crying scene, so I had to cry. What I'd learned from my acting coaches was to think of things that were sad to me. Well, my grandfather had passed away, so that's what I thought of. I cried and everything. They loved it. They wanted a girl with long hair—I have the long hair. So, I auditioned and the next day we went back to Texas—I didn't think of it. Well, I thought of it maybe a little bit.

Over the years, when I was acting, my parents were wanting to move out here to LA. When I left to go back home, my mom was like, "If you get the movie, we can move back out and if not, we'll go out for pilot season. And then we'll see what goes on from there." We had come out here before for a pilot season. Well, about a month later, my manager had called me and told me that I had booked the movie. I was so excited! It was the first big thing I had ever done. They sent me the script and everything. They told us what was all going to happen, where it was at. It was filmed in Stockton, California. A couple of weeks later, me and my mom came out here and did the movie. That made me SAG-eligible. After the movie was over, we went back home—this was Thanksgiving 2003—and then we moved out here in the new year, 2004.

What was it like going to LA for pilot season?

In my second pilot season, my first audition was for *Judging Amy*. I worked with a coach on it and everything. I went in, I was fixin' to start. I looked down to get my first line and the casting director said, "Wait. Stop." And I said, "What?" And she was like, "Look at me when you're saying it. Don't go down in your paper." I was just going down to get my line! I was going to come up and *then* say it. That kind of threw me. This is my first audition of the pilot season, and I'm kind of nervous. I still went on, I did my best. Then I came out and I just bawled. It was the first time I ever cried after an audition. I was like, "Oh, my gosh!" But then, maybe two weeks later, they asked me to come in again! The casting director loved me! Then I went in for producers—the same thing. I kept going in, going in, going to producers, and then I'm thinking whatever happened in my first audition, now this lady loved me. You kind of learn from that. You can't take anything too seriously.

How do you handle being a working actor while in school?

Ever since I started acting when I was ten, I did acting classes on the weekend, so my friends would always want me to go and do stuff with them and I couldn't. I had to go to Dallas and work on my acting. I was doing sports too, and we'd have tournaments on the weekend and I couldn't make it because of my acting. Then they kind of got like, "You think you're better than us." But it was just scheduling and something that I did. My parents and my sister would tell me, "Oh, they're just jealous." They were just always mean to me.

So, I'm homeschooled now. I've been doing homeschooling for about a year, ever since I got the movie and we moved out here. My mom didn't want me to go to public school in LA. I would love to go to school, just to be around people and have the social life and everything, but I'm getting to graduate earlier. When I have auditions or classes or something, it doesn't interrupt. My mom doesn't have to pick me up from school or anything. It's easier and my mom helps me with my school and everything. You can do work any time you want. I like it better.

Have you seen any part of the movie you did?

I have! Two months ago, we had an ADR for the movie. There was a scene in the movie that you couldn't hear the talking—there might be a plane or traffic or something going by and you miss the vocals—so you go back in and you re-record over the film. You have to get in character again—like you're really there, months later. I got to see little clips of the film then. When I first walked in and I saw myself on the screen, it was a crying scene. I teared up! I was like, "Oh my gosh! I made myself cry!" It was really funny. But I was kind of critiquing myself, like I should've done that a different way or something. But I guess every actor does that.

Are your friends in the industry?

Yeah. All my friends are actors. I hang out with my friends a lot. Mostly, we go out to dinner. One of my friends is on a Disney show right now, so we go sometimes on Tuesdays for the audience taping. We go watch some of our friends on set do their stuff. Or we go to movies, bowling, whatever.

I know a lot of young actors go through this: When you start acting, a lot of your friends are rude to you or mean or think that you think you're better than them. "You're better than me, just because you're an actor!" Just blow that off. There's so much more happening for you than them. They're just mad because they're not getting to do what you're doing. I went through that. All my friends that I know went through it. Don't let it bring you down. Find friends that support who you are and what you're doing. I did that.

Are you the only one in your family who is in the industry?

My older sister is twenty-seven. She already has a family in Texas. My other sister is twenty-three. She's in Texas too. It's hard being away from them, kind of. I stay in touch with them. But it's hard because my older sister is thinking about having a baby. I'm not going to be there all the time, so that's sad. Also, when we did move out here, it was a struggle. When we came to move out here, my parents sold everything in our house. We sold everything we had. All we had was two cars and our clothes. That's all we had. When we first moved out here, we lived in the Holiday Inn, in the suites, for about four or five months. My mom had all these things she could do for work, but she couldn't do them out here, because she wasn't licensed out here. She was a teacher, a technician, but she couldn't do those things here without a license here. And my dad couldn't find anything in construction because he had to have a license. So, we lived here, in the hotel, for like four or five months, and my parents didn't have jobs. It was getting down to the wire. We did not know what we were going to do. Finally we went out and found an apartment, but my dad didn't have a job, so he went back to Texas and worked there so that we could have money. So, me and my mom were just out here, living off of what my dad was making. I had been away from my dad sometimes, when I came out for pilot season or did acting stuff, but he was gone for five or six months, working in Texas. It was really hard. Now my dad is working out here in LA and my mom found some stuff she could do; home business stuff. Now it's working out.

How stressful is it to be the breadwinner at such a young age?

It's really stressful. I felt like I needed to book everything. It was really hard because, at the time, we didn't have any money. We didn't have anything. So everyone was in a bad mood. We were all down. It was just a lot of stress. I felt like it was my fault that everyone was in this position. I felt sad because my parents gave up everything that they had worked hard for. I'm sitting here going, "What am I supposed to do?" Friends helped me. My manager talked some sense into me: "You're here for a reason. People like you. That's why you're here. You're good at what you do. Your parents support you and they believe in you. They know that you can do something and you're going to go somewhere." That helped me. I've learned, when you're in that situation, everything is going to work out for the best. It ends up working out in the end. When we were going through the whole thing of not having money, I was thinking, "I'm not getting anything. What's wrong with me?" I went for maybe about eight months before I booked something. Everyone kept telling me: "When it's right, it's right. You'll get it." You just can't have the thought that you're not going to get something.

What is your favorite thing about being an actor?

Probably just the acting itself. Being another character. Being free to just be someone else and saying the lines. Coming out and seeing people like what you do. When I did this movie, I loved that people cried when I did this scene. I felt so good at what I did. That's what I love about it, making people laugh or cry.

What is your least favorite thing about being an actor?

Probably standing around on set. Usually, I listen to music or I do school stuff. But now, I've learned how to knit. So, I'm knitting! I'm working on a scarf right now.

How do you prepare for a role?

I usually work with my coach. That's all I really have to do. I don't really have to think about it too much, because you can't do that. I work with my coach on theatrical stuff, whenever I have sides. I really like drama. I don't know why. It kind of fits me more. I like doing comedy too, but mostly I like doing drama. I like doing films. I kind of want to do a series. Lately, I've been doing a lot of commercial auditions—I'm getting really good at those.

How do you handle rejection?

What my manager—Kristy Martin, of Calliope—told me is to go into an audition and do your best and then when you get out, just forget about it. That's what I do. There might be some that I really, really, really want and I can't get that out of my head, but there's always the next one. My thing is that everything happens for a reason. If I wasn't meant to get it, there's something better coming along.

Who are *your* favorite actors?

Johnny Depp! Because aside from the fact that he's really hot, he's a really good actor. Julia Roberts is such a good actor and she takes on so many different roles. Just like Johnny Depp. They take on the weirdest characters and it comes out awesomely. In every role Julia Roberts does, she is always herself. Not a lot of actors do that. I like her. I also like Brittany Murphy. She is *really* funny.

Stephon Fuller

Virginia Beach native Stephon Fuller began his acting journey on September 22nd, 1993. Thinking outside the box has been a major factor in helping him move forward in the business. From doing frequent drop-offs of photos and postcards to donating his time as a reader in casting offices, Stephon believes in making his career happen rather than waiting for his career to happen.

In addition to working in New York and LA, Stephon has traveled to Miami, Washington DC, Spain, and Japan for bookings. He has appeared on such shows as Frasier; Good Morning, Miami; ER; The OC; CSI; Friends; *and* Yes, Dear. *Stephon has also appeared in the feature film* The Terminal *and the Robey Theatre Company's production of* For the Love of Freedom: Part III Christophe.

Stephon maintains a journal on his website to share his journey with others at http://stephonfuller.com. He thanks Louise, Avis, and Jeff for their love and support.

photo by John Ganun
http://johnganun.com

When did you know you wanted to become an actor?

Originally, I wanted to get involved in music—not as a musician, but in the management side of the business. Living in Virginia Beach, Virginia, it was just difficult to find people that were really in it—although that has really changed now. It's a bit of a hotspot now. I guess I was a little early for that. A buddy of mine had told me about a teacher there in Virginia Beach. I had kind of procrastinated on the information and I finally, one day, got the courage to call her. She was a bit intimidating. She was a Meisner teacher. I showed up in class three weeks later and I loved it. We were doing the basic repeating, mirror exercises and I just thought it was the coolest thing—a bit confusing, but quite intriguing. We talked about the business and everything and what stuck with me was, "If you have tenacity, you'll make it." The teacher discussed that if you have the get-up-and-go and the staying power, you can do it. I'm like, "Okay, the mirror exercise is a little confusing for me right now, but I *got* tenacity. I've got a trunkload of that! So, I'm golden. I'm good." That was the first night in class. There was no question about whether I felt like I had "it," or "I'm going to give it a year," or anything like that. I still don't set time limits and I still have never questioned it. And that was eleven years ago.

I had a buddy who I met that first night in class. He saw it in me as I saw it in him. He came to me and said, "When are you leaving? On the downlow, y'know?" I said, "I don't know. I'm not going to put any date on it. I'm just going to bust my butt every day and it'll happen when it's supposed to." Eighteen months later, he and I were on the midnight bus, leaving from Virginia Beach to Port Authority. Didn't tell the teacher, because we knew that she would be totally against it. She would think we were not ready—and she would probably be right. But, my thinking is, "What would you tell someone that grew up in Queens? Move to Virginia?" She would also recommend that you have five thousand dollars to move. And she also recommended LA more so than New York. I was neither here nor there with that. I wanted to go to New York because I felt, if I came to LA first, I would probably not go to New York. And I wanted to go to New York not just as an actor but as a person. I'm from the suburbs and I kinda wanted that challenge of going to this place that was absolutely insane and seeing if I could last. I didn't want to run away. I didn't want to leave because I was scared or I got beat up. I wasn't there a tremendous amount of time, but I was there for like four years. That's long enough to get mail there and have an address and have a phone number. I did it.

So she would say you have to have five thousand dollars to make a move. I'd say, for me and my reality, that I would never have five thousand dollars, barring robbing a bank or winning the lottery. And I didn't play the lottery. Well, not that much. So, I had to deal in my reality. She drives a Lexus. I don't. She's got her reality. It's not mine. I had to deal with what my circumstances were. I left and landed in New York with two hundred dollars. I'm at Port Authority with two hundred bucks. I did have a place to stay, but no job or anything. We were at Forty-sixth between Ninth and Tenth in Hell's Kitchen, USA. That was in '95.

I had to find a job. My partner Greg—actually William Gregory Lee—he could go into a restaurant and lie and say he had experience waiting tables. I just couldn't do that. We went everywhere—gyms, restaurants—and just couldn't get anywhere finding a job. We had gone to the Harley Davidson Café, Fifty-sixth and Sixth, and we saw Scott Young, the GM. So, we tell him we're kids from the 'burbs—and he can tell—and we're looking for jobs. He asks if we have experience and we say no. He says, "We really need people with experience." I said, "Can we get applications anyway?" He kind of looked at me and then he said, "Yes." We took the applications, filled 'em out, put down references, and went back the next day. I'm thinking I'm going to get a call. No call. On Friday, we had gone to a TGI Friday's right across from Letterman and ran into some guy named Rocco. He said, "Hey, yo! Don't worry about it. We train all our people anyway. There's another guy named Rocco at another location. Go see him." We were supposed to go see Rocco on Monday. Sunday night, I start to sweat. We had stopped looking. Our life was hanging in the balance based on Rocco! And of course, Rocco dissed us beyond belief: "Hey, I don't know who sent you guys here, but hey, I don't know nothin' about it." I had to laugh. I thought, "I'm going back to Scott. What else am I gonna do?"

I said, "Scott, we'll do anything." He's like, "Oh, I know." I'm like, "No! You *don't* know. We'll do *anything*." He kind of sized me up and looked at me, went downstairs to talk to someone, came back up and said, "Come in tomorrow at four-thirty, wear black." I was just ecstatic. It was busing tables, which was the worst thing ever. We were making three dollars an hour plus tips. Theme restaurant in '95. It was just crazy. I had already made the decision that I was not going home—I had ridden the bus home a couple of times and it was just heartache—until I could fly. I ended up working more and hustling through, and made enough money to fly home for Labor Day. But I rode the bus. The thing was, I *could* fly. I had the choice. I saw all that money and I had to lock my dates in to fly, but to get on the bus, I could just go to Port Authority, buy a ticket, and go. Ride overnight and I'm home. The key was that I created a choice for myself.

Scott came to me and said, "We've been looking at you and we think you'd be a really good server." I had to trust this guy who was paying me three bucks an hour for the first forty hours a week and then dropping me down to server rate—like two thirty-five—after that. No overtime. And he knew I knew the deal. I was sure he was going to keep me on through the summer and then fire me because I made noise, I was a problem, I asked questions. I was skeptical, but respectfully skeptical, let's say. I just didn't trust him. Well, he knew I didn't drink. He knew I'd never drank in my life and that was a concern for him, having me as a server. He said, "We want you to get going on this," so I went and bought the *Mr. Boston Guide* for drinks. I didn't even know that beer was different shades. I didn't know the difference between a Beck's and a Bud Light. It's all the same to me: It's just beer, right? He ended up promoting me early and I actually bused tables, the morning shift. At 4:45, I was a buser. At 5:05, I was a server. That first day I worked as a server, my last table gave me four Mets tickets. I took Greg and gave the other two to some kids. The worst job I've ever had in my life became the best job I've ever had, outside of acting. That job was a complete dream.

How did you get your first manager?

I did workshops. I did mailings. I did drop-offs. And, in New York, I played the freelance game. I was freelancing with a dozen commercial agencies. I was working it like a girl on the corner. I was everywhere. There were some auditions, I'd get five calls. I just worked it to the hilt.

Greg and I had been getting ready to make our transition from Virginia to New York. We started doing mailings. He was mailing mostly to New York. I was mailing mostly to LA. It was kind of a toss-up, what was going to happen. He ended up getting a call from a manager in New York and she wanted him to come up for meetings. He wanted me to go, but I couldn't afford to just go as the cool friend. If I went, I had to go with the attitude that I was going to get seen too. I called that manager and she said, "Yeah, come on up."

So, we went up, we met her, we both did monologues which where completely horrible, and she wanted to sign both of us.

We had found out about her from the Conference of Personal Managers' guide and she seemed like a nice manager. She wanted to sign us, she gave us contracts, we were freaked out. She wanted us to move to New York in two weeks. It took us a bit longer. I'll never forget I was regularly going down to North Carolina to audition for the Fincannons. On the way back—on April 22nd of 1994—I was listening to Sandra Bullock in some interview. I remember her talking about her story. I just remember her saying, "So, then I moved to New York." I answered the radio and said, "I am too." I got home that night, I called Greg: "Dude, it's time." He was feeling the same thing.

As for signing with an agent, Buchwald was on my list from the very beginning. I met with Michael Raymen and they passed on me. And they should have. I was green. I didn't know what I was doing. But I knew that that's who I wanted to be with. Three years later, I ended up signing with Michael Raymen. I still don't think that he knows that I was the same guy. I had dreadlocks when I first met him in New York and when I signed with him, I didn't. And back then I was going by my given name, Bryan Fuller, but when I met with him again, I was Stephon. I had been doing the freelance game in New York and I was ready to lock it down. I didn't want to sign with any of the people I was freelancing with because I didn't want to compete with a hustler like me. So, I started to look at who doesn't freelance: Buchwald. That was the one.

I knew there was a workshop where I could meet Michael. I did that workshop and I said—and I kind of hated doing this—when we all introduced ourselves in the workshop, "Can I tell you what's going on with me in thirty seconds?" It was a really good time with a bit of stuff going on. I had the whole thing kind of rehearsed. He called the next day and I went in for a meeting. I had a mini-bio of what was going on. I had a page of all the casting directors that I had met, had callbacks for, or had booked through. I had six copies of them. I didn't know how many agents I'd be meeting. I went in. There was this oak table. I passed out these handouts like a Fortune-500 executive.

I remember what was supposed to happen when I passed out these handouts: I was supposed to hear, "Hm." And I heard that! It worked. They called within two hours of the meeting and said, "Stephon, we want to work with you. We want to do this." I was so happy.

What made you choose Los Angeles?

Greg and I lived with these two girls that we barely knew—there was a mutual friend that knew we were looking to move to New York—for what was supposed to be six weeks. It ended up being four months. We shared a bed in Hell's Kitchen for four months, which was interesting. We were working with this manager, and I gave her space, but I didn't feel hands-on enough. We were getting auditions, but I didn't hardly ever feel like I was right for the stuff that I was going in for. Greg was coming really close on some big things and he went out to LA. In the beginning of '98, I was in Miami doing a Wendy's commercial when Greg booked a pilot in LA. It got picked up in May and Greg told his agent he was going back to New York to visit an old friend. She asked him if his friend acted and he told her that I did. She asked, "When's he moving to LA? I'll meet with him." That got the wheels turning. A couple weeks later, I did a mailing. I got calls, I flew out, I had meetings, and I got a commercial agent. I had three meetings with theatrical agents and each offered me a second meeting when I actually moved to LA. They didn't seem to really believe I was going to do it. I told them I would be in LA September 1st. No one believed that, including me. Let me tell you, I was in LA July 28th. I got my agents from mailings and I'm still with them six years later.

How do you do make your mailings stand out?

It starts with the outside of the envelope. The party starts there. It's marketing. It'll make you feel something. I could use what everyone's using—the goldenrod colored envelope—or I could use a white one and put graphics on it: "New in town!" "From New York!"

"Just booked!" Whatever. Which one are you going to open? You want to see what's going on with this guy who's new in town and just booked. That envelope is buzzing.

Hopefully that, and the writing of the cover letter—even when I didn't have a lot of stuff going on—makes someone feel like, "Wow, let's give this guy ten minutes and see what he's all about." I think that is really what helped me get in the door in LA. Same thing in New York. I'd walk around and drop off my pictures. I didn't mail anything unless I had to. New York, you can cover the town easier, but it can still be done in LA. I just think there's a lot to be said for being "out there." You never know what you'll run into. But y'know, I do it all. I do the mailings, I do the workshops, I do the drop-offs, I do the postcards, I do all of it. And I don't tie results to any of it. I figure there's no way that I can put this much out in the Universe and not get what I'm after. It'll come back in whatever form.

What is your favorite thing about being an actor?

The playing. They can dress you up and give you a gun but no one really gets hurt. When I was in Spain, I shot an AK-47. It had blanks in it, but after I shot that thing, I felt dangerous. I was freaked out by the power of it. I had never shot a gun! I like the fantasy: being drunk on stage when I've never been drunk, going to these sometimes dark places, doing things that I would never do or have never done in real life. That's most of the joy for me.

I love the business. I don't ever remember not knowing how to do the business-side of this business well. I come from a family business. I'm not close to my dad, but I guess being around that—I worked for my family for fifteen years—I learned a lot. To be honest, from my father, I learned what *not* to do. The challenge of finding out how to do something that seems impossible is exciting. I'll start outside the box and I usually work with opposites. If *this* is the way it's done, I'm going start at the other end and kind of strip it down and see what works. That works so well for me.

I was talking to a guy at a get-together the other night and he was shocked that I would drop off a picture. It took me like twenty minutes to convince this guy. He had asked, "What would you do if you had auditioned for this show, didn't book, but they called you in every time after that—four additional times—straight to producers last season but you haven't been in at all this season?" I said, "Me? I would drop a picture off to them on Monday." He was like, "You mean, just go *over* there?" I said, "Yeah. Go over there," and I said the address, and he was shocked that I knew the addresses of casting people around town. I said, "Yeah, I know. It's kind of sick." He couldn't imagine going over there. Look, there's a lot of reasons why you won't get called in. Usually it's not because they don't think you can do the job. They have an infinite amount of choices and you may not be one of the first five people out of their mouth. But if they see you next week at Ralph's, maybe they'll stop and say, "Got a picture on you? You would be perfect for this thing!"

Now, I don't recommend anything I do, but I make no qualms about doing it. Someone that doesn't draw on the same things that I do—in deciding to try these things—could get themselves in trouble and do what actors aren't supposed to do. I feel like I'm the luckiest guy in the world. It definitely hasn't been easy, but it's been fun. And with all the hustling I do, I always pay the agency commission for the jobs I book on my own. Of course! There's no question. Do they come after me for reimbursement of courier fees when I bomb an audition? No. We're a team.

I remember calling a friend and complaining about a show like *Friends*: "They're in New York. How do they never have any Black people or people of color on *Friends*? How do they do that? Two of the creators did time in New York. They were writing theatre in New York. They know the deal!" Later that day I got an audition. For *Friends*. It was a couple of lines and I ended up booking it. Years later, I saw that episode of *Friends* on-screen inside the Hollywood Video. I got so happy. I thought, "Man, I am in the right business!"

What do you wish someone had told you at the beginning of your career?

Nothing. I made it a point to not ask anyone anything. I know what I know firsthand. Hearsay can be tricky. Learning everything firsthand helped me learn what's the setup at CBS Radford. It helped me know when to walk away without getting the job done. When I went to do my drop-off for *The Terminal*, there was a slot in the door. I didn't get to hand my picture off, like I wanted to. I didn't want to walk in and have someone say, "Did you see the slot in the door, asshole?" So, I learned firsthand that this was a place where I could slip the picture in the slot. Now, I thought, "They're gonna walk on our pictures!" Of course, I wasn't thinking about that when I booked the job and got to work with Tom Hanks and Steven Spielberg.

Who are *your* favorite actors?

Denzel Washington. His work just in *Malcolm X*, *Training Day*, and *Glory* shows you he's a chameleon. I like Kathy Bates. She plays with comedy like it's a drama. She's so serious, but it's always funny with her. It's that twist. Love Robert De Niro. Now, Denzel's Denzel, but watching De Niro's filmography, I just *love* what he does. Joan Allen is another great one. She's just really good at her job.

Angela Goethals

Angela Goethals is humbled to be in the company of the many amazing actors whose insights appear in this book.

A native New Yorker, Angela has appeared on stage in Blur *(at Manhattan Theatre Club)*, The Mandrake Root *(by Lynn Redgrave at The Long Wharf Theatre)*, As You Like It *(directed by Erica Schmidt at Fringe Festival NYC, Public Theatre New Works Festival)*, True History and Real Adventure *(directed by Michael Mayer at the Vineyard Theatre)*, Picnic *(directed by Scott Ellis at the Roundabout Theatre)*, Four Baboons Adoring the Sun *(directed by Sir Peter Hall at Lincoln Center)*, The Good Times are Killing Me *(directed by Mark Brokaw at Second Stage/Minetta Lane Theatre)*, and Approaching Zanzibar *(by Tina Howe at Second Stage Theatre), among others.*

She most recently felt the amazing grace of being directed by James L. Brooks in Spanglish, *has appeared in such films as* Jerry Maguire, Storytelling, Triple Bogey on a Par Five Hole *(directed by Amos Poe), and just finished the creatively inspiring* Behind the Mask *(directed by Scott Glosserman). Favorite television credits include* 24, Six Feet Under, Do Over, The Education of Max Bickford, Phenom, *and the great gift that was the truly magical ensemble of* The Brotherhood of Poland, New Hampshire *(created by David E. Kelley).*

Angela lives in LA and feels blessed to have in her life her new house, her cat, and most of all, her fiancé Russ. Thanks to Bonnie and Blake and best wishes to all who love and dream to act every day. More information is at http://us.imdb.com/name/nm0324462.

photo by Heather Laszlo

When did you know you wanted to become an actor?

I knew once I started doing it, once I'd been around the excitement and the strangeness of it. I was pretty young. I had the great fortune of growing up in New York City and being a part of this very rich theatre culture. My mom worked summers for a small company in the park and my sister and I would go and hang out and watch the women put on their makeup and we would touch all the dresses and look at the wigs. It was kind of magical to see this transformation happen in these people that ten minutes ago were smoking cigarettes and drinking coffee and then suddenly they're like princes and kings. We were just like, "Wow." That was my first exposure and my first kind of intrigue. Once I started doing it myself, I realized it was a very good fit. It was where I wanted to be.

What was your first paid gig?

I was an understudy in a production called *The Widow Claire* in New York City. It was at Circle in the Square downtown. I was nine. My godmother, who is an actress out here now, used to live in New York and took me to the audition as one of many activities we did. She thought, "Why don't we just add this as a possible fun outlet?" I never got to go on stage for that. It was actually a relief because I was so nervous and shy and scared. I loved it, but it was—and sort of still is—a conflict for me. I'm not all that comfortable with it all the time. It sort of freaks me out and can terrify me at times. I was kind of relieved that I never had to actually go up in front of people.

It's a big-time love/hate relationship. You try and get these roles and then suddenly, if you do, it's like, "Oh my God. Can I do this? Are they making a huge mistake?" It feels sort of complicated I guess. I talk a lot about it and I have a lot of great friends who are actors as well and friends who are not actors and family and great people in my life who are either very close to what I do or not close to it at all and therefore have a completely different perspective and different way of expressing themselves. Some people are like, "What's your problem? Just do it!" and some people are like, "Yeah, I totally get what you're talking about," and are very soft and gentle. I guess it's getting different perspectives and talking a lot and sitting with every emotion that comes up and existing in it for a little while that makes it go away.

What made you choose Los Angeles?

I moved out here two and a half years ago. Because I'm from New York City, I had that sort of "LA is evil" kind of bias. LA has been really kind to me and good to me. I've been really blessed and I like it so much more here than I thought I would. But I went to college on the East Coast and I grew up there. I have such deep roots there. After I graduated, for years it was kind of this specter of LA and knowing I probably should just go there and see what it's about, figure it out, and see if I could make a life there that I was comfortable with and happy with. I was sort of afraid but I kind of had this tough girl New York attitude like, "Screw LA. I don't need it. I'm a New Yorker!" My defenses were definitely way up.

My agents at the time—after years of gently suggesting that pilot season might be something to try—were finally like, "All right, look, you really ought to go out and just do it." So, the final push for me was a firm nudge from the professionals. My agents were on both coasts and they wanted me to come out. I booked my ticket, I had no job, and I was going to stay on Dan Bess' couch. He's really the reason I was able to do it. I credit him for that. I always tell him that, but he's very humble about it. Seriously, if not for him, I just don't know. I came out with my suitcases and nothing else except for Daniel every day being like, "It's going to be fine. Don't worry."

What's terrifying is that a week after I got here, my agents dropped me. I was like, "But I just got here!" It was a huge, crushing blow. Not only was it a big rejection but it was cutting the only line to anything potentially grounding out here at all for me. But I knew it was coming. They said they were downsizing. I'd been doing a lot of theatre in New York, not making a lot of money. I was very happy but not necessarily marketable in the way they wanted. Writers and Artists was a bigger agency than I think I really fit at the time. One agent there called and said, "I'm really sorry," and connected with me as a person, but nobody else did, even after I had been with them for three years.

I had managers in New York who were like, "Okay, this has happened and it's really bad. We're going to try to do something and set some things up. It's not the end of the world." Lots of tearful phone calls and panic. Super Dan, again, was with Abby Bluestone at Innovative and called her. He said, "Let's see. Maybe she'll meet with you and if nothing else maybe she'll talk with you." She likes to tell this story too. He called and said, "My friend's in from New York. Will you meet with her?" She said, "Absolutely not. It's pilot season. Absolutely not. I am frantic. No." He was like, "Abby, come on. She's a great friend of mine. She just got dropped by her agent." Abby said,

"No. Dan, I love you, but no." I'm like wandering around the living room while he's talking to her and I'm listening to his side, pacing. I don't know what she's saying or thinking. Then Dan said that it was me. Thankfully—I don't know if this was fate or what—but Abby used to be an agent in New York and she had seen a play that I did when I was twelve years old called *The Good Times Are Killing Me*. And it was her favorite play! So, she was like, "Put her on the phone!" I got on the phone and she said, "I love that play! It's my favorite play. Oh my God! It's my favorite." We're on the phone and I'm crying but trying to not because she's saying all of the right things that are just touching me and making me feel like everything is going to be okay. She met with me the next day and signed me the next week. I'm still with her today. Abby rocks.

Do you still do theatre?

It's definitely not as encouraged here in LA. I actually just had a difficult, tough decision with regard to balancing the *possibility* of getting a TV gig or a movie gig with the promise of some great play that I love and would grow so much doing. I was offered a part in a play that was going to go up in San Francisco. It was an amazing play. But it starts rehearsing in two weeks and it's out of town during pilot season. I said no, but it's not sitting well. Maybe it never will! It's not the first time that I've made a decision like that since I've been here. I don't do as much theatre as I would like but I know that's not why I came here, really. So, that's the only thing that I can say that sort of comforts me: I came out here for a very specific reason and I feel like I have to give it its due and really focus on that.

I think the timeline wasn't so much for me that I was giving *this* amount of time for *this* to happen, as I moved here kind of with one foot still in New York—my cell phone number is still a New York number—and there's still several vestiges of my New York self that I'm clinging to. We just gave up our apartment in Brooklyn this summer. That was one of the things that we were holding on to. For me, the timeline was more about not ever really saying that I was living here and being like, "I'm going to be out here for a year and then we're going to revisit the notion of staying or not and see how we feel," and it went along like that. The timeline was more about checking in with our inner peace with our surroundings and what we were doing. It was more about what was working right here and now.

Everyone's timeline is different. Everyone's story is different. Everyone's patience level and ability to deal is different. If you have a timeline set against the ultimate timeline of the Universe, it's not going to necessarily work out. The Universe is going no matter where you are and where you want to be so it's an internal timeline and checking in with it that makes you strong. I should take that advice more, I think.

What was your first pilot season like?

That first pilot season was very unique in that it was completely different from anything that I'd ever experienced in New York. The volume was so much greater. The constant motion of in and out of waiting rooms and sign-in sheets and the machine of it was something. It is a machine! I would call my mom that first two months I was out here and say that sometimes it seemed hilarious and sometimes it seemed devastating. You know how Barbies have "Eveningwear Barbie?" I felt like that. Today I'm "Slutty Barbie" and now I'm "Girl-Next-Door Barbie" and I would have all these outfits and ideas of these characters that weren't really fleshed out but that could be in keeping with the machine. Get in the car, get out of the car, lock the door, unlock the door, park. Everything was completely strange. Since my mom had been out here with me for a show I worked on when I was a kid—for about eight months—she kind of understood more than had we, as a family, not had that experience. She was the best person to talk to during that first two months out here. She thought it was funny, so I was able to not think it was freaky and intimidating. It was all about perspective that first time. It's so easy to lose it.

I was working at a bakery and at a movie theatre and had a weird schedule and was staying on Daniel's couch and then I moved in with some friends of mine—into their guest room—and I was living out of a suitcase and it was crazy. But it ended up being great because I had that one great chance that ended up getting me onto a pilot. The biggest reward about that was having this whole series of auditions for one thing. Of course, that's another bizarre thing to me, for my first pilot season, to have twelve auditions for one thing. You go and meet this person and this person then come back to meet this person and this person. As if it weren't hard enough, you have to sort of think about consistency in a different way and think about not letting yourself get in your own way the further you progress. Each time I went in at a different level of the process, I didn't freak myself out. I was so proud of myself because I'm very inclined to freak myself out and to sort of question what I do. "What did I do? How did I do it? When I went in that first time I really wanted to do more of this." You're in your head completely then. I was so happy that I didn't do that.

I called Abby after the final read. I was so emotional those two months. I was always crying. I would get in the car, get lost, and cry. I would call Abby and she would compliment me and I would cry. I would talk to my family, I was homesick, and I would cry. It was all kind of brimming up. I called Abby from the parking lot after the test and I was crying, saying, "Abby, I really think that you would've been really proud of me because I really did what I wanted to do in that room and I don't know what's going to happen but I just want you to know that I really thought that it was okay." She was like, "Okay. (Thanks, Daniel. Crazy actress. Thanks for giving me the lunatic from New York.)" Anyway, I got it and it was *Do Over*. It was such a great validation.

I was at an Internet café when I got the call that I got it. I got the call from Abby and Amy at Innovative and Krista LaFrenz, my manager back home. They were all on the phone and I was screaming in this public place. I was so, so happy. And strangely, they were apologetic about it. "It's a really cute show. It's not very challenging. So, we'll understand if you don't want to do it." I was like, "I AM doing this! Dude!" I called everybody. I called my then-boyfriend, Russ Soder. (He's now my fiancé). Called Mom. Called everybody. It was a great moment. It came right at the end of my time here. And I had a great time doing it. I had about a month and a half here of this growing sense of panic that nothing was going to happen and I was wrapping my brain around going back to New York after two months with nothing having happened. It's not that I would have failed, but there's so much that can cut into your self-confidence and your stability as a person here. Everything is riding on what happens during pilot season and that's weird. It's a loss of perspective.

After I got back, I went out to dinner with a girlfriend—Alexa Scott Flaherty—and I was talking about how I was so scared that I was going to come back and nothing was going to have happened. She was like, "What would've happened if that had happened?" I said, "Well, I don't know!" She said, "No, seriously. What would have happened if that had happened?" "I would've come back." "And?" "I would've gone back to Brooklyn and given Russ a hug." She kept on saying, "And? And then what would have happened?" She would do that for me periodically through college too. She did that until I was like, "Holy shit. Nothing would've happened and everything would've been really okay." She still keeps me in check and she's a wonderful actress. We went to Vassar together.

So, I had gone back to New York after we did the pilot and I didn't hear anything for a while and kind of thought, "Well, it's getting later and later and we haven't heard. It's April, May. We're probably not getting picked up." So, I was auditioning again for stuff in New York. I did a great workshop at HB Playwrights. And then at the last possible moment they called: "It got picked up and there's a party tonight," and there's this whirlwind and I'm in New York. So, Russ and I said, "Okay, if there's ever a time to commit to moving out there, we should do it." I had a job and Russ had been wanting to come out. He'd never been out here before and he's this wonderful actor with a great background in theatre and a lot of curiosity and passion about television. So, we did it.

What is it like being in love with a fellow actor?

I think it's so exciting and also just crazy. It's so up and down. When it's up—and really up—it's great. When it's down—and we're both down—it's pretty scary. What I've found is that usually we can kind of seesaw. If one of us is having one of those, "What am I doing? I'm questioning myself in everything," days, the other is like, "You know you're amazing. I feel stable enough to give that to you and maybe not leave as much for myself," and vice-versa. The best-best is when we're both inspired and working or just really feeling confident and good at what we do.

We met doing a play together but we had little or no interaction in the script. We had the very bizarre thing of making out with other people. Every night I was making out with another kid in the play and meanwhile Russ and I had a crush on each other. Every night I was making out with our friend Donovan Patton. Everyone was a really good sport about it, but it was really bizarre. It still continues to be, when I have to see him do that. I'm not going to lie—it's weird. I understand, but it's weird. I think being okay with the jealousy and having a little bit of a sense of humor about it helps. I think the more that it's talked about and communicated, the easier it is. That goes with everything. It's a really complicated thing. The connections you make with the people you're working with are—of necessity—really intense and they happen, usually, very quickly. Suddenly you're in this small world where these people are your closest people for a flash. That's what's expected of you as an actor: to be open to that kind of connection. When you see that, it's one of the most interesting and powerful things about what we do. Seeing the connections that people can make or not make when they deal with each other—to be able to sit back and watch that happen, which is a luxury that we never really have, is this voyeuristic thing where we're suddenly invited into this whole dance of people being with each other. It's a very weird thing! Russ and I still grapple with it. I worked with a wonderful actress who has been working for years. She's been married for 15 years and she said, "I've fallen in love with almost every single one of my co-stars to a degree. Nothing's ever happened. But for however long this created reality lasts, I've been in love."

It's about perspective. It's about not letting this job that we do become all-encompassing and become so hugely who we are that we get lost in it and suddenly that's everything.

What is your favorite thing about being an actor?

I think I've answered that question in the past too quickly. I think it's a shifting answer. It's different things at different times. Right now, my favorite thing about it is being inspired. From the perspective of an outsider, I just saw my friend in a play at South Coast Rep. The thrill of the talent in my life and how, because you do it, you can see it and appreciate it is wonderful. You know how hard it is. So, knowing the courage that it requires is inspiring too, right now. That's my favorite thing about it: enjoying the passion of it, the inspiration, the bravery from watching my friends, reading stuff they've written, being in shows.

Who are *your* favorite actors?

Adrien Brody because of his sort of sad, wise eyes and the fact that he played a role that primarily didn't rely on speaking. It was just silence and things happening in his face. I really responded to that.

Cate Blanchett is just purely, gracefully wonderful. I think that her chameleon thing is quite impressive. I have to confess to having read this somewhere, but I totally agree that you can't often recognize her in the roles that she plays. You really just don't know that it's her. I think that that's quite amazing.

Maggie Gyllenhaal is so young and so amazing and so just sort of full. If things trickle out, she doesn't try to stop them. She's not holding on to anything. The things that are happening in her are just coming out sort of without any kind of filter, necessarily, which makes it really powerful to watch. It's very honest and truthful.

There are a lot of others. I'm really impressed with actors that are around my age now. I feel like there are some great young actors that are navigating their careers very intelligently. I'm very impressed by that. I definitely aspire to that.

What do you wish someone had told you at the beginning of your career?

I now have this theory about relationships—and not specifically romantic ones but all relationships really—and it applies to acting. You constantly have to choose it. The responsibility of that is really just that it's not always going to be easy or make a whole lot of sense. Sometimes you don't feel up to the challenge. Sometimes your ego shrinks to the size of a pea. Sometimes you don't feel safe enough in your own skin to do what you have to do, go where you have to go, or be who you have to be, as an actor. And that plain sucks. Sometimes you don't feel inspired and that's an important aspect of our business to embrace. I find myself constantly saying, "If this is what I choose and I'm mindfully choosing this every day, then I'm going to navigate that." If I wake up one morning and I don't choose it, that's an important moment to listen to. As long as you keep choosing it, everything that comes with that is somehow okay.

James Hong

Born in Minneapolis, James Hong spent his early childhood in Hong Kong, later returning to Minneapolis at the age of ten, starting elementary school without speaking a word of English. James studied Civil Engineering at the University of Minnesota and graduated from the University of Southern California. After graduation, James worked as a road engineer with the County of LA, using his vacation days to pursue acting.

In the early 1950s, James teamed up with Donald Parker and established "Hong and Parker," a stand-up comedy duo. His day job ended when he was cast in his first movie, Soldier of Fortune, *with Clark Gable. Two films soon followed:* Blood Alley *with John Wayne and* Love Is a Many Splendored Thing *with William Holden and Jennifer Jones.*

Active in his pursuit to end discrimination in the entertainment industry, James co-founded the East West Players, the first Asian-American theatre company in LA. Known for his many small roles, James hopes he has laid the groundwork for other Asian Americans to be cast in major roles.

Some of James' best-known film credits include Big Trouble in Little China, Blade Runner, Chinatown, *and the voice of Chi Fu in* Mulan. *James' television credits include* Days of Our Lives, Switch, Marco Polo, The West Wing, The X-Files, *and* Seinfeld, *although to list even a few of his several hundred roles seems insufficient. James coaches actors in LA when not on the set himself. More information is at http://jameshong.com.*

photo courtesy James Hong

When did you know you wanted to become an actor?

I think it's one of those things like most actors have known, ever since they were small, that they wanted to be actors. You don't *know* it, but you do it. You're hamming it up. I guess it was back in Minneapolis, Minnesota, when I was a child. I don't know exactly how old I was, but it was during the Japanese-American war—World War II—or even earlier, when China was in battle with Japan, and my father was the head of a family association. He would take me as a small child and prop me up on a little soapbox or crate and say, "James, make a speech! We need some more money for the war effort." I would say, "Fight the Japanese!" and so forth.

My parents were purely farmers and such from Taison. It's a village not too far from Canton, the big city north of Hong Kong. That's where—during the early days, the first immigration from China to America—at least fifty percent of the people came from, I would venture to say. So, why Minnesota where all the Swedes are, yah? Yah,

I thought I was *Svedish*! Really! When you grow up, you don't know *what* you are. I think the story goes that my father came across the Canadian border in those old days and they went to Chicago, but there were too many Chinese at the time, so they went to Minnesota and said, "We hear you need some laundrymen and some cooks."

Was your family supportive?

By the time acting started to get a little serious for me, I was out here in LA already. I had hid acting from my parents all the time I was going to college because I was majoring in Civil Engineering at the University of Minnesota. They never knew that I took a sideline of entertainment and appeared in the University of Minnesota homecoming show and started doing stand-up comedy.

My mother died without ever really knowing anything about me being in show business at all. When I got on the Charlie Chan series in 1958—I was going to Europe to make that series, *The New Adventures of Charlie Chan*, starring J. Carrol Naish as Charlie—my father said, "Gee! You can make money with this." Then he approved. Prior to that, I think he was of the old-school thinking that being an actor was the last, bottom rung of any profession. His thinking would've been: "Why would you want to give up five years of engineering for the bottom rung?" The reason show business was considered the bottom rung was because it's considered very shameful and disrespectful to show your emotions in public, to display yourself and your expressions. I think my father adapted to American society's sense that this *is* a profession and you can make money at it.

How did you start off with stand-up comedy?

Well, being Chinese in Minnesota, what role could I play on stage? There was no such thing as the movie business or on-camera things for me there. The only thing left was stand-up comedy, but there were hardly any clubs. I was also too busy with civil engineering to really pursue this career. I did, however, appear in a couple of local radio shows. I teamed up with a fellow named Don Parker. He was a mixture of Caucasian and Native American Indian. We called ourselves the Hong and Parker Comedy Team. One summer, in 1953, we decided to come out to California and scout around—maybe knock on a few doors—with our comedy routine.

We started out in San Francisco. My family was going to come and move out to the West Coast. I had just come out for the summer and then I was going to go back to Minnesota and finish my senior year of college. I just wanted to be faithful to my university. The main thing that happened in San Francisco was that a comedy writer saw us in something and asked me to come down and appear on the Groucho Marx show *You Bet Your Life*. The writer pushed us as a team, but Groucho Marx said, "We want that Chinese kid who can do impersonations." I would practice and practice. I would talk like them day and night, all of the famous people of the day. I could do Groucho Marx. So, they put me on the show and Groucho gave me a cigar and I did my best Groucho. Everybody laughed and applauded. Then I did my best Marty Feldman, Jimmy Stewart, James Cagney, all of them! That appearance received the second most fan mail ever for the show.

From that fan mail, I got an offer from the club Forbidden City in San Francisco, where we had just tried out, previous to my appearance on the Groucho Marx show. Charlie Low of the famous Forbidden City said, "I like that Chinese young man—the one who could impersonate all of those people. Tell him that we will book him anytime." I still have that telegram. I didn't take him up on that offer because it was back up in San Francisco and I didn't know what to do about going there. I had transferred my credits from the University of Minnesota to USC and finished my Engineering degree because my parents did want me to graduate and I did obey their wishes. I got my Bachelor of Engineering in Civil Engineering from USC and I worked for the LA County Road Department. After a year and a half, I got so many offers, I had to go to my supervisor Mr. Thompson and say, "Sir, I would like to request a leave of absence." He asked, "What for?" I told him it was show business. He said, "James, sit down.

This is ridiculous. You're giving up education and a civil engineering career. You could be a *good* engineer. Why would you want to throw that away for Hollywood? Believe me, Hollywood is no good for anybody!" He was very obviously old-school. I said, "Well, I have to give it a try, sir. If, after a one year leave of absence, I don't make it, sir, would you please allow me to come back?" He said, "All right, all right, all right. I'll do it, but I don't like it." So he let me go and I never looked back.

I only went back to visit that office once in my lifetime. I was very glad I left. I saw my buddies there with the same calendar, crossing out the dates, counting how many days until sick leave or vacation time. It reminded me of a prison and how they cross out each day they're there. I don't see how I could've lasted as an engineer. James Hong's nature was not meant to be technical. Although, technicality and education has paid off in the sense that, during the slower years of acting, I distributed films for Roger Corman and produced a couple of films. I was able to organize certain things and stay above water. I was schooled to be very disciplined and reasonable and respectful. I never forgot that. That, together with my Chinese upbringing, has kept me above water. And staying above water is a great force of life, surviving through the bad times. I learned from my acting teachers Joe Sargent and Jeff Corey that, if you keep pursuing your goals—not only in acting but I think, in life—you will make it.

How did East West Players get started?

I literally sat Mako down at my little, crummy apartment and said to him, "There is no work here for the Asian Americans. Not enough." The roles we were getting were all the Chinamen being rescued by the White guys—not that we're not still doing that in films, but in those days especially—in all subservient roles. I said, "Mako, we have to do something." So, we got a couple of other people together and started to work. Mako loved the Japanese theatre, so he chose *Rashomon* as the play. He got his father—who was a great, recognized artist—to design the set. His aunt did the costumes. My sister did the artwork for the brochures. Everybody chipped in. We got that group started at a church basement. That was the start of East West Players. We banded together and that was the first Asian-American theatre group of any size to start. Now it's thousands of members and they've got their own theatre and people are doing a great job.

What is the overall impact of having worked on so very many projects?

You can only look at your memory—if you can look at it objectively—and know that the things that stay in your mind become the things you have learned. The things that weren't so important to you—maybe they were important to somebody else—have dropped out of your memory. Whatever you have retained has made you the person and actor you are today. It's intelligence and also a combination of emotions and subconscious. Whatever you have retained will come out in your acting.

I think I learned from Ridley Scott and Roman Polanski that you must explore every little small cell in your brain and emotions and the truth will come out. It's like that costume I wore in *Blade Runner*. It was a stiff coat that they had on me and they ripped it off in the middle of the scene. When I was first called for wardrobe, I tried on this stiff piece of what must've been deer hide. I said, "This is ugly. I can't even move around. Why would Ridley want to choose this?" I learned that when he planned that costume, he had something that was stirring in his mind. When you see it, then you say, "Yes. He explored some little minute cell that blossomed into this costume." It was just the right costume for that Chew character. It was a brilliant costume! But it's that attention to detail that went into every shot, every element of that film.

It has been a privilege to be in a few classics like *Blade Runner* and *Chinatown*. I loved *Big Trouble in Little China*. Each one of those films had some greatness in it. *Chinatown* is one of the most-studied films in colleges. Working with Jack Nicholson and John Huston, how can you *not* learn, unless you're just completely shut off? You can't be too egotistical in this world, and show business sometimes makes you think of yourself only, because you're pushing yourself so hard. You become so egotistic that you only see your career and you forget to listen and observe. That is a trap. You cannot think you're better than anybody else.

Do you feel a sense of cultural responsibility as an actor?

Definitely. When you eat rice every day, there's something else anchored to that life. The porridge your mother fed you was watered-down rice. That's what they feed babies in China instead of milk. Not that I was born in China, but my mother was from there, so that rice porridge was my main thing. That kind of stays with you the rest of your life. We changed the complexion of the business for the Asian Americans in certain ways. I was the president of the Association of Asian Pacific American Artists. We'd advocate for our rights as actors. We met with the Casting Society of America and tried to get casting people to have more equality in casting. We'd try to meet with producers and directors. In a way, we established that routine and it's still being done today, obviously by the wonderful young people with energy that push this issue at SAG and East West Players and all kinds of groups that are advocating for equal opportunity. I like to think that we were the first people to have done it. Certainly, we were the first to mount a protest to the so-called bad image of the Chinese in a film called *Confessions of an Opium Eater* directed by Albert Zugsmith. When I formulated that protest, it was because I looked at that script and said, "We can't do this. We can't even *allow* this." Practically all of the images were bad images of the Chinese. I said, "Somewhere, somehow, this has got to stop. We can't keep on, for generations, doing this. How can I be at peace if this happens?" So, I got together a bunch of people down in Chinatown and we had a meeting. Everybody was very fearful because, in those days, people didn't speak up at all. But, being from Minnesota, I was more liberal-minded than most. I didn't know real prejudice because I grew up playing with Norwegians and Swedes every day. There was prejudice in Hollywood. We couldn't move in certain areas yet. We couldn't buy on Beverly Boulevard, for example. I said, "We have to go see the director!" We called the director, Zugsmith, and he listened to us. He said, "I'm not going to stop making this film because of you. I'm just going to make this film the way I feel like it." And he did, but I know it gave us power to speak up in that way at that time.

I have to say, after all these years of being in the business, the opportunities for the Asian-American actors have not really increased that much. The SAG records show that the number of Asian Americans being hired as actors is really small. The problem is this: When the writers and the producers—even before the directors come on the scene—think of a series, they don't know what to do with an Asian-American character, if they even think of one! If they think of one, they say, "Let's make him a restaurant owner. Let's make him a butler." Of course, things like *Sideways* have shown us that you don't have to be an Asian character in order to be portrayed by an Asian actor! Sandra Oh, in a way, probably has done more for the issue of equality than that protest all those years ago.

I talked to Black actors earlier in my career when they were in the same situation and hardly any of them got recognized. We talked about the lack of opportunities for minorities in the business. Over time, they have freed themselves from that bond and increased their numbers on TV and features like crazy. It's great! For some reason, the Asian Americans are still left behind. I don't exactly know why, other than the Black actors knowing how to assert themselves to climb higher. After fifty-one years, I should see more improvement in our situation. I shouldn't even have to talk about it, but the issue is still there. It may take another twenty-five years to blow over, maybe.

Look at *Better Luck Tomorrow*, which was a feature picked up by MTV Films. Those actors have that film and they still, every day, are confronted with the same situation of not being able to get a lot of roles. There are no roles out there being offered. Why can't they cast them into *any* role in a TV series? They're very appealing, talented actors who proved their talent in that film and yet they still can't get jobs being "just American," only "American Asians."

We have to start from the root. The ones who are creating the projects have to be Asian American for it to start happening more. Certainly the Asian actors Jackie Chan and Jet Li and Chow

Yun-Fat have more-or-less created more work in this industry for the American Asians, but these people were stars in Asia first. I don't know whether they are using their star power to get more Asian Americans hired. It's not the nature of the Asian people—especially the ones that are from Asia—to speak out for themselves or for their own race. We revere our employer as the top dog. That is the respect given in Asia.

Are you ever asked to audition at this point in your career?

The jobs I have gotten recently are mostly through acquaintances and offers. However, I still have to go out for auditions a lot. I can understand a producer and a director—especially in a series, and especially if they're too young to remember my more important works—saying, "Yeah, let's see what James can do." Also, I'm growing older so I imagine they want to see if I can still walk. Walk? I can still break-dance! But I can understand that.

Auditioning can be important, I know. And to audition well, I would definitely encourage everybody to do as many aspects of drama and comedy as possible. In comedy—especially stand-up comedy—you learn how to play the room. That applies to camera too. It's not that much different because the camera is a member of the audience. To know how to, somehow, play to that person—the camera—is very meaningful. I prefer comedy because it gives me more freedom. Drama, of course, I love it also.

How do you prepare for a role?

I think it's almost second nature by now, having done four hundred and fifty roles in my life—possibly the most any actor has ever done. Some of them are very small, one-day jobs, but they are all different characters, different roles. I think every role I've had has been training for future roles. I used all my training from Joe Sargent and Jeff Corey and got into those earliest persecute-the-Chinamen roles using emotional memory. Even bad memories are the well of your talent. As an actor, you draw from that to create. You'll notice, most of the comedy I do has a little sadistic tone to it. I never do any villain without a sense of humor. Lo Pan is evil but what a sense of humor: "Now this really pisses me off to no end!" You are what you are. All those past experiences make you what you are. If you are a good actor, you learn how to draw all that back up and recreate it in the role.

I never accepted a role without putting my best foot forward. That's what you see on TV and in movies. I would like to have had more opportunities to play bigger roles. There will be no awards for such small roles, even so many of them. I take a look at my contemporaries, like Morgan Freeman, who has been given the chance to play big roles in American films. I have a life of only being able to play Asian roles, little roles. I have to wonder: "If I had been given some bigger roles, where would I be?" I've had to stay a "smaller" actor with many, many roles. That will probably be my legacy.

If look to roles I would like to play, I should be the head of a corporation. I should be a very important lawyer. I should be a politician. I should own a high-tech company. I should be a doctor or the head of the hospital on *ER*. These people in everyday situations are Asians, but the roles don't reflect that. Where are they in the portrayal of this society? It's a big quandary in the sense that you don't see actors on screen portraying accurately what it is that most Asian Americans do for a living. Of course, when they start casting like that, the rest of the producers will say, "Why didn't we think of that?" There just needs to be a start and then everyone will join in.

What is your favorite thing about being an actor?

Of course, being in a profession that you love. That's the main thing. I think that every actor loves the profession. Otherwise, they wouldn't go through all the hardships of being an actor—and there's a lot of that. I like that you take your feelings and you paint with your feelings and it's there forever. It stays in the vault and it's your legacy. Whoever you believe in—God or Allah or Buddha—gave you some talent. It has to be given that way. My mother was known as a "sand pan girl." She'd paddle her sand pan and deliver things. How else, from that, comes an offspring that somehow has talent and the ability to express it? I'm very happy that I have a venue to do so. That's the best thing about being an actor.

When I was in Communist China doing *Marco Polo*, some of the actors came to me and they said they could not be an actor because they didn't pass the test. I said, "What test?!?" When they start to go to university or college, they have to take this exam and only so many hundreds or thousands out of these millions of other guys that are applying go on to be in acting school. If you qualify, then you can study acting there. Otherwise, you have to study accounting or something. You don't have the freedom to choose your own occupation. Whereas, in this country, if you want to be an actor, try it!

What advice would you give to an actor starting out?

If I think back to my original drama class that I was a student in, I'd say, if not everyone, at least eighty percent of those students had a chance to make it. They got interviews, they got small roles, they had the opportunity. It depends on their talent and perseverance how far they got. The main thing is: "Are you ready? Did you prepare? Are you serious?" If you're not, then drop out—now—before you waste so much time. Once you get to this town, get yourself a professional teacher and begin to learn—no matter what you learned somewhere else—what acting is *really* about. I believe—if you set your goals high and you keep pursuing it—sooner or later you'll make it.

Ravi Kapoor

Ravi Kapoor trained at the East 15 School of Acting in London. He has worked professionally as an actor since 1990 in both England and America.

His film and television work in England includes the feature film Wild West *(the story of a Pakistani Country-Western band trying to get to Nashville), and various BBC dramas including* Blood and Peaches, Peacock Spring, Flight, *and* In a Land of Plenty. *He has worked with and at various theatre companies in England including the National Studio Theatre, Tara Arts, Tamasha, Theatre Royal, and the Gateway.*

His work in America includes regular roles on Gideon's Crossing *(ABC) and* Crossing Jordan *(NBC). Stage work includes* Rice Boy *(a Taper Too production) and work with the educational theatre company Will & Co.*

Ravi wrote and directed the play Oh Sweet Sita *produced by Tara Arts and performed in both London and Toronto. He also directed the play* Barriers *presented in San Francisco and LA.*

Ravi was also part of the steering committee of the LA South-Asian arts festival ArtWallah during its first three years. He was involved in the film and theatre committees and with the evening show production. He also directed, wrote for and acted in a multi-disciplinary piece House *commissioned for the festival. More is at http://us.imdb.com/name/nm0438500.*

photo by Rod Goodman

When did you know you wanted to become an actor?

I guess I knew when I was probably around thirteen, fourteen years old. I just started doing plays at school. We didn't have a Drama department as such—actually, we did for a year and then it disappeared and we just did a Christmas show. And then I started going to Saturday drama classes after that, back in Liverpool. For me, it felt like it was the only place I fit in. It was the only thing that I felt that I was halfway decent at as well. I was never really very good at sports. I was an average kind of student. It seemed to be the only place I got a bit of kudos and people seemed to like me. I got a kick out of it. I was very introverted as a kid, very shy. It was an incredible way for me to express some of the feelings that were trapped inside of me. At around fifteen or sixteen, I knew I wanted to give it a shot as a career.

Do you turn your accent on and off for acting?

The thing for me has always been, since Drama school, recognizing that I'm going to work more if I can play a great variety of characters—whether that's characters from different places, characters with different rhythms, or sensibilities. That was the thing for me, to try and expand my range as much as I could. I think, in terms of coming out here, I did make an effort to kind of find a very neutral kind of accent in some ways. In a sense, what I have right now is an accent which is very mid-Atlantic. I feel like I've found an organic accent which allows me to jump into places without such a leap. It's not so stark for me and it's not so stark for casting directors or directors when they hear that shift. When I audition, I'll try to go in with the accent I'm going to audition in, usually. Otherwise they start listening for it.

What made you choose Los Angeles?

Personal reasons. My wife was born in England but raised in California. She went back to England for Drama school post-grad and she lived there for six years after that. She didn't want to be there anymore so it was my kind of turn to be somewhere I wasn't sure I wanted to be. I was doing well in England. Things were going good. It was a move to follow my heart. It wasn't about acting, it was about my love. I actually came out here thinking that I wouldn't act. I was thinking I would write. I had just written a play back in England that went really well in London and we took it to Toronto, where it also went really well. So, I suddenly thought I was a writer after one play. It's now taken me six years to write another play. So, I'm an actor who writes occasionally.

I came out here and I was looking at the South-Asian parts. The kinds of jobs South-Asian actors were having to do out here seemed so regressive in terms of where I was coming from in England. It's a bigger community there, they've been there longer, there's a stronger history, and they've taken many years to get to that point in England. I'd seen part of that happen. And I could see that development was still in the early stages here. I didn't want to have to play those roles. I didn't want to have to go backwards. So, I thought I would write.

I started working with a children's educational theatre company here in LA called ArtWallah in which we do forty-five-minute versions of Shakespeare plays and take them around schools. I had done some educational theatre back in London as well and loved it. It's always been something I enjoy doing. That got me back into recognizing that I was an actor and I love to do this. This is what I feel strongest at. Then I did one audition, that was *Gideon's Crossing*. I had been hip-pocketed by an agent and that was the first audition they put me up for. That agent was representing a friend of mine I knew from back in England. I said, "I know you don't know me and you may not feel comfortable in terms of really representing me right now and pushing me, but if you ever see a role which is specifically South-Asian—I recognize what my selling quality is—all I ask is that you put me out for that. You don't have to try and push me for roles which are a little bit more of a stretch." I ended up with that agent for about four years.

What is it like being married to a fellow actor?

There's a real strong recognition of what we go through. There's a deep understanding in terms of what we're trying to achieve, and not just on the career level but in terms of the artistic level, in terms of what satisfies us and makes us happy. We recognize that often that's not a material thing. It's not often a career thing. It's just about needing to do it. There's a real recognition of that need. It's also interesting when one career is going better than the other. There's a great sense of joy for each other, but it's also a reminder of what you want. It's in your face a little bit more, suddenly: "I love you, but what about me?" And since we've had a son this year—and with us both being actors—there's a big issue in terms of our sense of security and the future. We're thinking about a house, but what if we're not working in ten years? That's the hard part: recognizing that there's no constant breadwinner within the household. I think having a child, you just know you're going to pay whatever you need to pay. You're going to do whatever you need to do to give that kid all that you can.

Do you ever feel like giving up?

Yeah. I think it's a constant thought. I often think, "What else would I do?" I've been working recently, so there's a little bit more stability. I wonder, long-term, should I do something at school so that I can teach way farther down the line? In the lean times, I have thought about giving up. I guess, when I came here, I was saying I wasn't going to do it for a while. I think more and more I recognize that, inherently, it is what I do. I am an actor. I don't know if I would ever really give up. I think I would find a way to do it.

Is your acting technique specific to your British training?

What I've found, specifically within the television industry, is that it's gone beyond the whole "working inside-out vs. outside-in" thing. I'm finding that doesn't explain the difference in the acting styles in some ways for me, between the American and the British. I feel there's a minimalism a lot more within the American television acting style. Minimalism doesn't necessarily mean that the actors are working from the inside-out. It just means the physical technique is so much smaller in some ways. I think that there's a generic acting style that seems to exist within American television that a lot of American actors adhere to that is about being minimalistic. What I tend to find with British actors is that often they are not as constrained by the television box. They're bigger in many ways. Often, a lot of them seem to be more expressive.

My thing has always been about: "Fuck the American acting style and go for it and don't be afraid to be theatrical." I find it more interesting when I watch it. I think it's given me a particular stamp. It's a certain form of expressivity which is unique to me. I see that as a difference. I always regarded myself as very "Method" back in England. It was all about living as the character, dreaming as the character, having every experience as the character. Probably getting married and having a kid, I realized that I couldn't work like that anymore. It required such a sacrifice to work like that where I wasn't able to give to other parts of my life. I needed to find a balance. I began to rely more on technique and I learned a way to not be so precious.

How do you prepare for a role?

It's so interesting now, doing a long-term television show, because I'm no longer preparing for a role. I'm in a role right now. Every role demands something different, every part demands a different approach to it. If the role is very emotional, I find I need to develop those character memories and build a bank of experience for the character. If the part is a little more comedic or expressive, I find I need to think more about the rhythm of the character or the piece. It becomes a little more about technique, in some ways. For me, it totally depends on the style of the piece.

What is your favorite thing about being an actor?

When you feel like you do something really well and you get that buzz from doing a great scene or a great theatre piece or just feeling in control of it, feeling like you made something sing. I think you get that less so in television—I think it depends on what you're working on and who you're working with as well. It tends to happen more on stage. But, with *Crossing Jordan*, we all go for it. We try to avoid this minimalism. We really try and play off each other. There are moments when the writing really helps us. I still get that sense of synergy. One of the other things I love about acting is the people. I meet some great, great people. I think the business is just filled with people who are self-realized in many ways, who are sweet, who are intelligent, and just a pleasure to be around and hang out with. All my friends are actors or writers, pretty much.

What do you do when nothing is happening in your career?

I try to write. That's a big thing. That's the part about being a South-Asian actor in particular. I do believe that we need to show the industry how they can use us instead of just always waiting for them to do it for us. We need to lead the way on that. I'm by no means prolific in any way, but when I try to write, it's a mix of something I wish I had a chance to do when I was younger and something I'd like to do now. That's one thing I do in the down times. Last summer, I directed a play. That was something that kept me busy during the hiatus. I like directing. It's such a different sense of satisfaction. I think the actual process of directing isn't quite as enjoyable as the actual process of acting. There's a massive sense of self-achievement when the process is over and you look at what you've achieved. Somebody recently said to me, "It's like running a marathon. You may not enjoy the actual running because it fuckin' hurts, but afterwards, you go, 'Ah! I just ran 26.2 miles!'" I think that's the feeling I get from writing and directing. It's something that I've done from scratch and put on.

How do you handle rejection?

I try not to take it personally. I recognize that it so much is about type. I work hard at recognizing that it's not about me. It's about how the director and the casting director see the character and fulfilling that. Sometimes they're surprised by new things, but often they want to fulfill their vision of something. It's not about me being good or bad. I try to deal with rejection by trying to think in those lines. I say I'm going to give up as well. I cry. It's such a mix of positive thoughts and negative thoughts. And sometimes I say to myself, "I'm a shitty actor and that's why they didn't like me."

Who are *your* favorite actors?

Gary Oldman because his character range is just incredible. You never get the sense that you're watching an actor putting on a character. You really get the sense of a completely different, fully-inhabited, twenty-dimensional character. It's so different and I'm so astounded by that. I just think he's brilliant. Al Pacino, though it's such a cliché to say that. Sir Laurence Olivier for his ability to create characters and play such a range of characters. Robert De Niro, I love for the incredible character shifts he makes. Daniel Day-Lewis is a lead character actor. He does play characters. He takes time out so that he can focus on the character and do it to the best of his ability and really explore the world of each character. It seems like he uses each job as a way to grow as a human being, to find out about that world. Another actor is Roshan Seth. He was in *Gandhi* playing Nehru. He was in *Mississippi Masala* playing the father. He was in *Metropolitan*. He's a South-Asian actor who just... I totally respect. I think he's brilliant.

What issues do you face as a South-Asian actor?

I didn't know I was a South-Asian actor until I left Drama school, until the business told me I was a South-Asian actor. Recognize that it's going to happen; the industry will define you. I think you have to start with the drive where you think you're going to change everything—and some people *are* going to bust through it—but you have to recognize that the color of your skin is going to be your selling point. I don't want to be limited by my race in terms of the characters I play. At the same time, it's sad when you see actors blacking or browning up. It doesn't happen often, but it still does.

What advice would you give to an actor starting out?

I wouldn't want to advise anybody on anything. I think it's bullshit. What's going to happen is going to happen. One person's advice is another person's poison. The thing that I've always tried to adhere to is, as much as possible, to focus on the work and not on the career. The career has so much to do with luck. The only thing you have control over is the work. Focus on the work, wherever you can get it. Taking gigs that don't seem to advance your career that are about doing the fifty-seat theatre or whatever is important, because you know the work will satisfy you. In the end, it only makes you a more interesting actor and a stronger actor and a better actor. It makes you more sellable in the end. Focus on the art as much as you can. Get the art where you can get it.

Tara Karsian

Tara Karsian has appeared recently on such television shows as CSI, Desperate Housewives, Six Feet Under, NYPD Blue, Everybody Loves Raymond, Complete Savages, *and* Reba, *among countless others, including* Emeril! *(often considered one of television's worst sitcoms. For the record, she didn't think it was that bad).*

Tara is a member of the LA-based Echo Theatre Company and has appeared in several of their productions, including the world premiere of Paul Zimmerman's Pigs and Bugs. *She also proudly teaches for Act Out, the Echo Theatre's outreach program for incarcerated youth. More information is at http://echotheatercompany.com.*

Tara is grateful she gets to do what she loves (to act. She hates writing bios). More information about Tara is available at http:// us.imdb.com/name/nm0440160.

photo by Erik Hyler
http://erikhyler.com

When did you know you wanted to become an actor?

I was basically raised in the industry so I knew at a young age and asked my parents. Friends of theirs would say, "You should try to get her an agent." And my parents would say, "Absolutely not." My mother—Pat Carroll—said to me, "When you turn eighteen, you can make the decision for yourself." My father was not as pleased about that. So, when I turned eighteen, I said, "I don't want to go to college. I want to start acting." They had to let me go. I just knew it was something that I wanted to do and at eighteen, I didn't feel that need to go to college. The first thing my mother said to me was, "You've got to find an acting class." I did. I was very lucky. I found a woman who was wonderful, Lynette Katselas. I don't know if she's teaching anymore. She was a brilliant teacher. Everybody in the class was young and working. I was the only one without an agent.

How did you get your first agent?

It took a while. It took four years for me to get an agent. I put together a showcase with some friends. I think we were all kind of sitting around talking about it one night and I knew I didn't want to do any of the pay-to-do-a-showcase things. I said, "We know enough talented people that I think we can do this." It was incredible. It was a great experience. I didn't quite know how showcases worked, but this young guy came up to me afterwards and said, "I think you're wonderful and I'm with an agency and there's no way they're going to take you because you have no credits." And I said, "Well, what do we do about that?" He said, "You keep me informed as to what you're doing." And I said, "I'm doing a play in a few months." He said, "Good!"

So, I was doing the play a few months later and he brought the whole agency to see me. They fell in love with one of the other actresses. I'd had a *shit* night. I was just so *off* that night. I'm thinking, "Here they come and they're going to love me and, hey, why are they talking to *her*?!?" The agent called the next day and said, "I'm so sorry. But I have an idea. I want to bring them back under the guise of seeing her again." At that point I'd already given up. The big thing was, the head of the agency never stayed for a second act—which I find incredibly rude—and there was a huge buzz outside after the show when I walked out the door. The agent said, "He stayed! He stayed for the second act." The head of the agency then came up to me and said, "We'd love to meet with you this week." They signed both of us actually, so it worked out for me and the actress they loved the first time.

My dad was an agent and then became a manager. He was actually my mother's manager, which I'm sure ended their marriage. I think my father saw all of the horrible parts of the business. Still, he was very compassionate with actors. He was at the William Morris Agency, so he was dealing with celebrities. He hated the bad parts about the industry and I think wanted to protect any child of his from having to go through that. I think, in a weird way, my father was against it until I started working and he saw other people saying that it was okay. My mother was the complete opposite. My mother was always supportive. The showcase I produced, she came to see. She had never seen me do anything professionally. Afterwards she called and said, "Can we have lunch tomorrow?" I thought, "Oh, God. Here we go." We had lunch and she said, "After what I saw, don't ever give up. If you do, I will kick your butt." And to this day, when I get depressed, she will call me up and say, "You know, the miracle is right around the corner!" So, I've had both types of input and that's a lot of how I see the industry. I see both sides. The question I ask of aspiring actors is: "Is it the only thing you want to do?" If it isn't, go do something else. You've got to want to be a lifer. It's not a hobby. I get a little bit annoyed with those who treat it as such.

What was your first paid gig?

Who's the Boss? A guy I had met who is now a big casting director, Greg Orson, was the assistant to Vicki Rosenberg then. He got me in on a general and I met with Vicki's associate. She told me about a part that I might be right for and I got it and it became recurring. I thought that *Who's the Boss?* was just the beginning and that it was like a corporate thing. I thought I'd just keep moving up the ladder from *Who's the Boss?* and that didn't happen.

The agency I was with explained to me what they were going to do. They said, "We're going to start you with Under-5s and we'll keep building you." And they did. There were years that I would work continually and then there was a two-year time when I couldn't book a callback. It freaked me out. I freaked out and thought obviously something was wrong. Desperation walks in the door before you do. I got to a very desperate point where every interview became so important to me. I was at borderline panic attacks because I couldn't figure out what had happened.

Looking back at it, I can say that the talent didn't change; I just wasn't prepared for the fact that the industry is cyclical. You can't explain that to someone, especially to a younger person. If this happens to you, don't freak out. You just have to get through it.

You have to keep walking through it. It's frustrating and scary. You begin to question everything. "How do I change things?" It can be an epiphany for some actors, but nothing had changed for me. I just kept walking through it.

The joke of it is, I said, "Somebody has got to give me a sign." I literally had not worked in two years and the phone rang. It was a friend of mine who was a producer on *Walker, Texas Ranger*. She said, "Can you get your tape here overnight?" And I said, "Sure." She said, "Great. There's a part for a man. But we've read everybody. They've seen everybody in LA. There's no one who can do it." Two days later, I was on a plane to Texas. Well, that's my sign! I began working again because I got my confidence back. I think that's a lot of it. Once an actor loses confidence, it's over. We all have egos and once that ego is bruised you start thinking, "I'm not doing something right. I need to do this. I need to do what everybody else is doing right now." No. Just walk through it. Just keep walking through it. There is light at the end of the tunnel. There always is.

Even when that light has been dim, I have always appreciated every gig. Sometimes the best part of getting the job is just getting the job. I have been on sets that are miserable but that doesn't mean I haven't been grateful for a job. I have a great lack of patience for those who aren't grateful. There are too many people out there who are deserving, who don't have agents, and who can't get in for the auditions. I've always said that casting directors should have a camera in the waiting room to see what they'll actually be getting on the set. You're going to get sunshine and lollipops in the room. What was going on in the waiting room? What do you want on the set?

Be grateful for the job. Go on the set, do your work, don't be a pain in the ass. When you have the job, it's the greatest drug in the world. When you're working, there's nothing better. When you're not, you're jonesin' for the next fix. Something has got to keep you going during that time.

I was talking to a young kid from my acting class. He said, "I just want it so badly right now." I said, "If I told you that in ten years it would happen for you, what would you do?" He said, "I don't know. I guess I'd go do something else." I looked at him and said, "I would love to hit my success later in life as opposed to early. I think it would be really scary to be twenty-six and washed up." We're not in control of it. I was supposed to have won an Academy Award at twenty-one. Didn't happen. If you're waiting for a job or a series to make you happy, you're going to be screwed.

Do you ever feel like giving up?

Twenty times a day! We're not in control. That's why it's so important to surround yourself with really good people who will tell you it straight. You need people who will let you know if it's never going to happen.

My sister's a casting director. I love casting directors who love their jobs. No, I love anybody who loves their job. I want to see that. I want the person who's doing craft service to have a great time. I want everybody to have a good time. I think we are ridiculously overpaid for what we do—not that I wouldn't take the money! I've been on some sets where I just want to slap people and say, "Nowhere else are you going to be getting this kind of money to sit around and play and have fun." I am constantly amazed when I guest star on a show and am grateful when Friday comes around because these people are miserable. They're making more money than God and it's embarrassing that they hate their jobs so much. I think, "Where were you raised that you aren't grateful for this?!?"

My mother was on a show and I was teasing her once because I had come to the set to get something. It was a Monday morning and the guest actor was walking on the set and my mom went up and introduced herself. She said, "Now, the stage manager is over there. He can answer any questions. Craft service is over there. Let me take you over." I said, "Hey, Cruise Director Julie McCoy, what are you doing here?" She said, "You mark my words. When you have a guest on a show, if you're a series regular on that show, Tara, treat them as if they're a guest in your home for a week." I will tell you, Tony Danza was that way. The lead on the first job I did stood up when we walked into the room. He introduced us to each of the cast members. Friday night taping, there were flowers in all of our dressing rooms from him. He was an absolute gentleman. How wonderful for that to be my first job! This is how it should be. I don't want to be *shocked* when that happens!

We, as actors, especially when we're guesting on shows, our job is just to go on the set and do the best work and not be the pain in the ass. I love working with actors I know are going to be there on time. And if you ask them to do something, it's done. It's not a big deal. These actors who want to discuss character for three hours, it's like, "That's homework, folks. Do it at home and don't waste our time." There's nothing more boring to me than watching an actor come on a set and want to talk to the director. "You're a guest actor. You were hired for a job because you did the job well in the audition. Do what you have to do before you get on the set."

I was working with a kid in acting class. I was doing a scene with him. Second week and he still didn't know his lines. He said, "You seem upset." I said, "If you were on a set, you would've been fired by now. You're wasting my time. I'm telling you this for when you go on to work professionally. Nobody's going to run lines with you. Nobody is going to rehearse with you. You'll get *maybe* one rehearsal if you're lucky. And that's for lighting. And if you think the star of the show you've got a scene with is going to say, 'Hey, let's run lines!' you're out of your mind. It's not going to happen. I just want to let you know what's going to happen if you do this on a set. You will be fired." Of course, this was in class and I believe every actor should be in class. But your work in class shows what your work on the set would be. Be ready. And say "please" and "thank you" on the set. I'm tired of the prop guy saying, "Thank you. You're the only person who said 'thank you' to me today." I'm tired of that.

In addition to keeping yourself in check in class, I think you should keep up with your feedback from casting. I think there's a problem if you're not being brought back in by casting people. If your agent says, "Bonnie doesn't want to see you on this one," or "Bonnie was a little lukewarm," you need to look at that. "Why won't Bonnie see me?" Most of the time, actors tend to be in a grey area. We don't know why someone isn't bringing us in. If you're an actor and you're not being brought in by someone you've booked with in the past, you need to look at that. Really be self-aware and then fix the problem. It really pays to look at that unspoken feedback.

My sister called me one day because her casting assistant was out: "Can you come in and fill?" It was final callbacks for this movie. I said, "Sure." It was the greatest thing I've ever done! I want every actor to do that! You see these actors leaving their power out in the waiting room. The girl who ended up getting the part came in, did the job, and left. Read the room! The girl who *could've* gotten it told this long, boring story. She just went on and on and on. The energy got sucked out of the room. There was no point, no punchline. I wanted to call this girl and say, "*What* was that story? *Why* did you do that?!?" She thought staying in the room so long was great. No, honey. Read the room! I wish actors were a little more self-aware.

What is your favorite thing about being an actor?

There's nothing I don't love about being an actor. I had a joke with my old agent. I'd call and go, "Ugh! Did I tank in the room!" and I'd get the job. It's the times that I go, "Whew! I was GREAT! I'll be getting that phone call in a couple of hours," that I'm then checking my cell thinking, "What's going on? T-Mobile must be out!" I think there are auditions that I've gone, "Ugh! I can't believe how embarrassing that was. Those people are going to take that tape home and laugh at it tonight with their family," and I've gotten the job. I don't think we know what goes on in a room after we leave. I think you walk into a room of seventeen people and you're like, "Which one of you is deciding?" Of course, you can't do that and this casting by committee thing goes on. And if someone thinks, "Well, she reminds me of my third grade teacher who I hated," you'll never know that. Instead they'll say, "She's not funny," or, "We went another way." And in a big room, how can you know who is really the decision-maker? I get so excited when I go into a room of two people. "Thank you! There's a chance these two will agree."

Ilana Levine

Ilana Levine starred on Broadway in Wrong Mountain; You're a Good Man, Charlie Brown; The Last Night of Ballyhoo; *and* Jake's Women. *Films include* Anything but Love, Kissing Jessica Stein, Storyteller, Just Looking, Roommates, Me and Veronica, Looking for an Echo, *and* Drop Back Ten. *Ilana made her television debut in Robert Altman's HBO award-winning series* Tanner '88 *and in 2004 filmed the miniseries for the Sundance Channel of* Tanner on Tanner, *the companion piece to the original series, co-starring with Cynthia Nixon.*

Other television credits include Law & Order, The Buried Secrets of M. Night Shyamalan, Seinfeld *(the infamous episode, "The Contest"),* Partners, Hope and Gloria, NYPD Blue, Lois and Clark, Hudson Street, The Job, 100 Centre Street, Law & Order: Criminal Intent, *and numerous pilots. She can be heard on the original Broadway recording of* You're a Good Man, Charlie Brown.

Ilana produced the original productions of Stephen Belber's Tape *in New York, LA, and London. More information is available at http://ilanalevine.com.*

photo by Lisa Franchot

You were a part of the inspiration for this book. Talk about the process of bringing working actors in to speak to your class.

I think we are driven to be actors because we're storytellers. We had actors come in at the start of class at Naked Angels to talk about their experiences because that humanizes the experience for us. This was a three-hour scene study class, but in the first half-hour, I had someone from the business come in and talk about how they got started as an actor. Everyone was nervous, no matter who they were. They'd want to know, "Who cares?" and, "What do I have to say that would be interesting?" And, similarly, I was thinking things like that in the car on the way over here for *this* interview. But ultimately, each interview was brilliant. There was a humility about it all.

When did you know you wanted to become an actor?

I would say that I knew I was interested in it when I took my first acting class. And I went to my first acting class because I had a crush on a guy. I had gotten a haircut by this guy who was completely Warren Beatty in *Shampoo*. He was this unbelievably handsome, sexy haircutter. He had a play on his station—one of those Samuel French plays. I don't think I'd ever seen one. We had read plays in high school, but they weren't in the Samuel French binding that we've come to recognize as a play. I think I picked it up and started asking him about it while getting my hair cut, trying to take as long as possible to stay in that chair. We started reading it together. And he said, "You're good! You're a natural! Your *hair* may not be, but your talent is!"

He invited me to come to the Terry Schreiber Studios in New York City to their one-night-a-month evening where you can audit a class. There was a teacher in there, a woman named Gloria Maddox, who has since passed away, and I immediately thought what was going on was fascinating. I thought the work was interesting. I thought the people were interesting. It was unlike anything I'd ever seen before. They were doing sound and movement exercises and sense memory stuff. She was a really inspirational person. That was my first mentor in the business. She had a light about her. She was also an actress and became a teacher at Terry Schreiber's studio. It was a place where I walked in the room—and I think people who come to religion as adults have the same feeling—it was like, "Oh my!"

I was just starting Fordham University at the time. My interest had originally been in advertising. I changed my major that summer. Some of the inspiring people who were there in classes ahead of me were John Benjamin Hickey, Patricia Clarkson, Julie White, and John Melfi (now a fancy TV producer). That was my first community. So, it was less of a "moment" in which I knew I wanted to be a professional, but I knew it was something I wanted to continue studying. And it was the first sort of "lesson" that I stayed with. I had done piano, ballet, a million things as a kid and never sort of stuck with it, but the minute I got into that room and got up on that stage, that was the beginning. I got a BFA in Theatre.

Was your family supportive?

Very much so! They were. I think that was a very lucky thing. I had an older sister who was a dancer and who I think was a trailblazer in my family that way. She opened doors for my parents and for me in terms of going a less-traditional route in life. Having her was a really important thing because she's the one who said, "Follow your dream." Having a sibling that was older and artistic was a really important thing.

What was your first paid gig?

What was kind of amazing was that, in the middle of all this, I got a job. It was also sort of why I committed to it as a career because I had something happen very quickly. I got *Tanner '88*, the Robert Altman series, which has kind of come full-circle right now because we just shot *Tanner on Tanner*. So, every fifteen years I work!

While I was in this acting class, some of us got together and put on a play. We did the Mamet play *Edmond* and for some reason, an agent named Steven Hirsh came to see that show. And it turns out that Steven Hirsh—who is now at Gersh—had been my boyfriend in camp, when I was eight years old. He became my agent.

I'm a freshman and I've got an agent. Now, at the time, the way things were cast in Robert Altman's world was his producer was the casting director and she would call a couple of agents that she knew—that she'd worked with before—and an actor who was with my new agent had just done *The Caine Mutiny Court-Martial* with Robert Altman. So she called my agent and said, "Cynthia Nixon may not be able to play the candidate's daughter. We need some young, eighteen, nineteen-year-old girls in case she can't do it. Do you have anyone?" And they did. They had me. So I was at the Terry Schreiber Studios and I called my service—of course, this is in 1988 when you had a service—and there was a message: "You gotta go right now to meet Robert Altman." And I called back and said, "I can't. I'm doing a scene today in class. I can't go." I had no idea who Robert Altman was. I was going to do *The House of Blue Leaves* in class and we had worked to get three people together and we brought all the props. I called my agent and I said, "I can't do it today." I happened to see Terry Schreiber and I mentioned to him that I was supposed to go to this audition and he said, "Oh, no. You're going to go." I said, "Okay, but I'll be back in time for the scene."

So, I went uptown, I met Robert Altman's producer, she thought I was really charming and funny, and she said, "Why don't you come back this evening and meet Bob?" And I didn't know that "Bob" was the same person as Robert Altman but I said, "Okay." I rushed from the Upper East Side back to the Lower East Side, did my scene—it went very well—I went back uptown going, "I rocked my scene!" It was so casual. I basically sat in the waiting room and then met Bob and talked about art for an hour. We talked about Modigliani and these painters that I really liked and that he really liked and we talked about acting and food and I had no idea what the project was.

It turns out that Cynthia could do the part, but Bob was so enchanted—as I was with him—that he had Garry Trudeau write in a role for me; a kind of a kooky campaign aide that I had no idea whether would be in one episode or what. It turns out that I went from New Hampshire, where we shot the first episode, to a nine-month gig, all twelve episodes for HBO. It was HBO's first series. It was very exciting and I made a lot of money, having never had a job before. I think I made like five thousand dollars an episode and it was amazing. So, here I was thinking, "Wow, this is easy." I went from that to doing Under-5s on *All My Children*. I thought, "This is so interesting. Life is very complicated in this area."

Right after *Tanner '88*, I auditioned for the nonunion summer company at the Berkshire Theatre Festival and worked with three amazing directors. One of them was Michael Greif, now of *Rent* fame. That fall, Michael was going to be doing a play called *Machinal* with

Naked Angels and he cast me. As an actor, you do this non-Eq thing and you just never know where it will lead. Through *Machinal* I got connected with these people at Naked Angels and I now realize that was the beginning of my New York life and my artistic life. The people I met through that production are still my closest friends.

And if that was the beginning of my life, *Tanner '88* was the beginning of my professional career. Michael Murphy who worked on *Tanner '88* with me said, "It's never gonna be like this again." It's true. When your first job is with Robert Altman, who is unlike any other director, you're spoiled. The man loves actors and you think then that everyone who is a director will love actors. His interest is in what you bring to it, much more than the script, much more than anything else. He creates an amazing world. Immediately you're having dinner at his house. It's all about a party. By the time you start work, you are so relaxed and so comfortable in the presence of each other, and that's what being in a theatre company is like. So, it flowed from Altman's world to the Naked Angels. And college is like that too. It made me realize that working with people that I know is an amazing thing. And now that I don't have that, it's harder. It's much harder. Usually you don't have that, but it has remained a constant for me, to always have that to come back to. Without that, I don't know what would've happened. Had I not always had a theatre that I could do work with when I wasn't being hired to do work, I would've really atrophied.

How has your affiliation with a theatre company allowed you to expand as an actor?

After *Machinal*, I came out to LA to do a TV show called *Second Chances* with Connie Sellecca. Soon after I came out, I had a recurring role and I thought, "This is so great." Once again, "I'm so lucky." And then the show got cancelled after I did three. It was gone. I thought, "Wow, that was really painful. I just spent a lot of money thinking that I was going to be on the show for a while. Luckily, the tags are still on the stuff!" I did a bunch of pilots and none of them got picked up. That was also a very strange phenomenon; to do all of this work that no one saw. I felt like I was working, and delighted to be making money at it, but it was all sort of going into a vacuum. Suddenly ten months have gone by and you've been on hold for six of them. I did five pilots in a row and I had tested for seven pilots before I got one. Talk about feeling like, "I don't get it!"

Every time I tested, I was so nervous. I really thought, "The only way I'm going to get one of these is if I just calm down. I have to figure out a way to fool myself into thinking that it's just not a big deal." But every time I saw the contract, it would freak me out! And the truth is, when I did get my first pilot, I was just as nervous as I had been every other time. There was no trick, but I really thought there was something I could master. And that's when I realized, "This has absolutely nothing to do with me. It's not because I'm nervous that I'm *not* getting jobs. It's not because I'm nervous that I *am* getting jobs." There was something so liberating about the fact that I was just as much of a freak going into the one that I got as I had been every other time I thought I'd derailed myself. That was really important.

Either I'm right for the part or I'm not. For me, either what I do is the right fit or it's not. If it is the right fit, nothing I can do can get in the way of that. If it isn't the right fit and I get the part, I have fooled them and then I have gotten fired. Maybe I do something really quirky, funny in the room to kind of deflect the fact that I'm not really the right one for it, but ultimately there's something they need to hang onto that the show needs in that character. Ultimately, if I'm not that person, it doesn't work. Twice now, I remember I was cast in something and they were like, "You're like the Betty White of the show." There is nothing Betty White about me. I can give you a little something funny and make you think the material is working even if it's not, but ultimately, it's not working.

The "I was not Betty White" thing happened when the one pilot I did finally got picked up. Basically, I couldn't make the material fit at all. It was a square peg and a round hole, trying to make it fit. I sort of rewrote it a little bit and I went into the audition, did all of these funny lines I had written. And they decided to test me. We got to the test and the casting director handed out some revisions for the character. The revisions were the lines I had done at the audition! I was like, "Wait a minute! That's my edge! Now all three of us are going to go in doing my thing?!?" And I looked at the casting director and asked, "I'm not crazy, right?" He kind of looked at me and said, "Don't worry about it. No one else is going to be doing your material." I got the job since no one else had a handle on it like I did and we got to the read-thru and I made a joke: "Am I going to get writing credit?" And the exec went, "What are you talking about?" I said, "Well, I'm very flattered that you put what I wrote into it." He was like, "You didn't write that." I had actually just been teasing—it was only about three sentences—but that was the beginning of a rough, rough scenario. We got through the pilot but ultimately my character didn't make it into the series. It was a perfect example of something not working and a committee trying to decide what it should be instead of just letting me do what I do, which is what they had been attracted to in the first place. The whole thing was hard and I was humiliated that I had been let go, but I did get some solace when I called an executive at NBC to try to get my job back. He said to me, "Ilana, why would you want to be on that show anyway? It's awful."

So, I went back to New York after four years and there was a play being cast on Broadway—replacements—for *The Last Night of Ballyhoo*. There was a part in it that I was really right for. I asked my agent to get me in on this thing. The role is a Southern, Jewish girl called Lala Levy who is very awkward and has a hard time in the world and has a real artistic light about her. She's just misunderstood and she's just living in the wrong time. I saw the play and I really responded to the character in a way that I thought, "I cannot believe I can't get an audition. This is crazy!" And my agents were like, "We're sorry. We can't get you in. Jay Binder won't see you." So, I finally decided that I was going to call Jay Binder myself.

Many years ago, Jay cast me as an understudy in a Neil Simon play called *Jake's Women*. I wasn't sure I wanted to be an understudy and Jay called me at home and convinced me I should take the job. He promised me I'd get to go on because the woman I'd be understudying had a deal to do a TV show and he knew she would be leaving. It wasn't a quote-unquote regular understudy gig. Ultimately, I was mostly glad that I took the part. So, I left him a message in his office saying, "Years ago you sort of called me at home and made it personal and I'm going to do the same now. Will you please see me?"

He actually didn't see me. He had his associate preread me. I went in at nine in the morning and read for his associate but got called back and that afternoon I went in and had the job. I had played a very different part in *Jake's Women* and I think, in his mind, I was not Lala Levy. Thank God I was right! The question is, "How many times can you cash in chips?" I feel like you've got to choose when you do it. I've definitely gotten in trouble from it, but I figure, "What do I have to lose? I'm not working anyway. What's going to happen? He's *still* not going to see me? Okay, he's *really* not going to see me now!" I think what's complicated when you do this career for a long time is that you become friends with the casting people and it's really awkward. When is it okay? When is it not okay? Why do people you know really well suddenly get weird on you? "You're the one who said if I ever needed anything, call. Did you not mean it? Then why'd you say it?" It's all messy. You just have to trust your instincts and sometimes you're right, sometimes you're not right.

But that started me on a four-year tremendously exciting run on Broadway. So, thank God I made that call. It went from there to *You're a Good Man, Charlie Brown*. And I don't sing, so that was a really big thing! Michael Mayer, the director, had seen me in *Machinal*. There was some quality about the character I did many years before that Michael thought was right. It's fascinating how you just have to trust that you keep doing what you do because you don't know where it's going to come back. The play for no money turns into a starring role in a Broadway musical. That's what's exciting about what we do.

How can an actor best handle bitterness?

I am so glad I was born with a sense of humor. You either are or you're not and I feel so grateful. It may make you lazy in certain areas, and maybe I'm less disciplined because I know my humor allows me to get away with certain things. But it really makes it easier. I know a lot of bitter people. The thing is: authenticity. At the end of the day, whatever you do, whatever your thing is, you just have to be authentically that. If you're truly bitter—I mean truly bitter—really own it. I think when I have embraced my envy or bitterness or jealousy and really let it just eat me up alive, I can get through it. It's when I pretend it's not happening that I'm a little out of control. If I really go there, and really feel the loss, I'm okay.

You have to trust that your path is your path. After *Tanner '88*, Bob asked me if I wanted to do this film called *The Player*. I had agreed to do a play at New York Stage & Film. My boyfriend ran the place at the time and he was directing a play that he had written for me. It was a really big deal in our relationship. I turned down *The Player*, which became Bob's biggest hit at that time and put him back on the A-list of directors. That was one of the times that I made a choice to honor a commitment. I understand why I did it, but everyone from that movie you can kind of track from that. Who knows what would've happened? You don't know. You just don't know. And that's what's really hard.

Sometimes you're right, but again, you have to do what's right for you at the moment. I look at that time and I say, "I'm a relationship person. I loved this guy. He wrote me this play. It was very romantic." It's not bad to be loyal. It just doesn't always get you stardom. It doesn't *not* get you stardom, but it's just a different way of operating. It is what it is. That is definitely a moment in my life that I replayed many times.

Do you ever feel like giving up?

I feel like, in some ways, I have expanded what I do into different directions, such as producing. I produced a play in New York that we ended up doing in LA and London. It's much easier for me to do these things that aren't about me. I couldn't ask for money if I were in the play. That's just me. I don't have that in me in some way. You make calls that you would never make for yourself. Being a woman is a very tricky thing. I feel like there are a lot of ways in which I have tried to not always be a grown up in my role as a female actress. I've tried to remain really young. There's a lot of ways in which the male/female dynamic comes up in casting situations, in social situations, in all of it—it's business. I never feel, in my role as a producer, that I have to think about who I want to be. Which Ilana do I want to be in this situation? Am I young Ilana? Old Ilana? Flirty Ilana? I'm just so completely myself and able to be a smart, whole, opinionated person. As an actress, sometimes you have to be a bitch or a diva or difficult. I'm not saying something new; it's just amazing how true it is!

A good producer ultimately gives people environment and opportunity to do what they do and to do it well. It is such a gift to get to do that: to give people opportunities to just be genius at what they do. Having had so many experiences from almost every audition I go to, almost every job I've had, where the environment is so set up for failure, and not to be creative and not to feel safe to do what you do—it's a great thing to be able to produce differently. It's a great thing when actors direct because of that. It's a great thing when actors write. It's a great thing when actors do anything other than act, because they bring so much generosity to it. It is so hard to do what we do and we don't want to recreate that nightmare for anybody.

What impact has acting had on your personal life?

I married an actor and it's been interesting, seeing the process. It's not that different for any of us. And falling in love with an actor is complicated. But you just fall in love with who you fall in love with and there's not a damn thing you can do about it. So, I married an actor and we have a daughter, Georgia. I've had a lot of great jobs since Georgia was born. I did *The Buried Secret of M. Night Shyamalan*, which was really interesting. This *Tanner on Tanner* with Bob came back again. I would say that the lucky thing is that both of these jobs were predominantly improv because learning lines for me right now is really hard. I'm so distracted. It takes really good writing to interest me more than playing with my daughter. It's really hard for me to focus on material that's not inspiring. I'm really aware now of having to choose how I spend my time and what feels worth it.

Camille Mana

Native to Orange County, California, this promising young Asian-American talent has proven her tenacity both on stage and off. Starving student by day, starving actress by... day, Camille Mana completed her Economics and Theatre studies at UC Berkeley in just six semesters, while concurrently managing to build the foundations of a professional acting career. This arduous process led to many plane trips, many failed midterms, and many *illegal stimulants. Kidding, mom.*

Recently, Camille was selected by Cannes and Oscar-winning director Adam Davidson to appear in Naked TV—*an innovative staged pilot series co-produced by Fox and the prestigious Naked Angels Theatre Company—sharing the bill with such talents as Melissa Joan Hart. She has appeared on the WB's cult fave* Angel *and the Fox hit* The OC, *for which she was featured in* Elle Girl *magazine. Camille's comedic credits include Comedy Sportz High School League and stand-up at the world-famous Improv in Hollywood.*

An active contributor to the Asian-American artistic community, Camille is a member of both Lodestone Theatre Ensemble and East West Players. She appears in the indie film Harlequin, *a selection in both the LA Asian-Pacific Film Fest and San Francisco International Asian-American Film Fest.*

She has accrued a handful of performance awards including the LAMDA Gold Medal with Distinction, honoring promising American high school students. Others include: Music and Arts Commendation for Youth, multiple honors from Southern California Educational Theatre Association, and Emerging Young Artist Award Finalist.

More comedy and the start of a writing career are next on her agenda. Currently, she's launching an offshoot of an entertainment industry startup, but if she told you what it was she'd have to do kung fu on you. Unfortunately, she doesn't do kung fu, so you'll just have to deal. Aregato that, Mister. More information on Camille is available at http://camillemana.com.

photo by Jeffrey Nicholson
http://theshotphotography.com

When did you know you wanted to become an actor?

I decided when I was thirteen. I guess I was watching *My So-Called Life* and—that sounds really dumb now—watching that show, for some reason I just made a conscious decision that this was what I wanted. I didn't start doing it until later because my parents were typical Asian parents. Typical parents, period, are not going to want their kids to go into this business, but Asian parents especially, this is like their worst nightmare.

So, I was thirteen and that's when I started researching the business. I read *How To Be a Working Actor* under my pillow with a flashlight in the eighth grade. I didn't want my parents to find out. I would go to the library and check out all of the industry books and read as much as I could. At that age, I had already absorbed somewhat of an understanding of how the business worked but I wouldn't be able to apply it until later when I had my driver's license and could actually do things on my own.

I started high school and I tried to get involved with the Drama program and my parents were not happy because when you can't drive, you have to get permission for all of that stuff. They were never going to start driving me to LA from Orange County to get an agent. But I didn't get into the first production my freshman year, after they'd let me audition for that. They felt sorry for me. *Oklahoma!* was on at my high school and they were doing *Oklahoma!* at the community theatre, like at the children's musical theatre. My parents said, "Poor her. She didn't get in it at school. We'll just take her to the audition on Saturday at the community theatre because we feel bad," and I got in and they were like, "Oh, no!"

That was the first show I did: *Oklahoma!* at the children's community theatre in Orange County. After that, I started to be really active in high school, professionally. As soon as I turned sixteen, I got my license and I drove out to American Academy of Dramatic Arts and I did the summer program. By that point, I had already done a lot of shows at school and I was emerging as one of the main people of my year in acting. I had to get really good grades, of course. You know *Better Luck Tomorrow*? That was my high school. Literally. My school was sixty-five percent Asian and we were number nineteen in the nation for academics out of all of the public schools. I had to compete on that level to keep my parents happy.

I continued to do classes in LA after the summer program at the American Academy, like on-camera classes. So, I started wanting to act when I was thirteen, but it took all those years of constantly training as much as my parents would let me and reading online and reading all of the "how to act" books. I did like ten shows at school and my parents would come, but when I started winning awards, they would not acknowledge that. I would compete in drama festivals and place and they would still not accept it. When I won an award for acting, they said, "Oh, good. Maybe you can be a lawyer."

What was your first paid gig?

My first paid gig was my first commercial. It was an Oakland A's commercial. It was actually my first union audition and I got my

SAG card on that commercial. I was pretty lucky, I guess. I was in San Francisco. I went to Berkeley and this was during my first semester. I knew that I wanted to have a normal college period and still build the foundations of an acting career. If I went to UCLA or NYU, I knew I would eat, sleep, and breathe theatre and I wouldn't be able to study and have a normal college life.

I had an agent in LA pretty much the whole time I was at Berkeley. I used to pretend that I lived in LA. My agent didn't find out until a long time in. I would fly down for my theatrical auditions. I never missed an appointment! One time I had to call from the plane to push back a few minutes, but I never missed one appointment, even coming from San Francisco. I got away with it forever! I had a really low-level agent in LA and there wouldn't be that much stuff for me, so I knew it would only be once in a while. I was ready, when those times happened, to not get caught.

Of course, the last week of one semester, my last test, I was going to cram. It was seven o'clock at night and I had a test at three the next day and I was going to study until the test and not sleep since I was so behind in the class. This was an Econ final. I got an email that said I had a producer session in Santa Monica at 10am. I was going to go home right after the test for the semester break. I was going to be home free. At first, when I got the email, I thought, "At this point, I can't possibly do it." And then I said, "Screw it! I'm getting in the car." I packed up my suitcase, I brought my test stuff, and I called my dad and said, "I'm coming to the airport right now. I'm in on the last flight. I have an appointment in Santa Monica and if you could just take me back to the airport right after, I'll go straight to my test." So, I got back and did really bad on the test. My grade dropped a whole letter for the class and I didn't get the job. But I said, "Y'know what, I did the right thing. I made the right choice and I don't regret it at all." Two weeks later, they ended up booking me for another role in that same episode. It was my first non-crime-reenactment show role. This was *Angel*. I didn't get the part that I read for, but they ended up writing in another part which had way more scenes. But even when I didn't get it, I thought I made the right choice and I always knew that this was my first priority and that school would always be there.

Did you do any internships while you were in college?

I did a couple. I also thought I might go into the music industry, so I had an internship in a casting office and at Capitol Records. I really wanted to create an acting resumé and also an entertainment work industry resumé in case I ended up doing that. I worked for eight months at a feature film casting office in Venice during a break from school. I started out as an intern but I was hired on my third day. I was still an intern, but I got paid. I was nineteen and I wanted to finish school so I didn't accept a long-term job there, but I learned so much from it! So much came out of that.

The most helpful thing about interning in a casting office is that you really see the big picture. I had a pretty good foundation of what the good agents were from what I'd read, but in the office, I saw which packages got opened. And that was a pretty name-oriented office too. That really taught me a lot. I used to sit in on the sessions. I would tape them. I got to watch all of these bigger actors come in. I realized how much less of a chance actors have if they're not at big management companies or *A*-list agencies with celebrity clients. You have to get *there* in order to get anywhere in a casting office. That was a big lesson. Even the really small roles would come from the *A* agencies. And if they hadn't cast something for weeks and weeks, they'd then go through the stacks and the boxes and boxes of *B*s and *C*s. It was really frustrating because it made me realize how far I would have to go to get anywhere.

How did you get your first agent?

My first agent was a referral from some on-camera class I was taking in LA. I had sent out tons of submissions throughout high school and I don't know what I was hoping to get. I was still pretending that I didn't really want to do it, but I was sending out a real headshot, resumé, and cover letter—but, oh, that headshot was so horrible! I looked thirty in the picture!

My San Francisco agent was the one I had when I first started booking. I had an agent in LA and that was the logo on my picture. I submitted to the top agents in San Francisco—there are only about a dozen—and I got one on my first round. It was my second appointment that I scheduled. The problem was, I was never really in San Francisco. I was always home and trying to work in LA. They got annoyed with me because I would book stuff but I would never be available because I had a final or I was in LA for an audition or something.

Are your friends in the industry?

Most of my friends are musicians. I'm not the person who hangs out with actors on weekends. I love actors and I'll keep in contact and hang out and talk business, but I don't go to parties with them or anything. I kind of don't like hanging out with actors. I've always been really into music. I've been to three hundred or more shows. I've always appreciated music, but never thought that I should be making music. But most of my friends make music. They're just kids. I don't even talk to my friends about my acting life, even though it's probably the biggest part of my life. I keep it separate from my friends.

What is your favorite thing about being an actor?

I don't even know why I knew I wanted to be an actor. It's just the first thing I think about when I wake up and the last thing I'm still thinking about when I go to bed everyday: my acting career, wherever it is. I can't stop! I have a degree, I could do a lot of things, but I couldn't quit. I can't stop. I don't know what is my favorite thing; it's just really exciting to know that you don't really know what's going to happen. There's just so much potential and opportunity out there.

How do you handle rejection?

It's still hard, every day. It's not hard getting rejected on a daily basis; it's hard when you're not moving forward at the rate that you feel that you've worked hard enough to earn. That's hard.

How would you describe the mentoring process?

I'm already a goal-oriented person, but having somebody keep me on track and push me more is really cool. I'm starting to look at people who are ten, twenty, thirty years older than me in the Asian community and think, "Well, if this person was working when there were less opportunities, then I can do it!" I look for people who are grounded in their lives and have been through it all. It's inspiring to see that someone has done it and been happy and given something to the community—not necessarily broken through, but they're working and they're happy and they're creating.

How do you reconcile the age issue?

I'm in a transition. I don't know what side of me to show. It's hard. I'm not even trying to be younger; I'm just me. When I go out for twenties, I never get called back! I know I have maturity, but I'm not enough of a woman yet. In class, I'm always working on older material but I'm in the middle right now! I'm with an agent in the youth department. I know they're going to submit me for whatever I'm right for, but it's really hard when I just went to producers for fifteen last week and a role for twenty-one comes up next week. "Dammit! I gave such a good *young* read, they're never going to see me *older*." I think that is the case with anyone in any transition between types or age or anything. It's hard and I'm still grappling with it.

I don't know what side of me to show—and there are so many sides to all of us anyway. It's all a PR game! I don't know if I can talk about it candidly because it does become the publicity you put out there. People don't respond to me as the age I am. But I don't know; am I allowed to hang out with people my age? I'm happy to go out older in my roles, but it's hard and it's going to be years before I can really be seen as my age. In the end, I go out for what I go out for one hundred percent.

What advice would you give to an actor starting out?

Give yourself permission to do a lot of different things in the business. I just started stand-up this year and I just started writing this year. I never thought that I could do those things. I'm just realizing that, putting in enough effort, I can do those things just as good as anybody who is doing them as their main thing. I realize I don't fit the prototype for the Asian stereotype. I'm realizing I'm going to have to write the roles for myself. I'm doing stand-up so that I can put what *I* know I am "out there." If I don't fit into someone else's storyline or whatever niche is already out there, I'm going to have to create that. I just wrote my first short film and since I have contacts with screenwriting people, I think I'm going to be able to produce and get funded my first short and be in it. I've written it for me. I don't fit into the narrow Asian female niche. It sucks. I've seen friends who are totally that prototype take off because they looked it. So, if I want to book the lead, I have to write it first. I'm not afraid of that.

Ed F. Martin

Ed F. Martin has been a willing slave to performance since the age of seven when he sang in a statewide vocal competition, coming in second place for his riveting rendition of "The Cowboy Mouse."

After graduating with a BFA in Theatre from the University of Arizona, Ed worked at the Arizona Theatre Company, the Kennedy Center in DC, and Westside Arts Theatre in New York, mentored along the way by such talents as Ed Sherin, Linda Lavin, Domini Blythe from the Royal Shakespeare Company, and Sandy Dennis at HB Studios in New York.

Since his move to LA, Ed's stage credits have included Rob in Twilight of the Golds, *Newman Noggs in* Nicholas Nickleby, *Erik Larsen in* Enigma Variations, *Paul in the Odyssey's world premiere of* Soundings, *and award-winning productions* The Nerd; You're a Good Man, Charlie Brown; *and* Clutter. *The recipient of the Robby,* Dramalogue, *Garland, and* LA Weekly *Awards for various roles, Ed is most proud of the Ensemble Ovation Award he received for his part in the Colony Theatre's hugely successful run of* The Laramie Project, *through which—with the help of audience donations—Ed and his cast mates raised over thirty-thousand dollars for the Matthew Shepard Foundation. Other credits include an encore run of* The Laramie Project *at the Laguna Playhouse and Lisa Loomer's* Living Out *at Theatreworks in Palo Alto.*

Television credits include Life with Roger, Chicago Hope, The Bold and the Beautiful, Family Law, Strong Medicine, Buffy the Vampire Slayer, *and the TV-movie* Annie. *Fluent in Spanish, Ed has appeared in numerous commercials for the American and Hispanic markets. Films include Josh Schiowitz's* Even Stephen *and* Crimes Against Charlie. *He will next star in* A Convoluted History of the Natural Biological Need To Be Loved by Somebody as Examined through the Courtship of Bentley and Max. *More information is at* http://us.imdb.com/name/nm0552232.

photo by Russell Baer
http://russellbaer.com

When did you know you wanted to become an actor?

Ever since I was a child: five, six. My family is half American, half Mexican and the Mexican side of the family is very, very dramatic—although none of them are in the arts. My sister and I are the only ones. But we were always singing and acting as kids at Christmas and Easter. I started primarily singing when I was like six or seven. I would say, by seventh grade, I knew I wanted to be an actor. I had just moved from Mexico and I still had a very heavy Spanish accent. In seventh grade I played George Washington, powdered wig and all. I've been hooked ever since.

Was your family supportive?

My parents were always very open-minded about it. I acted or sang all through high school. When it came time to go to college, my father said, "You can do whatever you want, but you should think about a grounding job." We considered maybe business and foreign language to work at the UN or that kind of thing, and a major in Theatre. But as soon as I got into Theatre classes, I started getting cast immediately. Everything else went by the wayside because I had no time: class nine to four, rehearsals four to eleven. There was no time for a double major or anything else.

Because we lived in Mexico so much during my childhood, my parents didn't really push the Ivy League schools. After I got out of college, I thought they were very important to an actor's career. Now there's much more perspective on what works and what doesn't. We were living in Georgia at the time I was choosing college and I went to Auburn University because that was my grandfather's alma mater. They had a Theatre department but no graduate department. So, it was a very humble beginning, but I started getting cast right from the first semester there and it never stopped. As far as an academic environment goes, I was always a big fish in a little pond. I was never told: "You should do something else," by anyone, ever. I've always had confidence because of that. There's lots of things to be insecure about, but I'm not insecure about my craft or my choice of it. That's a very comforting thing to keep me going at it.

What was your first paid gig?

That very first year of college, I went to one of those American College Theatre Festival things. And my first paying gig, for eighty bucks a week, was *The Lost Colony*, an outdoor drama, in Manteo, North Carolina. I had a part and I was one of the dancers. It all takes place on the sound in North Carolina about the first colonists ever to be in the United States. It was not as cheesy as they said it would be. It was actually a lot of fun. My first broadcast gig was a sitcom here in LA.

What made you choose Los Angeles?

I got out of college and went straight to New York and lived there for four years and couldn't get arrested. I tried everything including the Spanish. It's a much smaller competitive market. But, my father being American, I don't "read" perhaps as Hispanic as I should. I used to go out to Lynn Kressel for the first *Law & Order* a lot, but I didn't book it. I have a beautiful sister who is an actress here in LA who said, "Stop it. You need to come to LA. You'll start working immediately." She skipped the whole school route so she was already here. When I got here, I started working immediately. I started with Spanish commercials and that has been solid the entire time. Spanish and English, really. I keep my day job—working in finance for a major concert venue—because it's very flexible. I get to go on auditions and do whatever I want, and I can't really rely on commercials and television shows being steady. I would say that my income is eighty percent actor income and twenty percent day job.

What are the differences between Spanish-language and English-language auditions?

The difference is inherent in the copy. I work a lot as a dad: middle-class, middle-aged dad. The quality of a father talking to his fifteen-year-old daughter in English won't read the same in Spanish. Perhaps it'll be an eight-year-old boy. It's more the differences in the cultures and the way the ad agencies approach the material. Your acting is the same because they're approaching the Hispanic market in the United States. It's not a different culture that you're approaching, necessarily. It's really an American voice and an American product. I mostly go out for Spanish-language commercials.

In TV and film material, the Hispanic material is a lot more stereotypical. Commercials are addressing a sort of pan-Hispanic audience—so that's many Hispanic backgrounds. The television and film material is very specifically Puerto Rican or Cuban or Mexican or whatever. Physically, I don't come across with that edge. Although

I was "Eduardo" in New York. Here's how I became "Ed" Martin. I had a friend of mine go pick up sides for a Bob Newhart project that was being cast at Paramount while I was working. He said, "I'm here to pick up sides for Eduardo Martin." And they said, "There will be no 'Eduardo Martin' reading for this role." He literally said, "Is there an 'Ed Martin' or an 'Ed F. Martin' on your list?" They said, "Oh, yes. Here you go," and handed him the sides. It was that black-and-white. It was as though he was in the wrong office because "it was just not possible" that "Eduardo" would read for this. I immediately changed it—and not with insulted resistance. I just thought, "Well that's the way it's going to be. I'll let the fact that I speak Spanish fluently start to edge that other part out."

I've been on the other side of it. I used to work with a commercial casting director. I would run her sessions. In casting, you have a preconceived idea of what you want the spot to look like and people come in and it's very obvious, for whatever reasons in your head, that this is going to work or this is not. I don't know if it's the physical type or the sound of the voice or the actions themselves. There's so much that goes into it that it's very difficult to pinpoint. But working in a casting office was extremely helpful. It took the pressure off me, as an actor. You just do your thing with your take and if they want to see another take on the material, they're going to ask, and if they don't, don't worry about it. You're not right for it. And they're not going to sit there and mold and mold and mold your take on it when time is money if you're already not the right type for it. The perspective working in a casting office gave me was to not put so much pressure on the take that I choose. Choose it. Choose a couple adjustments in case they ask you for adjustments. And then go home.

Do you prefer theatre to film and television work?

Theatre has always been a passion. I think commercials and the day job have only funded that. I'm not big on acting classes, only because I've found through schools—going to two different colleges and HB Studios in NY—that teaching is very subjective. *You* are going to pick up something from that teacher that is different from what *I* am going to pick up from that teacher. And that's going to make him a good teacher for you or a bad teacher for me. With all of the expense that you already put in to maintain your career, I find that theatre—and I especially support the free theatre that's using you for slave labor—is my acting class. And, in my experience, agents and casting directors *are* seeing you when you're doing that. And you're learning as you do it. You can feel yourself burned when something doesn't work. And you feel when something works too. You're honing your own instincts. I'm a firm believer in that. Now, that's not to say: Don't take classes. If you like class and you get something out of it, take it. But waiver theatre in LA is plentiful and I've seen a lot of productions that I've found far superior to showcase productions that I've participated in in New York. I've also seen and been in bad stuff. The exposure is valuable. Work begets work. Some of those freebies have gotten me some great Equity gigs. They're all different, but there's value in all of them. And all the TV shows that I have in my credits are all based on somebody seeing me in a play. None of them were because of agent submissions—with the exception of that first sitcom. *The Laramie Project* at the Colony Theatre got me *Buffy: The Vampire Slayer*, *Strong Medicine*, and *The Bold and the Beautiful* when I didn't have an agent at all. That eight-actor ensemble for *The Laramie Project* was the best experience I've ever had in my whole life. That show was fantastic.

How did you get your first agent?

In New York, I freelanced, because it's so easy to do. Here in LA, it was nepotism. The very sister that asked me to move here was with William Morris, so I got in with William Morris. They were very patient with me. It took about a year and a half before I even started getting a good callback rate. You start to get the work—especially with commercials—when you have repeated contact, so you're not just a face. I now have a theatrical agent, a commercial agent, and a voiceover agent. The strongest way to get in, if you don't have an agent, is to start looking primarily for the commercial agent. A lot of them will take you across-the-board if you sign with them commercially. My commercial agent—Emily Hope at ACME—is a superwoman and I can't leave her, so when I *was* shopping for theatrical agents, I kept having to turn down across-the-board offers. I wouldn't leave my commercial agent—who I've now been with for like seven years. She's a machine! She's very accessible for that one-on-one. I've had agents where you're very afraid to bother them on the phone or whatever. We're big fans of the email, but I can contact her day or night and I'll have an answer. She's the best.

What is your favorite thing about being an actor?

That I'm able to do it. I have a lot of friends that have left the business. I have friends that have moved out of New York and LA because they just don't have patience for it anymore. I will confess that there was a passion in my stomach every time I would go into a dark theatre that there is less of now. When I was twenty-five, there was magic. I thought it was all a miracle. It still just completely turns me on though. It turns me on more than anything. I'm just very fortunate. I think you have to stick with it. The thing I like about it the most is that I've been able to sustain a career in it at all. I've only done two short films—no feature films—and a handful of television shows, maybe seven or eight. That used to be extremely important to me. It was such a goal, especially since I was in LA. Now, those jobs are just icing. I still pursue them, but they're icing. If I can do theatre all the time and support myself with the commercials, I'd be satisfied for the rest of my life. I would never turn down any television show; I like it, but it's not as fun as doing a play. I'll be doing that forever.

What is your least favorite thing about being an actor?

It's such an easy answer, but it's the lack of stability. Still, don't second-guess what's going to happen. Just go for it. It's just that now that I'm older, I'm trying to buy a house in this crazy market in LA and I've got to have something dependable. Always in the back of my head, I have, "Will I have a check next month?" I've been very lucky though.

How do you choose the material you work on?

When it's original scripts and they ask me to do readings or workshops of scripts, I'll do all of them. I'll do anything. But material that I am interested in is kind of in balance with who the director is. I seem to be very motivated, theatrically, by who the directors are that I haven't worked with, like Jessica Kubzansky. I would pursue working with her and would probably commit to working with her without reading the material if she thought I was right for it because I like mapping out connections with the directors in town that work really hard. You never know how material's going to grow. I go by the author and the director more than the material, actually.

How do you prepare for a role?

I go by what the author and director have in mind. I read the script. As far as acting homework, I like to do it on my feet. In my opinion, the table work that they do the first two days in theatre always makes me very self-conscious. It's like, I can sit in my room and write a four-page essay on what I think my character's about, but I haven't heard the other voices in the play or anything like that. Once you get up and start blocking and start hearing what the connections are, you automatically crave breaking down a scene into beats because you need to know why something is making sense or not making sense. That's where the homework comes in. I like to prepare and approach it while we're already in there, as we start to rehearse. I primarily work inside-out. Costumes, or whether the character has a limp, all that comes later. It starts with the way I approach the character and then we go from there. We braid the character traits into who I am. We braid what the director says into that. I hate it when my friends insist on coming on opening night because that show's like an adrenaline-filled pep rally. The show's not ready yet! The show really starts braiding "right" about a week and a half into it. Then things start to change on their own because everybody's not scared. Everybody is out of their own way. You're not thinking about it anymore. It's more natural. The last three performances, a line reading comes out and you go, "Oh, shit! *That's* the way I was supposed to do it!" It's hard to leave a character. I love them all.

Who are *your* favorite actors?

I love Jude Law. I love Sean Penn. I love Alec Baldwin. What they all have in common is they're very grounded. Their faces are very grounded when they're in a close-up but there's a lot of dramatic energy. That means to me they're being theatrical. The same thing with Anthony Hopkins: His face looks really still but the eyes are on fire. When it's time to break, you really feel them simmering. I think all four of them are great at that. I like what's cooking underneath. It's heightened language the same way poetry is heightened writing. In acting, you're conveying something that's bigger than just you in your living room, therefore there's got to be something bigger going on inside your head than just being realistic. That's why I love those guys.

What do you wish someone had told you at the beginning of your career?

You should not second-guess your instinct. You should not say no to any opportunity. You cannot second-guess your career. It takes a path of its own. You are wasting your time if you are going back and forth and really pulling your hair out as to whether you should take a gig that's out of town or stay in this waiter job because it's the most flexible thing. My waiter job was the least-flexible job I ever had! The nine-to-five jobs, if they understand you're an actor, are a lot more flexible. If you're bartending, you can't leave the bar for an hour. If you really are serious, put the career first and then let everything that is going to fall out from it fall out. It takes a life of its own and it's all meant to be.

I learned as an older actor that you just have to go for the big stuff immediately. I'd say: Find LA, find New York. If you're going to go to college, value that. But you don't really learn the business 'til you're in it. They spend those four years of college telling you, "When you're in the real world, this is what's going to happen." Three days in the real world teach you a lot faster than a whole year of school. Without saying that I don't value the time I went to college—because all those roles, making me feel like a big fish in a little pond, gave me the confidence when I was in the real world—I think I wish I'd been told I could go for the big stuff right away: "You can be on Broadway." If you think you're a good actor, go audition for the Broadway plays. Avoid the advice that tells you that you have to start at *A* and then *B* and then *C*. Go for the big stuff and when they say no, find the one that says yes. That'll beget work.

Michael McManus

Michael McManus grew up in Minneapolis and attended the University of Minnesota to become a teacher. It didn't happen. In 1964, he got his first professional job at Dudley Riggs' Brave New Workshop, a satirical revue theatre in Minneapolis.

In 1975, Michael and three other Riggs performers headed to LA. The group started a small theatre called the Hollywood Canteen, where they performed as the Comedy Corporation. Michael's first television role was as a woodsman in an episode of Mel Brooks' When Things Were Rotten. Other shows followed: M*A*S*H, Columbo, Coach, Happy Days, Laverne and Shirley, Night Court, Rhoda, Newhart, Baretta, According to Jim, Lewis and Clark with Gabe Kaplan, the first season of Baywatch, and Thicke of the Night. Michael has written for television: doing punch-up on Taxi and The Faculty, the Marie show, Night Wrap, and some Steve Martin variety shows. An NBC special, All Commercials, won a WGA Award.

Films include Mother, Jugs & Speed; Kentucky Fried Movie; Smokey and the Bandit; and Poltergeist. Through all of this, Michael always finds time for his first love, improvisational comedy. He performed with the critically-acclaimed group Funny You Should Ask for fifteen years. Michael wrote a television pilot and feature for HBO called The Chameleon. He was associate producer and contributed to the writing of Hot Shots: Part Deux. He also co-produced and co-wrote the screenplay for Touchstone's Mafia! (or its original, funnier title Jane Austin's Mafia!).

Michael lives in LA with his beautiful wife, television writer/producer Nancy Steen, and handsome son, Lake, who is smarter than both of his parents. Michael continues to write, act, and even improvise a bit when a local group needs a warm body. He spends his summers on a picturesque lake in Northern Minnesota where the fishing is pretty good. More at http://us.imdb.com/name/nm0573158.

photo by Sandy Simpson

What made you choose Los Angeles?

My background was improvisational comedy and sketch comedy. I worked in a theatre in Minneapolis called the Dudley Riggs' Brave New Workshop. I worked there a bunch of years. One of the guys moved out to LA—an actor/writer—and he encouraged me to come out. In '75, myself and a few other people in the cast at the theatre packed our cars, drove out, rented an apartment near Hollywood High. The place was filled with hookers; we didn't know! The apartments had a pool!

We took the stuff we had from Minneapolis—the sketches— and did the Comedy Store, Improv, Ice House, all those places. Eventually we found a place across the street from the Groundlings that at the time was a Country-slash-lesbian bar. There was a bar and a stage, we hung lights, we put in revolving doors that fit our comedy needs, we brought out a couple of guys that had worked with us in Minneapolis to do tech work. One guy made the place into a little restaurant, selling soup and sandwiches. And that lasted for two-and-a-half years. It was called Hollywood Canteen and our group was called the Comedy Corporation. There were four of us. It became a showcase. People would come to the show, we all got agents through that. This was in the days of variety shows.

We got really good reviews. One night, Jackie Cooper, who'd been doing a lot of directing, came on a Sunday. It was a dead night. Nobody showed up. It was just Jackie and his wife that showed. We apologized and said, "Sorry. Have a sandwich on us." And he said, "No, no. C'mon, do the show." So, we did this for an hour and a half, basically for them. They laughed their asses off, had a great time, and he ended up casting us. I did a pilot for him.

When did you know you wanted to become an actor?

I had a wonderful English and Speech teacher in high school that directed plays. His son is Richard Dean Anderson, actually. So this is Steve Anderson—a great guy. He was the cool teacher. He was a World War II bomber pilot. He drove sports cars. At night he played in a jazz band. He was the cool guy and we all wanted to be him. He got me doing state speech contests and stuff. Then I did the school plays. I think I just wanted to do something—I didn't know what.

Oh, before that, in junior high, there was a radio show—Top 40 kind of show—and the guy did a Dracula impression. He, as Dracula, and himself, as the disc jockey, would talk to each other. I would listen to this. I answered a contest question or something on the show. I hooked up with the guy and I would write jokes for him. I was about fourteen. I would call this guy up, tell him all these corny Dracula jokes, he'd use them on the air, and he'd send me movie tickets or albums. He never paid me, but I could go to the station and hang out.

Senior year of high school, we started going to Dudley Riggs and it was kind of in this hippie part of town—this was cool for us. My buddy and I would go and get espresso coffee—we'd never heard of that. There were cute girls on stage smoking and swearing. I liked hanging out there. So, later, another friend and myself, after starting at the University of Minnesota, went to another show at Dudley Riggs and they were doing parodies of Miss America and stuff. I started wondering how to get into these shows. So, I asked and was told, "Come backstage and read!" So, we did that and were told, "Okay, come back next Friday." In the meantime, we both got cast in *Romeo and Juliet* at school. We had to choose. I chose this and my friend chose *Romeo and Juliet*. I stayed with Dudley Riggs for a couple of years and did shows. I never actually graduated college. I was going to be a teacher and then I started down this path.

How did you get your first agent?

A friend of mine was a writer on *When Things Were Rotten*—it was a Mel Brooks' parody of *Robin Hood*—a pretty cute show. I got a shot on the show, so I did that. The guy who was playing the Sheriff of Nottingham was a pretty gregarious, nice guy. I said, "Gee, I need an agent. Do you know anybody?" He said, "Yeah, I'll give you a number." So, I went there—it was an agency called Jack Fields; it's been gone for a while. I met them, they liked me, and I said, "Y'know I'm in this improv group." And they said, "Bring 'em in!" So, I brought the other three people in and we all ended up with the same agent.

The next thing I got was a movie, because, when I was sitting on a couch at Paramount, waiting to see the casting guy for *When Things Were Rotten*, Mike Fenton walked by and said, "I think you'd be good for this thing." I read for it and it was *Mother, Jugs & Speed*. I got that. I love Mike Fenton. He got me a lot of work. It's about knowing somebody, almost seventy-five percent of the time.

How would you advise an actor on cultivating relationships in the industry?

Only get to know important people! Don't talk to the little people! They can't help you! They just want things. If you didn't talk to them and they *become* important people, *then* talk to them. Grow a mustache—they won't recognize you—and talk to them!

Ah, the guy I knew who was writing on *When Things Were Rotten* was a kid I went to high school with. In fact, when I did the show at Dudley Riggs and my friend went on to do *Romeo and Juliet*, we needed another person in the show and I asked my girlfriend: "Do you know anybody funny?" And the answer was, "Pat Proft," this kid from ninth grade. So, I got Pat, who went to Dudley Riggs with me, and subsequently went on to write *Police Academy* and *Naked Gun*. And he's still one of my good friends. It's a small circle, but you meet somebody, which leads to meeting somebody else, which leads to meeting somebody else.

What is your favorite thing about being an actor?

Not having to work in a factory. My dad did that, so I saw that. I think I like creating, whether I'm writing or acting. I'm not a big sit-by-myself writer. I like to work in a room with a few other people, bouncing ideas off each other. One guy says one thing and I say something funny and the next guy adds to that and I add something and the next guy says something funny and we are writing. It's very similar to my on-stage experience in improvisation.

What is your least favorite thing about being an actor?

I don't like the waiting around. If you've done a job and it's over with and something else isn't right around the corner, the little guy in your stomach says, "This is it! They found out! You're never going to work again!" I don't like that guy. But, it's been okay for me, I think. I've always worked. I've never had another kind of job—waiter or anything—in thirty years. Y'know I got out here and I got this job as the spokesman for Olympia Beer. They were going national at the time, so it was two years or so of those ads as the friendly bartender. That was a good start.

How do you handle the difference between improvisation and scripted work?

I think it really depends on who I'm working with and what my position is in the show. If I'm doing a guest shot on a show, I'm there to facilitate the show and they usually don't have a lot of time for the guest-star to develop a great idea. I've also done a million pilots and series where they'll have more time for me to come up with bits and ideas. It depends on who the writers are and the producers and the directors. I've been in situations where they don't want you to stray from the script. I find in the movies that directors will give a little more room to an actor to be flexible and come up with things within the context of the scene.

When you do your best work is when you bring something to it, when you make it yourself—whatever that means. For me, it sometimes helps if I can fool around with the lines a little bit. If you've got another actor who's comfortable with doing that, it's great. I did a TV-movie called *Dempsey*—it was about Jack Dempsey, played by Treat Williams—and I played Babe Ruth. They were contemporaries. In one of the scenes, he was thinking about quitting boxing and he went to see Babe Ruth on the set of the movie Babe Ruth was shooting during the off-season. They had this conversation basically about what were they going to do with their lives. Pretty heavy stuff for these two fellows who weren't real intellectual. They were having this conversation while walking through the studio lot. This was set in the '20s so they had showgirls and all kinds of people going by in costumes. We realized, in doing that scene, that these guys would not have just discussed this heavy stuff. They were players. So, we kind of rewrote the whole thing and improvised a lot of stuff about what happened around us—women going by—talking about how we got to play around in these lives. It made the scene better.

How do you approach auditions?

They're looking for people who are comfortable. If it's something that you're not going to get anyway, and you know that, you have to find a way to make them remember you. I remember a friend and I got called in for a Dockers ad and we were both like, "We're not going to get a Dockers ad! We're not those guys!" So, we went in for it, did the whole thing, and at the end of it, we mooned the camera. The casting director was laughing. You just have to do something to make it your own. How many actors do you know that just go in, do the words, do a really good job, and then that's it—they still don't get it? You're not just there to please that guy, that camera guy, that director, that casting lady.

Do you ever feel like giving up?

No. That's the nice thing about always doing a couple of different things. If I'm not acting, there is a writing gig I'll book. Sometimes I have to push one side down in order to work on the other—like when I was writing on the Steve Martin specials or something and would take weeks where I wouldn't act much—but that's fine. I'll come back. Writing helps a lot with acting. And I think so many years with improv helped while I was writing all the time. I would always have some place to go, every week. I think that's a smart thing to do, by the way. Have some place to go every week to do something. For me, it was improv every Saturday night. No matter what the week was like, if I didn't get an acting job that week, I could go and do my show and get a laugh. Another benefit to that was, if I got sick of the typecasting—if I got really tired of playing the dumb truck driver or whatever they saw me as—I could do this improv show and I could be the King of France, a waitress, a Thai valet parker. It was great. I could be whatever I wanted to be while keeping my chops up. Doing improvisation is like writing on your feet.

What impact has acting had on your personal life?

Maybe I'm special, but when I moved out here in '75 with three other people, I married one of them: Nancy Steen. She's a television writer/producer for sitcoms. We had worked at the Dudley Riggs show together and would do these college shows. We fell in love there. We're real normal people. We've written together—she doesn't like that, so we don't do it much. She's done a few different things than I have. I've been an actor a lot longer than she was one. She's been writing sitcoms since *Happy Days*. We've been together thirty years.

We like to blame the Midwest for us being together so long. We're grounded. We still have a place back on the lake in Minnesota. We go fishing. We have a son who has no interest in the industry. He's really smart: a brainiac.

Who are *your* favorite actors?

I've always liked Jack Lemmon's work. He had that everyman quality. Jimmy Stewart too. As for people I've worked with, Lloyd Bridges was great. He managed to have this great career and kept his great family together. He was just a cool guy to work with—a nice man. Richard Crenna was a really good guy. I liked him a lot. But in this business, it's not just the actors I like. It's people like Jackie Cooper, who gave me a break. Sheila Manning, who gave me my commercial break. She's great. Mike Fenton, of course, cast me in so many things.

What advice would you give to a performer starting out?

You can't always do this, but for us—my group I came to LA with—we had something we were coming here with. We had an act. We had a tangible thing where we could say, "Hey, come look at me." That was very helpful, I think. That, and having some place to be seen. Just have something. And find some truth in what you're doing, whatever it is. Even the wackiest character in the world has to have a thread of truth and believability for the audience to care.

Chris Messina

Chris Messina appeared in Salome *on Broadway. His Off-Broadway credits include* The American Clock *(with the Signature Theatre Company),* Refuge *(with Playwrights Horizons),* The Hologram Theory *(with the Blue Light Theatre Company),* The Light Outside *(with the Flea),* Blur *(with Manhattan Theatre Club),* Good Thing *(with the New Group),* This Thing of Darkness *(with the Atlantic Theatre Company),* Faster *(with Rattlestick Theatre Company),* Far Away *(with New York Theatre Workshop),* The Seagull *(with Second Stage), and* The Cherry Orchard *(with Williamstown Theatre Festival). Chris did* Late Night/Early Morning *as a part of the* Downtown Plays *which were first presented at the TriBeCa Theatre Festival and later at the US Comedy Arts Festival in Aspen, Colorado, where it won the 2005 Live Jury Award for Best Theatre.*

Chris' film and TV credits include Rounders, You've Got Mail, The Seige, Ordinary Sinner, Road, Crooked Corner, *and* Bittersweet Place. *Chris recently joined the cast of HBO's* Six Feet Under *for its final season.*

Chris studies at the Actors Center with Ron Van Lieu and Earle Gister. He is a lifetime member of the Actors Studio. More information is available at http://us.imdb.com/name/nm0582149.

photo courtesy Chris Messina

When did you know you wanted to become an actor?

My mom was a dance teacher, so she put me in dancing school really early. I loved it. I had danced up until ninth grade. Then I discovered girls and parties. I kind of realized that I wasn't going to be the dancer that I wanted to be. I wanted to go to LaGuardia High School but my mom wouldn't let me go. I grew up on Long Island and went to the public high school. I knew I wasn't going to be able to be Baryshnikov. The girl I was partnered up with in dance class was so into it that she would drive into the City and study with these great teachers. That didn't happen with me. But at my high school we had an amazing Theatre department. It was exceptional. I wish every kid had one. Living Theatre I was an English credit and then Living Theatre II was the company. We would improvise and put together plays about safe sex and drugs, and then put them on in front of the school. This teacher was taking football players and making them cry. They were opening up and crying. It was cool to be an actor. It was really cool.

I did so poorly in school and I was kind of searching for some kind of identity, like every kid I'm sure. Doing those plays allowed me to see that I could be all of those different people and kind of run away from myself and be somebody else. I remember doing a play where we would improv these characters. I improvised this really swishy gay guy. This was ninth grade so I did the stereotypical limp wrist kind of thing. The class laughed and I thought, "Oh, that's good. They laughed." I didn't realize that the teacher was taking these characters and developing monologues and then they were going to be presented. I guess, as we were getting closer to them being presented, I went to the teacher and said, "Look, I don't want to play the gay guy." I was scared. I didn't want to do it. And she was like, "Why? It's a great character you came up with. I think you should pull it back—it's getting a little cartoony—but it's a great character." She talked me into doing it.

I remember the first day. We're sitting there. I'm in the ninth grade and there's all these seniors and I started the monologue— and I had pulled it back to not-swishy at all—and if you were in the audience, it wasn't quite clear if these kids were talking about themselves. So, the monologue was like, "I don't know. I feel really weird sometimes—like I don't fit in—because I'm gay." The audience was silent and this was a packed room, a black box theatre, and some kid yells, "Faggot!" And in the monologue I said, "Fuck you." The crowd went crazy. All the kids were clapping and yelling and there was this rush. I just kept going with the monologue. And afterwards all the kids backstage were like, "You said, 'Fuck you!' You said, 'Fuck you!' *to the audience!*" And the teacher wanted to talk to me. She said, "I liked what you did with that, you broke the fourth wall, but you did it in character. You stayed in character. You kept going. You used it. It was interesting." Well, then the second period came where we presented it again—it was probably everybody's lunch period—and I got to the part in the monologue where I said, "I'm gay." Somebody just snickered. Nobody even said anything. And I screamed, "FUCK

YOU!" I was looking for that same thing. It didn't work. The teacher said, after, "Come here. You said it again and it was uncalled for." We talked about repeating things and trying to hit things and that was the beginning of something really cool.

I went on to do those plays in high school and we weren't doing *Grease*, we were doing these improv shows. It was great. I was doing so poorly in school. The teacher would turn around and I'd be standing on the desk or something. A lot of the kids took me as a funny guy and I'd get up there and try to do serious stuff and the kids would be laughing. These were really great lessons in learning to control your audience: "We're going to be funny now. Now the material's turning." It was really hard to do with a bunch of kids who know you as "Messina, the guy who was doing a keg-stand." But that's how I got going.

I applied to one college, Marymount Manhattan College. I didn't have good grades at all. My teacher had studied with the head of Marymount Manhattan College. They'd let me in if my parents would pay extra money to have a tutor constantly working with me. I got in on a theatre scholarship but I left after one semester. I dropped out. Because of the kind of background I had, I wasn't into some of the stuff they were teaching. I felt like the kids weren't as lucky as I'd been in doing all the improv in high school. I didn't like "acting." It turned me off. So I went back to Long Island and worked on a lobster boat and delivered pizzas and landscaped and saved money to become Jack Kerouac. I was going to come to California and smoke a lot of dope. And then by the time that whole phase passed, I remember standing outside of the pizza place waiting to do a delivery and it just hit me. I wanted to go back to the City and become an actor.

I first started commuting and going to the Lee Strasberg Theatre thinking that Lee Strasberg was still alive and teaching and that I would be in *The Godfather: Part V* with him or something. He would tell me about Brando. Of course, he wasn't alive at the time and I found that out when I went there for my interview. So, I commuted in and studied there for two years. I learned some interesting stuff. I moved into an apartment on Gold Street, which is in the South Street

Seaport. I lived there in a studio apartment—there were three of us. It was a bad lab experiment with one other actor and a photographer. I used to go see plays in the City every night or every other night. I'd be doing it to learn. I'd be studying. I wasn't going to NYU or Juilliard; I was going to put myself through the Rocky Balboa School of Theatre. I was going to see everything.

I guess then I did a play in the City. The guy I was living with was doing this play and he told me to come join in. It was cool. This was at the St. Marks Theatre, which is still there, and it was a play called *Plato* and it was based on Plato in *Rebel Without a Cause*—the Sal Mineo character. A friend of mine was in it playing Buzz, the guy who challenges James Dean, and I played Crunch, the sidekick. I think I had one line: "Down there, Buzz." I think I really milked that line.

How did you get your first agent?

My father called up and said, "A friend of mine's father is Howard Feuer and he's casting a movie." I didn't know who Howard Feuer was, so I looked him up: *The Silence of the Lambs, Bad Boys, Dead Poets Society*. Okay, so he's a big casting director. So I went and met with Howard Feuer and I was twenty years old or so. He said, "Do you want to read for a small part in a movie with Meryl Streep?" I had never done any films. I had done this one play and had been studying at the Lee Strasberg Theatre. So, I said, "Sure." It was only five lines, but it was fine, perfectly fine. It was a Barbet Schroeder movie. I read with him in the office and he said, "Come back tomorrow." Perfect. I came back the next day and I got the job. He sent me over to Paradigm, which is like God sending over one of the disciples. They signed me. They said, "Do a monologue." I did *Does a Tiger Wear a Necktie?* as Pacino. I think I slammed my fist on the desk and maybe knocked over some paper clips. I walked out of there and the whole office was like, "Who's that idiot?" And I guess somehow I made it through the door—most likely because Howard Feuer set me up and because I was very excited and eager. I worked with Paradigm for seven years.

It was tough going though. Because of that movie—by the way, I was edited out of that film—I was going out on all this stuff I wasn't ready for. I really wasn't ready. I didn't have the chops. I didn't have the skills. It was frustrating because I was having these great opportunities and I kept blowing them. I first thought I was Ethan Hawke, I thought I was Johnny Depp. In my mind's eye, I was Dean. I thought I looked like Dean. Maybe Dean's distant cousin from New Mexico is more like it. I think there was a moment where I thought, "Oh, I get it. In order to work at my size and how I look, I've gotta be good. I've gotta go into the room and be real good. My goatee or a cool haircut is not going to cut it." Some guys can work off the goatee. I was not going to be one of those guys. I had to get good.

I went to every acting conservatory I think there is in Manhattan—from HB to Circle Rep to Circle in the Square—I ended up with private coaching, some Shakespeare. I went to the Actors Center—I think I was there the day those doors opened and I've been there ever since, whenever I can. I was lucky enough to meet Ron Van Lieu and Earl Gister who really changed my life as an actor. They took what I was throwing out to the next level. Then I started booking. I think when I was with Paradigm I had done some *Law & Order* and a slew of studio films: *The Siege, Rounders, You've Got Mail*. But those were like glorified extras. Four lines. Work one day, two days tops. But then I started booking plays. The first Off-Broadway play I booked, I was blessed enough to be in the room with Arthur Miller and he cast me on the spot in *The American Clock* which was at the Signature Theatre Company.

From there, like anything else, it's a clique Off-Broadway. The audition doors started to open. From there I did a play called *Refuge* by Jess Goldberg with a really great cast including Catherine Kellner, Chris Bauer, Mandy Siegfried. Neil Pepe directed it for Playwrights Horizons. It was a really huge lesson for me. I was really able to put this stuff that I was learning all these years and focus it in and figure out how not to say, "Fuck you," twice and try to get the same reaction from it.

I was doing a lot of plays that weren't getting received all that well. I kind of blew off pilot season every year. If I was in a play, that was where I was. I wasn't going to be the type of actor who left a play to go out to TV or anything. Then I got into a play called *Far Away*, a Caryl Churchill play with Fran McDormand and Stephen Daldry and that was my first time in a play where they were lining up down the block. Then it got extended and it was one of those phenomenal experiences. That led to changing agencies. I went to Endeavor and got a management company and then did *Salome* on Broadway with Pacino and Dianne Wiest and Marisa Tomei. I played a very small role, I was just in twenty minutes of the play, but it was cool to work with those extraordinary people. The lessons are amazing. Right around *Far Away* and *Salome*, I started to get more into the cinema. My film auditions really had picked up, so I started to investigate filmmaking. I bought a camera. I'm very much into the theatre, always will do it, but I'm really into film acting right now: watching it, dissecting it. I'm really interested in that medium for storytelling, the size of it.

What made you choose New York?

I will always be a New York actor. This year is my first pilot season in LA. I came out last year to do a short film for a friend and I went on a bunch of pilots but it was like a two-week thing. This is the first time I've come out and I don't know if I'll make it the entire season. I have nothing against it, but I miss New York. It would be cool to do an interesting TV show, but I'd rather do films. Things have changed. When I did *The American Clock* and *Refuge*, they were offering some roles in those plays to star names, but it wasn't as ridiculous as it is now. It wouldn't surprise me if Paris Hilton was doing *The Glass Menagerie* next year. I wouldn't be shocked by it.

How do you handle having come close on some really big projects?

The thing is, I don't know. You're catching me at a really interesting time where I'm really trying to find that balance. I've never had balance in my life. I've always been very obsessed and I've spent a lot of time really depressed and really angry and comparing myself. I think, it's beginning to change and I think it has to do with some things going on in my personal life-slash-getting older. I used to say, "It isn't fair!" But I started to realize that this business isn't fair, that's what it is. It *isn't* fair. I think that having more of a life, whether that's having a family or going on a hike or having other hobbies and other loves helps.

I love the craft of acting. I don't love the business of it. You don't succeed because you work your ass off or because you paid tons of money to study. I've been trying to figure out: "What is success?" I'm trying to change my perspective. It's great that I've had really great near-misses. I can look at them as, "This could've been," and "Why me?" I've done that. I've been practicing—and believe me, it's not easy—saying, "I'm blessed and lucky to have those near-misses, to have these opportunities. I have great agents and great mentors and friends around to bounce these things off." I work on that and I do go to the shrink as much as possible. If I die today, I had a lot of great moments. I guess the last thing I would've wanted to have said is, "Why didn't I get that pilot?" I don't want my last words to be bitching about that show I didn't get.

What impact has acting had on your personal life?

It fucks with you. Being an actor, you're just constantly looking at yourself in the mirror: "You're just funny looking. You're just too short. You're not interesting. You're boring. I wouldn't buy you." It fucks with your perspective of yourself. You're constantly battling that. You've got to come out of that going, "I'm okay." You've got to keep open. There's that quote that you have to have the inner life of a rose and the shell of a tortoise. I think Stella Adler or Uta Hagen said that. But you have to have this open heart *and* this armor. It's hard to have both, but you've gotta.

I'm recently separated and my wife was an actress. There's a lot of things in there that I don't need to get into, but acting was definitely a mistress for both of us and something that got in the middle of life. And certainly more for me. I think a relationship between actors can definitely work. It depends on the individuals, first of all, and then where they're at in their careers. I ended up many times going to bed bitching about an actor and his career and then I'd wake up in the morning bitching about another one. I think somebody can only be attracted to that or want to be with that for so long. I know *I* don't want to be with that. And I don't want to be that guy. Who the hell would want to hang with that all the time?

Doing theatre, you miss weddings, you miss funerals. I missed a lot of stuff and had a lot of people become annoyed with me. In the past I was abiding by Uta Hagen's *Respect for Acting*: shut off the telephone, take a long walk down the beach alone. I was very much: "This is my life. You want to be friends with me, you want to be hanging with me, this is what I'm going to do." And I still feel like that when I have work to do. It's hard when you're playing a character to just let it go without shutting the world out like that. It's not a nine-to-five kind of thing.

What is your favorite thing about being an actor?

The thing that I connect to most is getting to be other people. I'm not tied down to just being Chris. I think we all have a lot of people within us and we're being allowed to have them come out and it's somewhat safe. I've been under the title of "actor" for about nine, ten years. Now I'm beginning to play the role of "Chris," which is an interesting role. I'm hoping to get some good reviews and play the part for a while.

Baadja-Lyne Odums

Baadja-Lyne Odums has kids (check), has grands (check), has two cocker spaniels (checky check), and is waiting to be cast in her own television series (double check, please). Baadja is a very spiritual person, meaning God and all of His glory controls her existence. She not only loves what she does, she lives what she does and that is to act.

Baadja started acting when most people reading this were spiritual dots in a microcosmic time warp. Uh, don't try to "figger" that out. Just roll with it for a minute.

Many, many, many years ago, being shy and unpopular, acting became Baadja's escape from reality. It was just her and the characters she created within her: a perfect world where she was in control of her life, her loves, lovers (some poor choices) and her future; where the curtain rose daily as to who she was going to be. Fast-forward: today she still creates within herself, but now she gets paid for it.

Baadja's body of work includes The Ladykillers, Judging Amy, Without a Trace, ER, Philly, Strong Medicine, The Shield, Charmed, Clubhouse, Joan of Arcadia, Cold Case, *and the NAACP-Award-winning play* The Marriage.

Baadja has just gotten into sewing and she loves it. She has made some cute and some not-so-cute fashions. Be that as it may, they are her fashions and she wears them sometimes against her own better judgment (ha ha). Baadja will be hiring a PR person to write her bios as soon as she signs her first ten million dollar contract. Peace out. More information is at http://us.imdb.com/name/nm0644172.

photo by Kevin McIntyre
http://kevinmcphotograph.com

When did you know you wanted to become an actor?

It was actually by fluke. Growing up, as a child, I was always an outcast. I didn't really have a lot of friends. I was always the biggest one, the one that didn't have good clothes. Me and my girlfriend were sitting around and we saw Bill Cosby on TV on *Room 222*. They were looking for extras for the classroom. We didn't know what an "extra" was. All we heard was that they would pay us and we'd be on TV. We went and we stood in a line that wrapped all the way down Hollywood Boulevard. This was back in 1972, '73. We stood out there and we waited and we got called in. They asked for headshots—we didn't know what headshots were. We were just *there*! We didn't get selected, but it sparked something in me. When I went home and started looking at TV and started looking at these actors, it was as if I wanted to do that.

I started inquiring about taking classes. I ended up at a place called Inner City. At that time, that was where every actor went: Black, Hispanic, it didn't matter. That's where you were. A lot of talented people came out of there, including Sumi Haru. That was the place where you broke your teeth or your teeth started growing. You had to take dance. You had to take voice. You had to do all the things that now, a lot of the actors are missing because they just want to act. I wasn't used to working. I wasn't used to being disciplined. But when you got there, you had to be disciplined or you were out. There were no second chances. When I got there, there was an instructor, Beah Richards. The first time I got on stage, I thought I would never come back into acting. She told me the truth and I couldn't accept the truth. She told me, "No one's gonna believe what you just did. *You* don't even believe what you just did! To be an actor, you do *not* have to act." I went home and thought about it and said, "If this is really what you want to do, you gotta come out of your shell." I stayed with her for maybe two seasons and then I went on to Ed Cambridge's Negro Ensemble Company. I stayed there for about five years, at the studio on Santa Monica Boulevard in Hollywood.

I started on stage. I didn't get to film and TV until about five, six years ago. A lot of actors were leaving their agents for whatever reason and when the actors' strike was going on a friend of mine, Bill Brown, said, "Why don't you contact my agent?" I did, and he didn't contact me back right away. I was working a temp job in Long Beach and he called me and told me to come in. I came in and I did a monologue. I signed a contract that day and ever since then it's been going up, up, up. About two years ago, I got a manager. She's really been grooming me. A lot of things that you think you know in this business, you don't really know. The people that have actually been where you're trying to get start guiding you and showing you different things. I used to have a hard time interacting with people. I can't just go into a crowd and say, "Hi!" I have to stand back and size everybody up and then *maybe* I'll go in. My manager says, "Don't be pushy, but let people know you're out there." I've met almost every casting director now, when five years ago, nobody knew who I was.

Now people are calling me in. I got one job called *The Hard Easy* with Peter Weller and Gary Busey. The casting director called my agent and asked me if I wanted the job. It wasn't a big part, but she called *me*! I didn't even have to audition! I just sat there crying. That's never happened to me before. It's always like I was begging for a job and now people are calling my agent. It's just been a blessing.

What were your survival jobs?

I worked for the government for thirty years. I was a physical science technician. We analyzed hazardous waste for disposal coming off the ships or coming out of the harbor. It started getting political where it was time to shut down the base at Long Beach and everything was going to go to San Diego. I didn't want to go to San Diego, so I was forced out. I had to do an early retirement. I couldn't live off unemployment, so I had to get a temporary job. The first job I got was in a warehouse. It was the most god-awful job I have ever experienced in my life. I had to go get safety shoes. They'd reproduce CDs and we had to pack 'em and then we had to lift 'em and by the end of the day my butt, back, teeth, *everything* ached. I said, "Lord, just let me be an actor! I will do anything you say, just let me be an actor." The next job I got, I worked in Long Beach at an up-and-coming computer company. They were going on the Internet, having teachers put their lesson plans up so the kids would come online to do them. I was basically the housemother because what I did was answer the phone, I cleaned the kitchen, I kept the bathroom in order. I didn't have to use my brain. I left there during the actors' strike, and I couldn't get any more work. I didn't know where the money was going to come from. My daughter was helping me the best she could, but I didn't have any money.

What do you consider your first break?

There was an ad in the *Dramalogue* for Bonnie's play, *The Female Perspective*, and I didn't have money. I didn't have any gas.

And I went to this audition. I was scrapin' pennies to get there. I did a monologue for Bonnie that I made up on the spot. I didn't have anything! I wanted it so bad. I wanted to work! I was at a point where I didn't want to exist anymore because nothing was working for me, I thought. I did that play and I was getting the bug back to perform, but I still didn't have any money. I think everyone was going out somewhere one night and I wanted to go, but I didn't have any money. I said, "Oh, I'm going to pass. What I really need to do is look for a job." Well, one of the cast members, Lisa Lefevre, said, "What kind of work do you do? My husband is looking for someone! Let me talk to him." It was almost a month, but then her husband and a coworker came to see our show.

That next day, he called me in for an interview. I said, "Lord, I have less than a fourth of a tank of gas. I don't have any money and I have to have money to park downtown. But I'm going on faith." I went down there and I parked in the wrong place—I didn't know this at the time. I went in and I did the interview and they said, "We'll get back to you." They asked me for my parking ticket as I left and said, "Oh, this is not our lot. You're going to pay a good fifteen, twenty dollars." I was crushed. But then they said, "Can you start to work next week?" I said, "Can I start now?" They said, "No. You start next week." So, I started that next week, but they advanced me money because my house was in foreclosure, my car was behind. Sometimes, I would sleep in my car so they wouldn't come and take it. That's how bad it was. I said, "Lord, something has got to give. I'm coming out here on faith." They kept me there long enough for me to pull myself out. When 9/11 came, things started going bad for everybody, so they had to let me go. By that time, I had gotten *Philly*, I got *ER*, things had started picking up. And now, my house is out of foreclosure, my car is paid for, and I'm just so happy. When I think back on that, I wanted to leave this Earth. That's how bad it was. And I know it's a sin to even think about committing suicide, but that's how bad it was. God has been good.

How do you handle rejection?

You really have to have patience and faith. I've been doing this for thirty-five years and the last five years, it's really been paying off for me. I think once I got on stage and I saw how people received me—because I've always been self-conscious of my body and everything—I knew people weren't looking at that. They were reacting to a character. People don't judge you when you're on stage. They're relating to that character and where that goes in their life. If I make someone stop and realize, "Hey, that made me feel good," or, "That made me feel sad," I can just let all of this out. I don't have to worry about what I look like. I just get up there and do the best job that I've been trained to do. It has been a blessing. Every day I get up and I pray and I just thank God. My faith is stronger—not only in God, but in myself—because of what I've faced. I used to say, when someone would ask me what I do, in a whisper, "Uh, I'm an actor." And now I say, "I'M AN ACTOR!" I can say it now! It took me to get this old to realize that I'm at a young place. I feel great about it.

What do you wish someone had told you at the beginning of your career?

I did some extra work maybe about five times. I knew it wasn't for me. If I had guidance where I would've started in this business—although I'm glad I started in theatre—maybe I would've started in film and television a little bit sooner if I had known where to go. At the time, there were a lot of Black-exploitation movies out but there was only a handful of Black actors. Either you were one of those actors or you were an extra. I knew I didn't want to do that. I was married at the time and I was working so I wasn't going out for a lot of work anyway, I figured, "Oh, I'll wait for my big break." Because I wasn't in the union, the few extra jobs I did, they treated us like dirt. We worked eighteen, nineteen hours and they barely wanted to pay us twenty-five dollars and even then they had the nerve to ask us, before we even got paid, if we could come back the next day and work another eighteen hours before we could get that little twenty-five dollars. I said, "Y'know what? If this is how you get into acting, I don't want it. There's got to be a better way." So, I gravitated toward these theatre ensembles that were like family. If something happened to one, everybody knew about it and they would all come help you out.

How do you choose the material you work on?

Most everything now comes through my agent or manager. They'll call me and say, "What do you think about this?" And sometimes I can't see the vision. I'll say, "If you truly see the vision, I'll work it for you." But we try to get a balance. One thing came through that they called me on—and it's not that I've never heard curse words—and every page was full of curse words. I said, "I can't do this. I just can't do it." My agent sent me out for a Howard Stern movie and I said, "I can't do this. I cannot be a mammy." I just don't want to be a mammy, and that's what they were looking for: a loud, bodacious Black woman. I just won't do that. I said, "I came to you guys so that I can clean up that stuff. I want to do judges." I'm not like, "Oh, they said, 'Damn.' I can't do this!" But morally, I'm looking for the right fit for me. I have to think, is it going to help someone else? It's not about me, it's about helping other people. That's why this is my ministry. This is one of the reasons I've gotten into acting, because sometimes it helps other people. I did a play called *The Marriage* and it's about Alzheimer's. I played Dawnn Lewis' mother and I had Alzheimer's. We were doing this scene together and we heard this woman in the audience crying. When it was over, she came up to us and said that her mother has Alzheimer's, and that's the way she was acting and she couldn't understand why. But when she saw me in the character, she understood her mother more. It gave her more compassion for the illness. She never took the time to find out what it meant before. It taught her not to label people until she found out what was going on in their hearts. I thought that was most profound. When you're on stage, that audience isn't looking at you. They're looking at their life.

How did you feel about being asked to play God in *Joan of Arcadia*?

To play God is the ultimate call without trying to be God—because no one can be God. But just to represent Him was a blessed feeling. Then when they called me back again, I said, "Okay, Lord. I hear you. I got it. I got it this time." I love the show because it doesn't drive it in and beat you with, "You've got to repent or you're going to Hell." It's like everybody can be God. Blake can be God sitting here doing this book. That's God there, because what you two are doing is going to help somebody else. That's God. People have their own concept, but that's my concept. What you do to help somebody else, that's your God.

What's your favorite thing about being an actor?

Even if I were to stop acting today, I've done more in my five-year lifetime than a lot of people have done their *whole* lifetime. I can take that to my grave. I'm happy with that. I get to hang out with other actors with like minds. They know what the struggle is. You love your family, you love your friends, but they don't know. I like hanging with actors. They're so cool. They're in a world all their own and I like it because they're non-judgmental. I do have actor friends that are negative. Now, I love 'em, but I gotta leave 'em where they are because they're not growing. If you keep up with them, they're going to pull you down and you're going to have to start over. Keep yourself surrounded with people that are doing the same thing you're doing, love the same thing you're doing, and if you didn't get that audition, so what! You'll get the next one!

Who are *your* favorite actors?

Nowadays, it's Johnny Depp. He is so versatile. He can play an inchworm and make you believe he's an inchworm. He is so remarkable. He wowed me in *Edward Scissorhands* and in *Ed Wood.*

That's when I really started watching him. He makes good choices. He's up there with the best of them. He's a "real" actor. I like Tom Cruise, but Tom Cruise is more for show. Depp can act the pants off of Tom Cruise. Favorites from the "old movies" are Tyrone Power and Linda Darnell. Those are two of the greatest actors.

What do you do when you're not acting?

I spend time with my two Cocker Spaniels. I say, "Look! Momma's on TV! Watch! Watch!" and they say, "Okay, Momma." They're always: "You're happy, we're happy!" I write. I'm writing a play right now about alcoholism. I've taken up sewing. I go see all the free movies I can. Between SAG and Cinemark, I can see a lot of free movies. I work on my yard. I ride my tricycle. My sister died and her husband was selling the house. The trike had been sitting out. I said, "What are you going to do with that?" He said, "Give it away." I said, "Can I have it?" So I took it to a bike shop and they cleaned it up and I went to Sav-on and I got a basket for the front. I put my radio in there. Then I bought a canopy to go over because it would be hot. I go on the riverbed and I will pedal my tricycle from Compton to Long Beach in the riverbed—that's about twenty-six miles, roundtrip. My daughter has a hot dog stand called Snooky Doggs on Sixth and Pine in Long Beach. If you ever go down there, you'll get better hot dogs than they have in New York. Sometimes I go down and help her out. And every Friday they have a Farmer's Market in Long Beach and I'll go down there and get my fruits and vegetables and then I'll come home. I'll pick out some old movies—some black-and-whites—and I'll watch them. I love being an actor!

Danny Pino

The talented Danny Pino easily transitions between film and television roles and can currently be seen playing Detective Scotty Valens in the hit CBS drama Cold Case, *which was the number-one new drama on television in 2004.*

Danny recently wrapped production on Andy Garcia's directorial debut entitled The Lost City, *which was shot on location in the Dominican Republic;* Between, *which co-stars Poppy Montgomery and Adam Kaufman; and the independent film* Rx, *which also stars Colin Hanks and Eric Balfour.*

Danny's television credits include the critically-acclaimed telefilm Lucy, *in which he starred as Desi Arnaz, and the series* The Shield. *Danny's other television credits include* Point of Origin *and* Men, Women, & Dogs.

Danny has an extensive theatre background. He starred opposite Madonna in Up for Grabs *in London's West End. He also starred with Billy Crudup in the New York Shakespeare Festival's productions of* Measure for Measure *and* The Winter's Tale.

Danny was born in Miami and currently lives in LA with his wife Lilly. More information at http://us.imdb.com/name/ nm0992694.

photo courtesy Warner Bros. by Nigel Parry

When did you know you wanted to become an actor?

Everybody has stories of doing a play for the family at three years old. I don't have that. I pretended more playing army and being a soldier and protecting my house. I would play like my house was our castle, our fortress. I would hide in wait to ambush cars that would come by as I pretended to shoot 'em up and run back, retreat.

I was acting. I didn't know back then but that's exactly what I was doing. To me it was so real. When you're doing it you're not thinking, "I'm doing this to prepare for my acting career." You do it because you are a kid. I think back and think about what is the foundation of what I do now. I look back at that and I was always sort of the dramatic one. My older brother and I would do that all the time. We would play *CHiPs* with our Big Wheels. Nobody ever really died in *CHiPs* but every day when I played it, I'd die. I'd die *every* day in that role. For me, Poncherello would die every day. I'd be like, "Go on. Go on. I can't make it." I'd roll my Big Wheel over. I was always sort of the guy who had a penchant for just pushing the dramatic. Always.

It was sixth grade when I did a play. I was involved in sports my entire youth, growing up. I was always playing baseball or soccer or football or something. I was always doing extracurricular things. It was always school and then everything else. Acting and being on stage was part of that. I kind of lumped them all together. In sixth grade, the play was called *Tracers of the Lost Parts of Speech*. It was an educational piece. There were nouns and verbs and pronouns running across the stage and nobody died, which I found very disappointing. I tried to change the script but of course the writer would not budge. I played a professor. I'm there in sixth grade and the professor must've been like seventy. They colored my hair silver. It was a musical. I had been in choir and I was singing and always involved in a bunch of different things. That was my first experience on stage. I realized that I really liked it. It was fun.

I was recruited to go to a performance magnet program for middle school. My mother and I—and my father—we sat together and talked about it. My mother, who was a teacher, said, "I think it's really important that you not limit yourself right now. I think it's really important that you don't give yourself a title. I think it's important that you have a very broad education." I said, "All right. I'm not going to go to the magnet school. I'm going to go to a regular school and I'm going to take all the courses and do sports and all of those things you can do at a regular school and not at the magnet school." So, that's what I did. Same thing with high school; there were these magnet programs that were ideal for an actor or musician. My mom advised me the same way: "You want to play football in high school. You want to play baseball in high school. When else do you get to do that?" I was like, "Y'know what, Mom, I think you're right." So, I did that. Of course, I went out for the football team. I didn't play. Of course, I went out for the baseball team. I didn't play. The reason I didn't play was because there was a play every single time and I always chose to do the play. So, back then I always thought, "I'm such a quitter. How can I not play football when I love playing sports? How can I not play baseball?" I wanted to play sports but the play was there and all my friends were in the Drama department and so I just felt compelled to do the play. Back then I felt like such a quitter: "I'm *just* doing a play."

I think for me it was like I didn't have enough time in the day to do everything. I was a typical overachiever. I was vice president of student council, I was president of the law club, I was the typical sort of guy who was a seemingly borderline nerd but had these parents who raised me in such a cool way that I was able to come across as more mainstream and I was friends with a lot of different groups. I actually had a lot of different interests. I always felt that high school was pretty stressful only because I was so involved with so many things that I always felt bad saying no to something. It's still the hardest thing for me now. The hardest word for me is *no*.

Was your family supportive?

Yes. They were and they are. It's important for me to say that my brothers keep me grounded. They're all in Miami. We're five boys. My wife also, of course, does that job well, but if anything slips through the cracks, they are there for me. Other than my wife, they really are my best friends. When they watch something that they don't think is what they expected, they—in a very supportive way—will let me know. Mostly, they've just been there to congratulate me, support me, and encourage me. I've been extremely blessed and fortunate several times over for several lifetimes. I've been given a very fortunate situation with my family.

With my family, it was never a professional thing: "Oh, you want to be an actor? Let's get you out there, do commercials, earn your money." It was never like that. In fact, I remember watching a movie—I think it was *The Good, the Bad, and the Ugly*—I remember seeing it and thinking, "That would be so cool; to do what they do, to have the attention of an audience and to really (for an hour, two hours, three hours) transform their lives into whatever world it is that you're putting into their living room or putting on the big screen in that theatre." It's almost like that hour of playing outside and defending your house. It's not your house anymore; it's the castle. You're giving them that, hopefully, for that bit of time. There's power in that. That helps people see what it is we're all going through: what this life is about and why are we here and what's our identity. Who do I really want to be and who am I and how do I appease that gap between who I want to be and who I am? Essentially, that's what the characters go through in the arc of a story. It's a very universal thing to explore.

I must've been thirteen or fourteen and must've watched a movie like *The Good, the Bad, and the Ugly* or *Young Guns* or a coming-of-age story like *The Karate Kid*, where it's inspirational. And I'd be like, "I really want to be involved with something like that." I remember picking up the Yellow Pages in Miami. My mother had said, "If you want to do it, it's totally on you. I'm not pushing you to do this." I looked up agencies in Miami and started making phone calls. I'm sure they realized they were talking to either a thirteen-year-old boy or a forty-year-old woman. My voice hadn't started to crack yet. I was pursuing it like that. Nothing ever came of that; it was just an afternoon making phone calls. My mom just let me go through the motions of that. She never got on the phone, she never made any phone calls, she just let me go through what I was going through. That slowly died away and I played sports and I continued to do my thing and just be a normal kid.

I did a number of plays in high school that got a lot of attention. We won a bunch of awards in state competitions and stuff like that and that caused Florida International University (the school that I ultimately got my BFA from) to take notice. They came over and watched some of the plays and they offered me a scholarship. I was still using theatre to achieve something else. I was taking theatre courses to have my scholarship in order to study law or in order to study engineering. I was always looking at something else. Theatre was always an after school thing. It was never *studying*. It was a sport or an extra curricular activity or belonging to a club. It was an interest, a hobby. And this was all without knowing that I was actually learning a lot from it. It was actually informing my life.

I think the more characters you play, the more masks you play, the deeper and more textured your fabric is, the more texture you add to your own character because you have put on that life and you have learned, hopefully, something from the choices or the mistakes that that character has made and it informs you. So, totally as a tangent, I was learning these things but I was pursuing scholastically something else. I was in the honor society and in the honors college, but the Theatre department was paying for it. It came time for me to choose a major and I was like, "Man, I don't know." I couldn't decide if I wanted to go into Engineering (which ultimately, probably, I wouldn't have been able to do because those guys are much too smart—lots of math—which I wasn't bad at, but there's too much. Too much math) or Law. So, the law part of it I started pursuing and I remember filing for an emphasis in pre-Law, so I graduated with a Bachelor of Fine Arts with an emphasis in pre-Law.

I was studying for the LSAT when my father and I sat down. My mother was always a big fan of whatever I decided to do. She was always a cheerleader for anything as long as I really wanted to do it. My dad, not so much. My dad was very practical. Both my parents are Cuban. They were both born in Cuba. Their parents, my grandparents, came to the United States without anything. They really had to abandon everything. So, my grandfather came from Cuba being a sugar engineer and the vice mayor of their town, Union de Reyes, to assume a dishwashing job in Miami and he died as a security guard at the Miami Sea Aquarium. My grandmother, who is an inspiration, was a secretary in Cuba and came to Miami and worked in a sweatshop. The same story applies to my father's parents. They were prominent in Cuba—they were middle class—and they came to the United States and had to start over. So, it was very important in my family to take on a practical profession, especially if you were going to study it in school. Make it count. Earn your money. Something stable. Something that you can fall back on as something solid. My parents did the same. But given the choice, my mom would've still chosen to be a teacher. She still followed her passion but in something practical. My father got his Bachelor's in Psychology but ultimately went into investing and banking, something also very practical. They knew they needed to build a foundation for us, which I'm so grateful for every day.

Acting is not a practical thing. It's not a practical field. At FIU we were asked—as part of the requirements to graduate—to do something called the senior project. It was something we did on our own. We could take an existing play and put it on ourselves and produce it and direct it and act in it or create something on our own. And I chose to write a one-person play about the last hour and fifteen minutes of Edgar Allan Poe's life. The project was only supposed to be half an hour, but mine turned into more like an hour and fifteen minutes. Poe was found in a gutter. Supposedly alcohol had an adverse effect on his brain, which caused him to go into hallucinations and convulsions and they found him in the gutter and he ultimately died from that. I took that last portion of his life where he's in the bed in a hospital and made those hallucinations part of how he went in and out of his short stories and poems. So he was literally in bed and immediately the lights would change and the music would change and "The Raven" would start happening and it was all just part of his life. All these characters that he made would start up. With the help of a lot of friends, I was putting it together; writing it, performing it. I had a friend direct it. Doing that—it made acting not a hobby.

That was the beginning of opening the door to thinking acting was what I was going to do. I think the sheer investment, the time, the emotional aspect to put all of that together, that's what did it. I'm sure I could look back at the tape and think, "Wow, that really was awful," but what actually is on stage at that time and what your perception is of how important it was are sometimes really different. So it's not really all that important what the actual performance was as much as what it meant to me in my development as an artist. To me, it's one of those times I look back on and know was one of those moments that was a defining moment for several different reasons.

Personally, I was able to invest in something so much that I was able to see myself being much more serious about it. Also, I got the attention of some of my teachers at FIU and, most importantly, I got my dad's attention. There was a teacher at FIU who said, "Danny, I think you need to go to graduate school. I think what we prepare you for here is graduate school. I don't think you can come from here and go into the profession without getting serious training." I took that advice very seriously. I was studying for my LSAT at the time and I started looking into graduate schools on my own for acting.

And then I had a meeting with my father, sitting down for breakfast one morning. He was like, "How's the LSAT going?" I said, "Yeah, it's going really well. I'm studying. It's coming up in a few months. But I really want to talk to you about acting." He was like, "What about it? That show was great, by the way. That show was really wonderful. I was very proud of you." I was like, "Thanks, Dad. I really appreciate that. If I get into one of the three schools that I want to get into, I'm going to grad school instead of law school." He said, "Okay." He left it at that. I thought it was going to be much harder than it was.

So, I auditioned for graduate schools and I got into the graduate school I wanted to get into. I went to New York University's Tisch School of the Arts' Graduate Acting Program. I auditioned for Yale and UCSD—and a fair amount of them actually—University of Minnesota, I auditioned for a bunch of schools. I went to NYU and studied under Ron Van Lieu.

For me, every single project I work on, every character, has Ron's stamp on it. He has that kind of effect on an actor. Ron will tell you how it is without anything personal—you can take it personally and often times I did—but having distance from the school and having several professional credits and projects that I've worked on, I see he was right. He was right. He's sort of the Yoda of acting. If you met him, you wouldn't know that. In fact, he would hate that I said that. He is so unassuming. He would think that I'm silly and ridiculous and I'm completely over-blowing the whole thing. I remember one day in class, we were doing *A Streetcar Named Desire* and I was in my first year. I really wanted to prove that I deserved to be one of the people that got into the program. I'm up there with Nadia Bowers and he says, "Okay, stop, stop, stop, stop. Stop the scene." I'm into it. I'm playing Stanley and probably my shirt's undone and I'm all sweaty. He says, "What were you thinking there, Danny?" And I said, "Well, Ron, I was trying to come over to Nadia so that I could deliver this line." And he said, "So you could what?" And I was like, "Well, I was trying to come over and deliver this line." And he was like, "What?" And I said, "Deliver this line?" And he slowly stood up, *slowly* stood up, just ever so slowly started walking toward me and said, "So you could what?" And I started backing away going, "Get away from me, Ron!" But from that point on, I realized what he meant: You're not delivering lines. There's no script. There's no stage direction. None of that. That's all bullshit. None of that exists. It's the interpersonal relationship between those two characters that exists at that time. If there's blocking, it's secondary to the connection between the two characters. It should not be something that dictates what you're doing. That's just one example of Ron. When I say I was intimidated by this man, backing me up, asking what I was doing, let me say that he's like five-seven, five-eight and a buck-twenty dripping wet. Yoda is the perfect example. He is the Yoda of acting. Yale's really smart to have brought him on to their team. He definitely changed me as an actor and a person.

What do you consider your first break?

NYU. But, you know, it's hard to say that there is a break. I don't necessarily see it that way. I think it's all a process. To say that there's a break, there's an unbroken line from imagining you're defending your house to being on the big screen or being on television. There's an unbroken line. To say that there's a big break, everything prepares you for the next step. Everything prepares you. If you're smart enough and you realize that no matter how small your role is, or however small your school is, or however little experience you have, if you can take any of those little experiences that *you* consider little—but that *I* think are as monumental as being cast in a Steven Spielberg movie—I think each and every one of those carries its own weight. So, to say that there's a big break, I think that is sort of shortsighted.

I don't think of the business. I don't know how the business perceives me. I really don't. I don't know. I'm always surprised when people say, "Yeah, we'll have him on board." I'm like, "Really? Cool. All right. Let's do this thing!" Absolutely. It's just another opportunity to play. I don't know if I can point at one thing and say, "This is my big break." I know that NYU is one of those places where you're surrounded by such talented people in your class—as well as in the faculty—and you're also living in New York City, so you're seeing all this live theatre and you're surrounded by all of these directors. It's a melting pot of all of these talented people and everybody's kind of feeding off each other, being inspired off of each other and you just want to create. You can't *not* create. It's infectious.

What made you choose Los Angeles?

I stayed in New York for about a year and a half after I finished the graduate program at NYU. Not that long. Many different things made me choose LA over New York. I'd done a few plays; I went to Williamstown (that was a great experience), I've done Shakespeare in the Park twice, I did a workshop at Lincoln Center. I was working steadily in New York, but I was also waiting tables at night. Doing workshops during the day, waiting tables at night. It was the typical actor's journey: having to grind it through and have your survival gig so that you can be asked to play again. I thought I wanted to be in New York because I felt it was less of a name game than LA, but an experience in New York made me feel it was also a name game in New York. I felt like that was being played there as well. There are a lot of productions in New York that are very expensive and they need names to fill the seats to cover the production. That's a very real situation. I thought, "Well, if I'm going to play the name game in New York and struggle with the opportunities potentially being less in New York than they are in LA—at least that's what I was hearing—let me go and see what LA has to offer during pilot season." This is what a lot of actors do. A lot of New York actors come out here for pilot season.

I came out with a bicoastal agent and I signed with a manager out here. I felt I was being covered in New York by my agency but that I needed to have an ear to the ground on the West Coast so I signed with a manager out here. My manager facilitated me flying out. In fact, the management company paid for my trip out because I didn't have the money to pay for it. I had to reimburse them, of course, because it is a business. I came out and I was very fortunate.

When somebody says, "Aren't you happy that you've been able to achieve what you've achieved?" I just look back and I'm like, "Y'know what? *I* didn't achieve anything. There were so many points along the way where other people contributed so much that without those people it would've never happened. Or maybe it would've happened but it would've never happened the way it has actually transpired." It's not *my* achievement. The reason I say that is because when I came out to LA, I had a friend who let me stay at his place for four months. That allowed me to audition. My wife (who wasn't my wife yet—we met in junior high and have been together the entire time) came out here with me for pilot season and she taught English at a university so that we could eat. We had a place to stay, but I wasn't going to ask my friend to feed us. If anything, I was going to try to feed him because we were staying at his place. So, she went to work while I went on auditions.

When we came to LA, I went to Rent-A-Wreck and got a Ford Festiva. I'm trying to go up La Cienega in this reddish, rusted out Ford Festiva with racing stripes. And there's always this guy who pulls up right on your tail in a Mercedes Bens automatic V-12 and you're just looking back going, "I'm going to nail you when I roll back!" I don't think it had an emergency brake. This thing was a wreck! We went to Universal Citywalk and went to the movie; we had valeted the car. When I came back and everybody's waiting—a huge amount of people waiting for their cars—there's Seal waiting for his car and down the ramp I see four dudes pushing my car. They're trying to start the damn car. They opened the hood, I swear the car's aflame. It's on fire. The battery, the foam flowing. I called Rent-A-Wreck and they replaced the car. You get a very reliable car, sometimes. And it's very cheap. It got me from audition to audition until I was able to book a pilot my first season out here. It made it, it got picked up. It was a WB pilot called *Men, Women & Dogs*.

Before that, the first thing I tested for they actually flew me out of New York to test out here. That was trippy. I was at CBS and there's a big picture of Elvis. I'm thinking, "Man, this place looks kind of familiar, where he's standing. Oh, man, I'm standing where Elvis was standing. Wow. This is LA. This is what the west coast is about. It's celebrity. But I want my art! I'm studying theatre! I'm a trained actor! But, man, that's really cool." Literally, you go down into the basement and it's like a little home theatre. They have maybe twenty seats in there and it's raked for the audience, it's very dark, and there's like four or five guys. Sometimes we all look the same, sometimes we don't. This first test, we didn't look anything alike. We were a bunch of different looking guys. We all go in and do our thing, we come out, we call our agent, and hear, "We don't know anything yet but I'm sure we will soon and we'll give you a call." I didn't get it and I was very disappointed because I was sure this was "it." But that's how there's no break. What it did was inform what the next network test was going to be like. The next time I was in that room, I was a lot more confident and the next time I was in that room, I booked it. It's about learning from those experiences, not necessarily whether you succeed or fail in that particular experience. It sounds a little cliché, but it's what I believe and that's what's helped me.

My first pilot season, I remember I auditioned for this movie. First of all, the casting director didn't necessarily want to see me because the director was with my agency and the agency went directly to the director and the director brought me in which made the casting director feel a little bypassed. But I came in nonetheless. I read. I think I gave an okay read. I know I prepared a lot for it. Well, the director and the casting director couldn't even sit down. They looked like little kids. They were like, "You're perfect. You're just perfect. I love the way you did that. Let's do this again. Let's try this." It was playing. It was so energized. The room was so energized. I thought, "I got my first thing." I'd been out here for about a month and a half and I was so ecstatic and I knew my wife Lilly would be ecstatic because she was working just as hard as I was. I knew my friend would be happy because he had given up a lot of his comfort having us there. It just all came together for this movie. They were so excited in the room that they said, "We've got to be quiet. There are still guys outside that are auditioning for this, but we just know you're perfect." So I left the audition and I called my agent and my manager and I said, "I think I got my first job." They were like, "Not so fast. Let's call. Let's make sure."

"But they *said*!" I had been to enough auditions to know that it never happens that they tell you that you have it in the room with guys still outside. Unless it was *Totally Hidden Video* or something, I had it. They *told* me! Sure enough, three days later, they were like, "They really loved you but the producers don't know who you are and they're giving the role to an *A*-list actor." That was really hard. It was a hard lesson. But there are several hard lessons. As long as you know that even that audition is part of informing who you are and the power that you have in that room, you're okay. That's the only thing you can control: how you prepare for an audition, how much you prepare for an audition, and how—when you go into that room—you make it your own. When you walk out of that room, you want to feel like you gave your best.

I used to call my family and be like, "Oh my God, this is it. I think this is the one." I would tell them all about the project. I don't tell them anything now. They don't even ask anymore. There's a code. "So, are things going well?" No specifics. I think they get even more disappointed than I do. I've learned to make my time the time that I'm in that room. If you're looking for work, the time that you're in that room is your chance, your opportunity to act. That's your opportunity to go in there to work, go in there and play. Those two worlds should cross paths. That should apply to auditions as well as the bookings.

How do you handle being recognized?

It doesn't really happen that often, to tell you the truth. I have run into some people that recognize me and like the show, they like *Cold Case*, or they recognize me from *Lucy* and start quoting Desi lines. Those who do recognize me usually do from *The Shield* because Armadillo Quintero was such a memorable character. I usually know by the way that they look at me where they know me from. Armadillo gets a very unsure, uneasy kind of stare, but still it really doesn't happen that often.

I did a play in London with Madonna. That's fame. People were coming after me at the stage door because I was on the stage with her. That's fame. We couldn't go to dinner. My wife and I, and Madonna, we couldn't go out. It seemed like a thunderstorm because there were so many flashes going off from the photographers.

It makes me feel good when somebody recognizes me for the work that I've done. You do like to feel like you're affecting people and that people appreciate you and that you're not doing your work in a vacuum, although you probably would if you were given the opportunity anyway because it's what you love to do. But that is a huge component. You can't forget that there's an audience out there and you can't forget that there are people out there who love your work or maybe even hate your work and that that exists. And sure you want people to like your work. You want to feel appreciated. You want people to give you a pat on the back. But that's certainly not why I do it. I think that if you're a good actor and you focus on your craft and with every performance (if you're on TV, every episode; if you're in film, every movie; if you're looking for a job, every audition), if you take every chance you have to improve yourself and push your craft, then fame and notoriety and the acknowledgement and the awards and all that, that's just residue of hard work and some luck. And it's hard work from a lot of people, sacrifices from a lot of sources. From your manager, to your publicist, to your lawyer, to your agents, to your mom and dad, to your brother, to your best friend, to your wife; I mean the list is endless. And then all of a sudden, people might know you. But you're the figurehead of an iceberg that goes much deeper.

What is your favorite thing about being an actor?

There are so many favorite things about being an actor! I think you're a student of humanity. I think you're a student of why we're here and what we do with the time we're here, what other people choose to do, what other characters choose to do with the time that they're allotted. I think you're literally studying choices and that's fascinating. Every time you read a script, even if you have no part in that project, every time you read a script, every time you do a reading, it's like you're putting on the shoes for an hour. Just to read through something to help a friend out who just wrote a script, you're stepping out of yourself. And you're stepping out of having to pay the phone bill, having to put dishes in the dishwasher.

I feel like that psychology, the feeling of taking something from an idea—even if it's someone else's idea—from the black and white of a page to the three-dimensional presentation of who that person is (or was, if you're playing a historic figure), there's something that informs you. You can't help but feel changed at the end of a project. You can't help it!

I remember doing Desi; I wanted to continue doing it. It was huge for me. I remember wanting the role so bad. That's really one of the first auditions I went into the audition as the character. I didn't want them to know that I didn't have a dialect, that I didn't have an accent. I didn't want them to know who I was. I didn't want them to know anything about me. I wanted to go in as Desi. We would talk about all kinds of stuff but I'd be talking about it with his dialect, with his cadence, with how I saw him move. I was studying a lot for that audition. I really gave into that. I thought, "This is the role you've got to cast a Cuban American in. You've got to stick with that." I wanted it so bad. Once it was offered to me I thought, "What have I done? What am I going to do now?" It turned from this aggressive desire to do the role to this wanting to run away fear. It was pretty amazing. But it was a study.

How do you prepare for a role?

While I was auditioning for the role of Desi, I was looking at tapes. I bought the DVD of some of the first season of the *I Love Lucy* show and I recorded his voice. I would just listen to his voice all day. And it was well written, the scenes that they gave me to audition with. I studied the scenes over and over again. I was really prepared for that. He wrote a book, thankfully, and I drew a lot from that as to who he was and what his principles were from his own words. I watched a lot of film, a lot of tape, a lot of video, anything I could get my hands on.

People would think, "Oh, being Cuban you'll be able to do the dialect 'cause you're Cuban and he's Cuban," but I'm two generations removed. On top of that, going to school where they sort of beat any regionalism out of you, I was totally neutral. That actually helped. When I was in speech class, I was thinking, "What am I going to use this for? I'm never going to use this! Let's do some acting!" But now I have a technique that I can anchor into. Even with Armadillo, I was playing a Mexican, much different from a Cuban dialect. Now playing Scotty Valens, somebody who's from the northeast—from Philadelphia no less—and a Philadelphia accent is really difficult to get. I'm still working on that! With any accent, I usually work at it on my own only because I know what those accents sound like. I've met people from each place and recorded their voices. I spent so much time in speech class that I know the difference in the vowels and consonants and cadence. And when, occasionally, I do have a question, I can call NYU. I know where to go.

Everybody was really enthusiastic about Desi. I learned how to play the congas, the guitar, I learned about his family's exile from Cuba, which parallels my family's. His was twenty-five, thirty years prior, but still, having everything and then coming to Miami with nothing. It gave me a soapbox. Whenever I was asked a question about Desi, I was able to pay homage to my grandparents from a personal place. My grandmother, who is still with us, was able to hear it on different Spanish radio shows that I was talking on or read in different newspapers or magazines in which I was interviewed. I would always mention her name and let her know that her grandson could've never decided to pursue an artistic desire had she not been in a sweatshop. She gave me that choice. I always remind her of that. That's one of the perks of the business; that I can do that publicly.

•

Who are *your* favorite actors?

Andy Garcia. I think he has a way of being. Most great actors do. They're not acting, they're being. They just are. I remember watching *Godfather: Part III*. He was, in my opinion, one of the best things of the movie (if not the best thing in the movie). Taking the role of Sonny's son and making it believable that he was Sonny's son with the aggressiveness, the impulsiveness that he imbued the character with was reminiscent of Sonny and yet he made it his own. He wasn't replicating anything. He wasn't indicating that he was the son of Sonny. He was just it. He was it. He was being. That's a difficult thing. It looks easy. That's the amazing part. When you watch a baseball game, the best players make it look easy. When you watch a football game, the best players make it look easy. He makes it look easy. I had the opportunity to work with him last summer. He directed. He made it look easy; even the directing. He's just one of those guys that is infinitely talented. He's a musician, he's an actor, he's a family man, he's a writer. He's a renaissance man. He's one of those guys that you look up to and you hope to emulate.

Raul Julia for the same reasons. His career was so diverse, just so infinitely diverse. He did everything—from comedy to musicals to drama to Shakespeare—so well. He's like one of those guys that if I had to audition against him, I'd hate him, but he was so damn good that he would up the ante. He'd raise the bar. He'd make everyone else want to be better. Andy does that too. Working with Andy you're like, "I want to be better." That's cool. It makes you feel less prone to be complacent, which is easy to do in LA. It's difficult to do that in New York. The energy of the City, you're out there, you're doing it. But in LA you can be complacent.

Robert Duvall. He's great. Daniel Day-Lewis. These are people that I'll go watch their films just because they're in it. People that are my contemporaries: Johnny Depp. I think that he pushes himself. Javier Bardem is bold, both with his choice of material and within a performance. He continues to challenge himself and the way the public sees him. There's so many good actors out there and I get inspired by a lot of them. To mention a few, I'm leaving out others who inspire me for other reasons.

James Rebhorn

James Rebhorn is a veteran character actor of over one hundred television shows, feature films, and plays. Born in Philadelphia, Pennsylvania, James moved to Anderson, Indiana, as a child. He attended Wittenberg University in Ohio, where he studied Political Science. His alma mater honored him in 2003 by naming him a University Fellow. After graduation, James moved to New York City, where he earned an MFA in Acting from Columbia University's School of the Arts.

After making his television debut on the NBC soap opera The Doctors, *James starred on* Another World: Texas, The Guiding Light, *and* As the World Turns. *He had a recurring role on* Kate and Allie *and is widely recognized as the DA that put the* Seinfeld *gang in jail for the show's finale. James has recurred on* Law & Order, Third Watch, Now and Again, Hack, *and* The Practice. *His telefilms have included* Sarah, Plain and Tall; North and South; Skylark; From the Earth to the Moon; *and* Reversible Errors.

A sampling of James' many film appearances include Regarding Henry, My Cousin Vinny, Basic Instinct, Scent of a Woman, Lorenzo's Oil, Carlito's Way, Guarding Tess, I Love Trouble, Up Close & Personal, Independence Day, If Lucy Fell, My Fellow Americans, The Game, Snow Falling on Cedars, The Talented Mr. Ripley, Meet the Parents, The Adventures of Pluto Nash, *and* Far From Heaven.

Between film and television appearances, James spends much of his time on stage at Manhattan Theatre Club, Playwright's Horizons, the New York Shakespeare Festival, the La Jolla Playhouse, the Ensemble Studio Theatre, and Lincoln Center. After earning rave reviews in the Roundabout Theatre's production of Arthur Miller's The Man Who Had All the Luck *with Chris O'Donnell and Samantha Mathis, James returned to the Roundabout for their hit production of* Twelve Angry Men. *More information on James is available at http://us.imdb.com/name/nm0714310.*

photo by Timothy Lampson
http://timlampson.com

When did you know you wanted to become an actor?

I don't think I really knew until after I was nearing the end of my course study at Columbia University where I was getting an MFA in Acting. When I was a senior in college, I didn't really know what I was going to do. I had a job tentatively lined up with the YMCA in Chicago and I thought I would apply to some Drama schools. All of the ones I applied to were accredited programs, thinking that I might teach. The three I applied to—University of Minnesota, SMU, and Columbia—I ended up getting accepted at all of them and I thought, if I was going to study it seriously with an eye towards maybe getting involved in professional theatre I should go to New York. So I went to Columbia.

My teacher there was a fellow named Ted Kazanoff and if it wasn't for his influence, I don't think I would've thought about pursuing it. It wasn't that he didn't encourage me any more specifically than he encouraged any other actor, but he gave me a respect for the craft of acting which I had hitherto been unaware of that inspired me and made me think that it was something I could actually do as opposed to creating simply based upon inspiration. He gave me a system that I thought I could work from. That was why I decided to stay in New York and pursue it. And much to my chagrin, even though I thought I had a firm grasp and understanding of the system, I did not get a job right out of the chute. I was a little surprised. You work hard, you understand something, you got a system; it should all happen and fall into place.

What was your first paid gig?

I got my MFA in the spring of '72 and that summer, I went down to Atlantic City and worked in a theatre called the Viking Theatre which was on the thirteenth floor of what was then called the Chalfont-Haddon Hall Hotel, which is now the Resorts International Casino. It was a real theatre and had been pretty much underused, unutilized until about '71. I did the lead in *Star Spangled Girl*, *Lovers and Other Strangers*, *Plaza Suite*, and I was Dracula in *Dracula*. We got thirty-five dollars a week, room and board, and we had to share a bathroom. And I thought, "I could do this forever!" I loved it. That was my first paying theatre job.

It happened because the director was in the directing program at Columbia and he knew me. That was how most of my first jobs the first few years happened: because friends knew me or friends of friends knew me. Ironically, it's pretty much how I get jobs now too. Friends or colleagues either know me or have worked with me before. Fewer and fewer jobs happen because of auditions, which is just as well, since there are fewer and fewer auditions going around for people my age.

Cultivating relationships was never high on my agenda, but working with people and encouraging them to work with me—folks who I liked and who I had a good relationship with, had a friendship with—I wanted to promote that. I still to this day send out postcards and Christmas cards to a handful of directors and casting directors who I've known and worked with—or for—over the years. But I was never very good at particularly fertilizing relationships. It only happened because these were friends and colleagues who I felt I had already had a relationship with. I've tried to keep those active, certainly. I think that's important.

Early on in my career, I was doing *Are You Now or Have You Ever Been* and the role of Lionel Standard was frequently recast with relatively notable stage names. At one point, the late Mike Kellin, who was an actor I had long admired, came in. I saw him backstage one night before he was going on, busily writing away and I said, "Mikey, whatcha doin'?" And he said, "I'm sending out cards to people, letting them know I'm in the show, hope they come see me." And that for me was a real lesson. This was a guy who had done, well, *Midnight Express* was probably his most recent movie at that point and to me, this was a guy who had it made and he continued to send out cards and letters. It was a lesson to me.

What do you consider your first break?

I think I can point to a couple of events. One was in '79. I did Roderigo in *Othello* in Central Park at the Delacorte. Although I was not all that happy with my work—and I don't think I was alone in that opinion—I did manage to get a manager out of that. It wasn't that I was looking for a manager, but I was looking for representation that was a little more high-powered, higher profile than what I had up until that point. Jimmy Greene, who was an actor in the show, said he'd be pleased to introduce me to his manager. Her name was Yvette Schumer. She passed away a couple of years ago, now. She had launched Richard Gere's career and a number of other careers. She and her partner offered me a chance to sign with them, so I did. They made it possible for me to have the confidence to say no to dinner theatre and summer stock, those kinds of things, which I had always said yes to because I just wanted to keep working.

And sure enough, that fall I did my first movie. It was also Tom Hanks' first movie. It was a slasher film called *He Knows You're Alone* starring Donny Scardino. That was my first film. Joe Beruh and Edgar Lansbury who had produced *Godspell* and *A View from the Bridge* and *Waiting for Godot* produced these films. They did one or two every year and they were sort of a tax write-off for them. I had done a number of commercials before that time and I had done an occasional educational film or industrial film, but essentially, that was my first film.

What do you wish someone had told you at the beginning of your career?

I don't know. Things change so rapidly in this business. It's hard for me to even assume that I would know anything that would be of value to somebody who is twenty and starting out in this business. I don't know. Maybe I wish I had auditioned for a school that had a higher profile that would've gotten me in some bigger doors faster, but I never really thought that I had the chops to get into anything like Juilliard or Yale or something like that. It just didn't occur to me. And maybe if somebody had said, "Well why don't you just try auditioning?" who knows? Maybe that's the only thing, but I don't hold that against any of my advisors or any of my teachers or friends or counselors. You never know unless you strive for something higher where you might end up. Sometimes I wish somebody had told me just to shoot a little higher. That having been said, the business has been very, very good to me. Who knows? Maybe that would've been a huge mistake. You see a lot of people who get in the door early in their careers and end up flat on their faces in about five years. I don't know that I would ask for any advice other than what I was given which was, "Be true to yourself and do what you want to do. Try it. Do it."

What is your favorite thing about being an actor?

I would guess the opportunity to continue to explore the human condition, which is what I think got me into it to begin with and what continues to reinvigorate my interest. As long as there are complexities to the human state, then I'll be attracted to it, I think. And that's what I hope to do in my acting; to explore that, expose it, and help people to understand the human condition better and leave the theatre or the movie theatre or the television screen thinking about their lives and the world in a slightly different way because of what I've done.

What is your least favorite thing about being an actor?

The insecurity and lack of control over your career. In some ways, I feel more insecure now than I did when I was starting out. When you're starting out you're young and you're stupid and you think you're going to live forever and everything's going to be fine. As you get older, you realize that life is far more complex than that.

Most of the jobs I get now are offers, which is very flattering. But on the other hand, in me, anyway, that can create a great deal of insecurity. As I worked my way up through the business, I got my jobs through auditions so that when I was hired, I was hired with the director and myself both knowing that we were sort of on the same page because of the audition. And now there is this great responsibility thrust on me that I over-inflate, admittedly, because of who I am, my psychology. It creates more insecurity.

Twelve Angry Men is a cast of extremely gifted, talented, skillful professionals, all of them. When I was offered it, how could I say no, but I thought, "Uh, uh, uh, sure!" This is also to Scott Ellis' credit, he cast the show—I don't think anyone auditioned for it—with a group of guys that he just knew, who get along on and off stage. Nobody was a diva. Nobody was overly needy. Nobody was into criticizing someone else's work. It's truly a remarkable situation to have twelve people—well, thirteen with Matte Osian who plays the guard—on stage who are so genuinely happy to be working with each other and very generous. But still, I have this insecurity.

Also, you start developing a lifestyle and I've always tried to live modestly in that I have never really borrowed any substantial money. When I've bought cars, I've bought in cash. When I've bought houses, I only borrowed what I knew I could write a check for tomorrow if I had to. Even though we've lived relatively close to the belt, we still have houses and cars and kids going to college and all that. You wonder if you'll continue to make the money you need to keep all that afloat.

What are some of the family sacrifices of being a working actor?

They are huge and they are unknown. I can't say for sure that the business has been good *or* bad for my children. It's the only business they know their daddy has ever been in. They see the world in those terms. I think if your father was a policeman or a garbage collector or an accountant or a president of a corporation, that's the way you see the world. You tend to mirror your parents' values and your parents' reality.

I'm sure they have been damaged at times by what has happened in my life. I remember one time both my daughters (they were very young at this point; Emma was eight, Hannah was four) were asked to be in a bridal party for a second cousin and we went to Laura Ashley to pick out some matching dresses for them. At this time I was on *The Guiding Light* and at that point I was playing this fellow who was a blue-collar security guard who beat his wife and ultimately raped his stepdaughter. We're in Laura Ashley in Shorthills Mall in New Jersey and these two women come into Laura Ashley. One woman was the customer, the other was her buyer and the buyer turns to me and says, "Oh, you're the rapist on television!" in front of my two little children. I remember that as a particularly chilling moment in my career. Now, of course, she meant this—in her own twisted way—as a compliment. But who knows where that lives in my children's hearts? So, I can't tell what the negative effects are.

There's an actor friend of mine, Tom Mason, who has referred to his relationship with his children as sort of one of being a grandfather because he's not there all the time. He kind of pops in and it's all jolly and then when he is there for an extended period of time, nobody really looks to him for parental advice because mommy has been handling the reins for so long. It's understandable, but it is unfortunate too.

How do you handle being recognized?

When it first happened, it was a novelty. I can't say I ever felt that it stroked my ego, ever. But I do say when it first happened I thought it was very interesting. Now, it's pretty much just an intrusion. It's not that people are intentionally rude, but they frequently are, without meaning to be: yelling out at you on a street, interrupting you when you're having dinner with your family, shoving photographs or pictures up into your face. I used to get phone calls from people, collect phone calls, until I took my name off the phone bill.

Frankly, the only thing that really is flattering is when someone comes up and says, "Excuse me. Are you James Rebhorn? I know your work." If they come up and say, "Hey I know you, don't I?" or "What have I seen you in?" or even more peculiarly, "What is the last thing I saw you in?" I have no idea! I don't know what you're watching. People respond as if they're talking to their television sets as opposed to talking to a human being who might be running late for a doctor's appointment or who is trying to pick up his kid at school or who wants to go home and rake the leaves so that they don't pile up.

I'm walking out of the theatre the other night with Larry Bryggman, who is a good friend, and this Korean family stopped me and said, "May I take a picture with you?" and we're back and forth with the wife and the daughter and back and forth with him and with her and all of these pictures and at the end he says, "And what is your name?"

I remember one time getting into a fight with somebody who was convinced I was James Woods. It became an argument!

I'm frequently mistook for Jamie Cromwell. I know Jamie and there is a similarity in our physiques but we are very different people. It's gotten to the point where people say, "I loved you in *The General's Daughter*," and I say, "Well, thank you very much," and walk on. I just let it go.

Do you prefer theatre to film and television work?

First of all, I feel I have been blessed. I have had opportunities to do quality work in all the media: very interesting roles, very interesting stories. And I've worked with some wonderful, wonderful people in all media. I think though, in the end, what is the most exhausting but also the most satisfying is stage work. It's the only medium that really is the actors' medium. Television is very much the producers' medium. Film is the directors' medium. On stage, it's really you and the audience. If you look back historically, initially that's all there was; there were actors and there were audiences. It came out of religious ceremonies. Even the playwright was a later event and the director is only about a hundred and fifty years old. The primal experience for the actor, it seems to me, is stage. Being able to play something from beginning through the middle to the end is very, very satisfying. And to know that you've landed on the audience is something you can experience right there at the moment. You don't wait for the film to come out or, if it's television, to be broadcast. It happens right there, in real time. And that's very stimulating. That having been said, a good film, the work on that is no less challenging or interesting for me as an actor. It certainly has proved in my experience to be considerably more lucrative. I've been very fortunate to be able to ply my craft in all the media.

How do you choose the material you work on?

In the best of all possible worlds, I choose the material because it is really good and the character is interesting. But there are always other considerations. Will it fit with my schedule? Will it make sense with what family plans I have? Will it pay the bills? Will it keep me out of town for only one week instead of three months? All of those other considerations come into play as well. How long has it been since I've done a play? I like to do a play once a year if I can. Those are the kind of questions I ask after I read the material, after I figure out whether I've really responded to it or not. And sometimes it's just: I need a job.

How do you prepare for a role?

That depends on the role. This experience at the Roundabout—Blake knows this from working with Scott—we do an awful lot of research in the course of the rehearsal. We read an entire book on this one jury foreman's experience on a trial and that was tremendously helpful. Whenever I'm working on any role, I start with what's in the script and then kind of work backward and forward from that. There are several details in every script that give you an idea of who that character is. In *Twelve Angry Men* it's interesting, everybody in the course of the play, what they do for a living is revealed, which is interesting. Out of that, for instance, that can spark the imagination of all the kinds of things that can start to be created. I'm a stockbroker in the early '50s. What did that mean? It wasn't quite the career path that most upwardly-mobile people would take because, in many cases, you went into family businesses. It would suggest other things: who my family was. Maybe we've been investment bankers for generations. That's how I begin working on a role. Of course, in a play, in rehearsal, you're fed all kinds of things every day with your other actors. They give you other kinds of ideas just by simply rehearsing. That's how I develop it.

When I audition, I look at an audition experience as a performance experience. I don't go in there fumbling around. I make clear, strong choices in the hopes that it will either land and be exactly what they're looking for or that it will be strong enough that they will then want to redirect me and have me audition again. I look at it as a performance.

I must say my own ego is either big enough or fragile enough that if somebody is paying me thirty-five thousand dollars a week for a film, I'm considerably more willing to do anything anybody tells me. My choice has already been that I'm doing it for the money. Hopefully I can get other pleasures and satisfaction out of it as well. Theatre, I'm doing it because I love it, because I love the play. If somebody is going to make that experience unhappy for me, I'm less likely to want to go along with it because I'm investing so much time and energy in something I love and if that love is sucked out of it, it's no fun.

What made you choose New York?

I've always been in New York. The irony is, my two least favorite places in the world are LA and New York, in that order. But, if you're an actor, you have to be in one or the other. I think, on balance, New York for me is a healthier world. LA, for all of its strengths, is essentially a one-industry town. No matter what you're doing for a living there, it's all focused and dependent on the entertainment industry. New York is not. I think that—for the human soul—is better for me. That's why I've always stayed here, and I'm lucky.

I was in *Scent of a Woman* and *Lorenzo's Oil*, two movies that came to New York to cast, which they do less and less of. I was in both of them and they were released within a week of each other. Both were hits in different ways. *Lorenzo's Oil* was a big hit with the industry and *Scent of a Woman* was a big hit at the box office. I think—and this is conjecture on my part—at that point I became a known quantity to Hollywood. So that when they said, "What about Rebhorn?" they would say, "Now who is he?" "Well, he was in *Scent of a Woman* and *Lorenzo's Oil*," and they'd go, "Oh, yeah, yeah, yeah." So they could pass judgment or give me a shot early in the process. I've been fortunate that I've been able to stay in New York, I think, because of those two movies.

Who are *your* favorite actors?

I'm working with twelve of them right now! Larry Bryggman, who is a very good friend, is one of my favorite actors both to watch and to work with. Debra Monk is another one. She's just sensational. Deb's won a couple of Tonys and Larry's been nominated several times. They both have Obies. They both have Emmys as a matter of fact, too. They're two of my favorite actors. An actor I would love to work with sometime is Robert Duvall. I think he's brilliant and I've seen him on stage as well as on film.

Blake Robbins

Best known for his role as Dave Brass on the HBO series Oz, *Blake Robbins' other television credits include a recurring role on Joss Whedon's* Firefly, *guest appearances on* Medium, Cold Case, Crossing Jordan, Law & Order, Third Watch, 10-8: Officers on Duty, Strong Medicine, *and* Charmed, *among others. Blake has appeared in over sixty theatrical productions. On Broadway, he appeared in Arthur Miller's* The Man Who Had All the Luck, *Tina Howe's* Disorderly Conduct *and* The Elevator *by Rinne Groff. He has also worked at the Atlantic Theatre, EST, New York Stage & Film, Naked Angels, the Huntington Theatre, and the Evidence Room.*

Blake's films include Love Comes to the Executioner, Going Under, Alice, Blackout, Never Surrender, Gun Control, About the Cello, *and* An Actor Prepares. *He has also appeared in a number of commercials, including Maxwell House, Colgate Total, Lowe's Home Improvement, Saturn, Connecticut Lottery, Ameritech, Ford Motors, and Giant Eagle Supermarkets.*

He is a graduate of the American Academy of Dramatic Arts where he was selected for the Academy Company. He studied with Ron Van Lieu, Earle Gister, and Peter Francis James at the Actors Center as well as studying with Terry Schreiber, New York Stage & Film, and Naked Angels. More information about Blake is available at http://us.imdb.com/name/nm1083077.

photo by Brigitte Jouxtel

When did you know you wanted to become an actor?

The moment that I knew that I wanted to be an actor was in Boston, after I got out of college. My parents, for my birthday, took me to see *Les Misérables* and I was so blown away when I walked out of the theatre. I think, at that point, I had already started taking some classes; I had done theatre in junior college. I was now a graduate of college and had decided I wanted to be an actor. I saw that performance in June and that was the moment I knew that's what I would be for the rest of my life. It was a good show. I was blown away. I couldn't even get up for intermission. I've since seen it about four or five times and I love the story and the show, but it was so pure when I saw it. It was the first tour and it had a magical element that these people were just doing their thing. These people were doing the show from their heart and it was beautiful, powerful.

What was your first paid gig?

An episode of *Law & Order* is what I consider "first," although I did do a six-week summer stock show when I got out of the American Academy for a hundred and fifty bucks a week in Courtland, New York, of AR Gurney's *The Dining Room*. I had just gotten out of the American Academy's two-year program and then did the third year, which is the company year where you do productions. The whole angle becomes about introducing you to the community and to the industry. Where else are you going to get a chance to do five plays, fully-produced, right in a row? You wouldn't that soon out of school, even if you hit it big.

I got that summer stock job sort of right out of school, and then from there it was seven years before someone said, "Oh! Blake," for a role. I went to one of those NETC cattle calls and literally over the course of the weekend they saw five hundred actors do monologues. I got hired out of that for *The Dining Room*, so it didn't feel like I went into the casting room for the specific role and got cast. So, I consider *Law & Order* as my first paid gig because it was more the result of the pursuit of a job.

With *Law & Order*, I was in an acting class that I'd pursued because I knew that that theatre company had a lot of young actors and that if I did that class I'd meet a lot of their actors. It was a celebrity-driven company, but with talented, aggressive people who just wanted to impact their careers. Here are these television actors just wanting to do theatre for themselves. I got into that class through word-of-mouth from a friend. The guy who ran that class—Jace Alexander—is just one of those great people in the industry that if he has something for you, he'll call you. He put myself and another classmate together to do this scene in *Law & Order* to play German tourists. It was a one-day guest spot. What I had to do was be trained, be able to immediately pick up a German dialect, work on the scene with her, go in there and win the job. But I got the job because I put myself into a class where I knew people worked and people would get to know my work.

I didn't have an agent, and I think it's really important for young actors to know that you can work in this business without an agent. I feel like not having an agent stops many people. It becomes their pursuit. Instead of pursuing jobs or theatre companies or apprenticeships or places to go do readings, they start to pursue mailings and chasing down their friends' agents. I really feel that you'll have the right agent in the right time if you pursue the people you like and the work you love. I went eight or nine years without an agent and had a career by the time I had my first agent. I found solace in learning that a lot of actors had the same situation. I think there's an advantage to going a while without an agent because you learn how to survive in this business on your own. Even when you do have an agent, you have all these tools in place to pursue the business. I've had an agent for four or five years and I've brought them more work than they've ever brought me. That's just the way it is. The agent will do the submissions and negotiate the contracts.

What do you consider your first break?

I think the "first break" has to be the thing that changes the industry's perception of you as an artist. You know when that happens. In my case, I was the perfect person for the job that no one else could get and I happened to be there at the perfect time. This was the twelfth hour. They had seen hundreds of actors and were in desperate need of an actor to play this guy who could convince everyone that he could possibly have played professional basketball—and I played basketball in college at a high level—and that was when Tom Fontana decided to put me on *Oz*. That was my first break. I was in a play, playing a professional basketball player at the time that I convinced them to see me.

In my situation, no one knew me from anything and they were just trying to cast this role. It happened to be a storyline that was in the last three episodes of that season. The storyline was that I get involved in this prison basketball game and they cut my Achilles' tendon so that the prisoners don't lose the game to the prison guards.

It kind of all converged that summer. I started to realize that the only way I was going to be happy was if I started putting priority on the things that made me happy outside of the industry. I started planning a trip with my wife and we focused on ourselves, our lives, our marriage. Karen got pregnant that summer. We were going to have our first baby and then this opportunity for *Oz* came up. I operated outside of the box. I didn't have representation, but I asked this producer of this play if I could get into this audition, how would she recommend I go about it. She started advising me, giving me ideas, and then she said, "Wait a second. I know those casting people from my days as an agent. I'll call over there and, if they're still seeing people, I think I could get them to see you." And she did.

I got a call from the casting director saying they wanted me to audition on a Thursday. On Monday, they had me come to the set to a basketball court to see me play at the level they needed. Interestingly enough, I didn't hit any shots at the callback because the rims weren't at the right height, the ball was this, that, the other thing, it takes a while to warm up to play ball, whatever. But, the producer who wrote the storyline for the show was a basketball player and he knew from looking at me that I was a ball player and that was the most important thing. The writer-producer-source of power in the show was Tom Fontana. He was the one that saw my taped audition and said, "That's the guy," for whatever reason. Tom had already decided—which I found out later at the cast party at the end of the season—from watching the tape that I was the guy.

My last scene was me being back in the prison system with the obvious injury and them saying, "What's going to happen to you?" So, it was guaranteed to be a three-episode arc, but I could've disappeared because that final scene—if they decided never to use it in the last episode—it could've been that Dave Brass got cut, he went to the hospital, and we never see or hear from him again. I started to hear rumors from some people I knew. I saw Terry Kinney—who I worked a lot with—at a screening of a film and he said, "Oh, I talked to Tom. Did you know he's bringing you back?" And I didn't. I got these weird phone calls from casting for a while. "What are you doing next spring? Are you going to be available? Would you be available?" I was twisting in the wind. All I could do was go back to the classes I was taking, the things I was doing up to that point. I had no idea what the future held. All I knew was that I had done three episodes.

I know that was my first break because no casting situation since then has been the same as it was before. Some go better, some go worse, but the people I'm dealing with now deal with me as if they may really need me sometime soon. Whether I nail that particular audition or not, on some level, they deal with me as an entity that's of value. I don't carry myself the same as I did before because I know what it takes to get good, big jobs. I know it came out of a freedom of being that I had. Even though sometimes I'll slip out of that, in a certain sense I still have that. I know that I'm going to get the jobs I'm supposed to get.

What do you wish someone had told you at the beginning of your career?

I wish I had known that I should pursue my life—and my happiness within my life—as aggressively as I was trying to get acting work. I was always pushing the envelope of, "How do I get better? How do I get more people to know who I am? How do I move forward as an actor?" I wish that I had known that more probably would've come to me if I was pursuing my own happiness and my own life as aggressively as I was pursuing those connections and auditions and classes and things. I really think that I could've *let* more happen than *make* more happen.

There's so much you can't control, but you can control how good you are—and you know it. If I could put my finger on my talent, I know when I'm full of crap and when I'm good. I don't need anyone else's opinion to tell me that. So, I've been able to always get better. I feel like, if you're better all the time, people will eventually know it and the roles will come. People will look for you, people will remember you. Some people are ready to work in their teens, some people are ready to work in their twenties, some people are ready to work in their thirties, and so on. It's just the way it is. And you won't know it until it happens.

I'm a much better actor now that I have kids because who I am at my core is someone that needed to be a dad. I feel like I own what I do and own who I am more now that I know who I am—which is, predominantly, a father and a husband. I never would've known that. I didn't anticipate that that's how it was going to be. It just turned out that way. Like a lot of young actors, I always thought I was ready, all the time, for years before anything ever happened in my career. I assumed that I was going to get every job and that I was right for everything and that people were just not giving me a chance. The industry was just conspiring against me. I felt that. I felt that all the time. "They don't know! They don't know me! If they would only give me a chance. If they gave me that job." But in hindsight, *I* didn't know. I don't pass judgment on that being right, wrong, good, or bad. It's just how it happened.

I also wish I had been told at the beginning of my career, "You can and you will work without representation. You've just got to figure out how." Also, if it's not fun, you're doing it wrong. It won't always be fun, but on some level, the work, the auditions, the life—if that's not fun, you're doing it wrong.

What is your favorite thing about being an actor?

I love the possibility of it. I love the possibility of every audition. I love the possibility that every day is going to be different than the day before. I love the possibility of the people I'll meet along the way. I love the possibility of the people I'll get to research and play along the way. I love the freedom I've had. I truly love that it's worked out that I've gotten to spend a lot of time with my wife and kids. I don't think that guys that work a seventy-hour job get to do that. That doesn't happen for every actor. I've lucked out that way. A lot of actors have their career success and it takes them away from their family. I've just been lucky that in my beginning, my breaks were working on shows that shot close to where I was, working at theatres that were close to where I was, so I got to come and go to my family.

What made you choose Los Angeles?

We all knew we needed to do this. The industry informed me that it was time to be in LA as opposed to being in New York. My wife is always up for anything. I highly recommend that people marry people that could support their choice to do this with their lives. By marrying people that don't support your choice, you're sort of acknowledging that you are not really behind your choice to do this in your life. I do think you can have whatever you want in your life and make it work. There are people who will support you doing what you want to do. I thought for a long time, as an actor, that I couldn't have a relationship like the one I have with Karen. I thought it was an either/or equation. I went a long time not thinking that existed. I found that I've gotten my career *out of* my relationship with her and *out of* having kids. I married someone that was always going to support me being who I needed to be. A lot of actors think they have to choose. I would say they're wrong and that they're living a very narrow life and therefore acting in a very narrow way. You *can* have it all. There will be compromises along the way but you *can* create the life you want.

Do you ever feel like giving up?

From the moment that I saw *Les Misérables*, I knew I was born to be an actor. It doesn't mean that I haven't at times had doubts along the way, doubts about my own ability to make it happen, but I can't say that I've ever known that I was going to leave it, even for half an hour. I know I'm supposed to be a storyteller. That to me opens the possibility of being a producer or director or writer. Telling great human being stories is what interests me. It's how I operate as an actor. I see myself as a part of the whole. A lot of actors succeed by just being able to focus on the task at hand. I had a great acting teacher—one of the best—Ron Van Lieu. He's now the master teacher at Yale and he was, for many years, the master teacher at NYU. I came across him at the Actors Center. That was the only place he taught outside of those Master's programs. I went in there and I auditioned for them and I didn't get into his class right away. I took other classes and I kept angling for his class and eventually got into his class. I've now taken four or five and I've met some of my most favorite actor-peers who I know are going to be names for years to come there.

He helped me find that I was the type of actor that was going to have an overview as well as be in the moment. I had to marry that as I worked and not judge that I must not be in the moment if I can see the whole as I do it. I remember for a lot of years, it didn't kind of work for me. I was trying to turn off this part of my brain or deny its reality because I could see the whole while I was doing the work. I had acting teachers that would try to beat that out of me. Ron taught me how to run on both rails at the same time and not to judge that. He did teach me to play the moments instead of my ideas that I had about the moments, so I did have to make a flip. It's great to have a whole bunch of ideas, but then it's time to act. And acting doesn't happen in a set of ideas you bring to it. All my ideas are what I have to bring, too. As long as I don't play them in the moments, if I don't judge them, some of them stick. Some of them don't. They make me an inventive, problem-solving type of actor who sees the bigger picture and can therefore fit into the whole. It opens up a whole bunch of possibilities about who I am as an actor now. It was a liability that has since become who I am.

How did you get your first agent?

I got out of the American Academy in '92 or '93 and did the third-year conservatory program. Part of that year is also a showcase. We did a bunch of scenes: my very first scene night. It doesn't work for me. I went many, many, many years without an agent. I was in New York seven or eight years without an agent. After I got on *Oz* without an agent, I learned the lesson of, "Don't be afraid to ask people to help you because it's the only way people can help you." Be prepared that they can respond in whatever way they're going to respond and that doesn't mean anything either.

Because of my type, when I went to inform the world that I was now a working actor to be taken seriously, they still didn't see that. The agents that I did meet—and I was able to get some meetings—didn't know how I fit on *Oz*. To explain the part wasn't enough. Agents needed to see it to believe it. They need to know you're "money." An agent's job is to make money and the easiest way for them to do that is if you're already making somebody money somewhere. They'll take you then. Or, if you bring them money and they say, "Oh! I'll take a cut of that." Or, they come to see you in a show or a play or a showcase and absolutely know that that's "money" and no one else knows, but they have to be visionary for that to happen.

I got some meetings after the three episodes of *Oz* and a lot of people looked at me as an oddity. One agent at Don Buchwald said, "You've had an amazing career without representation. I have a lot of clients that don't have the credits you have. You're a rarity. You're in your mid-thirties and you're having your first break now." I *am* an oddity and that's why agents passed on me. They didn't get it. When *Oz* started airing and I got invited back for the second season, then I got a few more meetings. I went into EWCR and I met Renee Panichelli. She and I just connected on a human level. I got her. She got me. She understood that I was an actor's actor, someone that was always getting better, someone that had made a lot of stuff happen for himself. She just liked me. She liked me as a dad, she liked me as a person, she liked me as an actor. They asked me to do a monologue, which I took as a good thing. It earned them a lot of respect from me because they wanted to get to know me more as an actor, not just what they could see on *Oz* or from my theatre credits. I know my monologue blew them away, but to seal the deal I went to Tom Fontana and asked him to write a recommendation. I could've done that at any time along the way because I had known that he was willing to help me. But instead of pissing that opportunity away on all these other people that had passed on me, that had seen me,

I waited for the one that I connected to and where I thought, "I'll be home with these people. They'll get on the phone every day and say, 'If you haven't seen Blake Robbins, you're crazy.'" I was with EWCR until last year.

Who are *your* favorite actors?

I've always loved Kevin Kline. He's so adventurous, and bold, and surprising, and can do it all. I love watching actors who surprise me. I'd rather be drawn into a performance than to have a performance pushed at me. I love vulnerability in performance. John Travolta has amazing vulnerability and generosity and you can tell, whether he's playing good guys or bad guys, that as a human being, he's generous. He's generous with the other actors.

How do you choose the material you work on?

I wish I could attribute it to someone, but some veteran actor said, "There are three things you base taking a job on and you can prioritize however you choose. It's the script, the people, and the money." Since I haven't worked for very much money along the way, that's always come third for me. I also fundamentally believe that if you do things you're passionate about, the money will follow. For me, always, "script" is 1A and "people" is 1B. When I've used that, I've done some projects that maybe business people—agents and managers—would've asked me not to, but they've always turned into wonderful experiences. People have got to get to know you, and for them to know you, you've got to know yourself. And part of knowing yourself is what you do have passion about and what you don't have passion about. Trust that you're going to get the jobs, but don't do anything that you can't have some passion about. Along the line, I've realized that when things happen for me is when I truly believe I'm doing something of value, something that I have a voice about, something that I have passion about. I seek that out. Value your time on Earth and value the time of those around you.

What do you do when nothing is happening in your career?

I would tell any young actor that you don't have to do everything today or tomorrow, but you should always take a step. And any time you find that nothing's happening, there is a step you can take. Whether it's send out one headshot to someone you're really passionate about getting to know, volunteer to work on something you know is going to teach you about the industry, go to a reading series, or get in a class, one step in any one of those moments when you feel like, "What's going on here? Nothing's happening," moves the ball forward. It always leads to another step and eventually it leads to a journey.

Faith Salie

It's a safe bet that Faith Salie is the only Rhodes scholar doing sitcoms in Hollywood. She starred as the lovably intellectual Eleanor in the critically-acclaimed improvisational comedy Significant Others *for NBC/Bravo.*

Faith grew up in Atlanta and began her career in musical theatre. After graduating magna cum laude and Phi Beta Kappa from Harvard (where she performed the lead roles in Cabaret, Lysistrata, *and* Grease *and also tangoed with Matt Damon in* A... My Name Is Alice*), she won her graduate scholarship to Oxford University. While completing her MPhil in Literature, she performed at the National Theatre of London and at the Edinburgh Fringe as the lead in* Antigone, Chess, *and* Assassins*. In 2002, she was part of the Ovation Award-winning LA premiere of* The Laramie Project.

On the small screen, Faith has appeared in both dramas and sitcoms, most famously wearing nothing but gold lamé on Sex and the City*. Having been beamed up on* Star Trek: Deep Space Nine, *she is proud to be a "tradable life form" for Trekkers. A busy voiceover artist, she can also be heard on the animated series* Astro Boy*. In addition, Faith is a stand-up comic who appears regularly as a pop culture pundit on a variety of VH-1 shows.*

Behind the scenes, Faith is the co-creator and executive producer of the new VH-1 reality show Spin Cycle*. She has written for the Oxygen Network shows* Girls Behaving Badly *and* Guys Behaving Badly *and created a reality pilot for Endemol USA called* The Done Thing.

Faith's hobbies include baking Coca-Cola cake and giving it away before she can eat it. More information is at http://faithsalie. com.

photo by Alexandra Hedison
http://hedison.com

When did you know you wanted to become an actor?

My parents would say I wanted to be an actor all my life. I would place it at about eleven years old when I took an acting class in Dunwoody, Georgia. I was playing soccer and had Sunday School class—well, when you're Catholic, Sunday School is on Tuesday night—and my parents always encouraged us to do whatever we wanted. I said, "I want to take an acting class." I had been cast as the judge in a play in the sixth grade. It was all in rhyme. I liked it and I think I was probably the most successful because I was the loudest. At that age, they're looking for someone who can articulate, read, memorize, and be loud. It's all about projection! I'd been dancing since I was three, taking tap and ballet, so I knew I liked performing.

I would not be where I am today without my parents. I probably sound so cliché, but it is the truth. They were never the least bit "stage parents." I remember being frustrated, wishing they had been more "stage parent-y." I remember getting into a professional children's company at the age of fourteen and thinking I was old. I felt like I was a late bloomer because there were these people who had been doing it forever and they could twirl batons and they had sashes and they would come into auditions with their tap shoes on and their sheet music. I was like, "Oh my gosh, I can't believe my parents didn't help me more!"

When I wanted to get an agent, I was fourteen and I sat down with a phone book and I opened it to Theatrical Agencies and I wrote these letters—I gave them to my mom to do on the typewriter and she'd do them verbatim—and signed them, sent them off, and followed them up with phone calls. And then if I got an interview, my parents would drive me. But I remember going to auditions and feeling just sick and nervous: "I don't want to go." I remember my dad would slow down the car and say, "Oh, I'll just turn around." And then I had to say, "Oh, no, no! I want to go!" And he'd say, "Okay." They were that sort of chill about it, which I think was pretty smart of them to do. I had to be the one to say, "I'm choosing this lifetime of rejection." I'm only kidding! A lifetime of alternate rejection and success.

How do you handle rejection?

I can't conceive of how I would deal with it or whether I would still be acting if I hadn't had the family I had, because, I think if you want to be an actor you just have to think you're a little bit special. That's not "better than" other people, but you obviously think you have something to say that people should listen to. Or you think that you have a way of expressing what other people want to say that people should pay attention to. I understand that some people come to acting because maybe they never felt loved enough and seek that approbation from the public. I had the opposite story. I was insanely loved, made to feel very special and smart and pretty and all those things. Who knows if I was "all those things" as much as my parents told me I was, but in my mind, I thought, "I can do this." I feel like that sort of unconditional love comes from coming home and saying, "Mom, the kids at school said I was fat," and her telling me, "You're not fat. You're athletic. They're just jealous." That whole mentality, if you instill it in a child from day one, it kind of sticks with you.

It's always hard to deal with rejection. Something gave me healthy calluses early on. You carry that through life: "They didn't like me? Somebody else will. They didn't like me? I like myself. They didn't like me? My parents adore me." I feel very lucky. I really don't know how other people do this career. I don't understand that. An actor without healthy calluses is a walking wound of a human. They're just raw. When you're given compliments and approbation, it feels wonderful, but it must be such a temporary psychic hug.

What was your first paid gig?

I was fourteen. I did a voiceover for a cartoon and I think I made like seventy-five dollars for about an hour's work. My brother was eighteen and he had to work at a pizza place and mow lawns to make that much money. When you're fourteen and you make seventy-five dollars—that is pretty amazing. There's a theatre company I was involved with called the Atlanta Workshop Players. They had a children's touring company. It was teenagers mostly performing for kids in other schools. I think we made twenty dollars a show. That instilled such dignity in me: "I'm a professional." It encouraged me to act professionally: to show up on time, to practice at home, to know my lines, to go over it in my head on the way to the performance. It's not mercenary. It really is about instilling professionalism. I think that getting paid at that young of an age—even though it wasn't much—affected my whole adolescence: "I'm a working professional. I go to school and then I leave school and I go do my job." There's a sense to knowing that what you do is worth something, literally.

What makes someone a "professional" actor?

There is a very literal sense in which you can say a professional actor is someone who gets paid for it. What if you felt like you were a professional actor but you weren't getting paid for the work you were doing? That's a minefield and way too pat to say. I do sometimes look around at people who are thirty-five, don't have health insurance, moved to LA ten years ago, go to scene study class twice a week, call themselves actors and I don't know if they would be called professional actors. I don't mean to sound condescending; I just don't know where that line is. You almost want to say, "You could move to Montana and you could star in every community theatre play and have a house and not have to wait tables." So, I guess I don't have a good answer to that question.

However, *professionalism* is being on time; it's having a strong sense that what you do is important and not just that you speak a part in a play. Professionalism is doing things on your own time—not showing up to rehearsals thinking that's where all the work takes place—being there for everybody else on the team when it's really a scene about them. I'm on a TV show now and I feel like every member of that crew is family. Maybe that's because I'm on a show where there isn't a huge star. It's very much an ensemble—and for the most part people think "an ensemble of unknowns" although we've all been working for years—and the sound guy is my buddy. I think that's part of being professional: being part of a team. You're not more important because the camera's focused on you. Guess what, if the guy behind the camera doesn't want you to look good, you're going to look bad.

Who's to say what defines you as a professional actor? Is it the day you earn your insurance through SAG? You know it's changed so much. Didn't it used to be that you had to make six thousand a year and now it's eighteen thousand dollars or something? And next year it's going to be like twenty-seven thousand dollars for Plan I? I got my insurance in 1998 and I had been here two-and-a-half years. I had dental, which was all very exciting. The thing is, I had been acting professionally as a teenager and then happily put the professional acting on hiatus while I was in college—where I was doing tons of theatre—and then grad school. Neither in college nor grad school did I want to major in Theatre, but I was doing tons of theatre. It was the greatest experience of my life. It was amazing. I knew that I had this amazing creative outlet and became a much better actor and singer and dancer during college and felt like the same thing would happen during grad school. It did. So, I was in England for grad school—I won a scholarship my senior year of college that I couldn't turn down—and right before I left, I auditioned for this TV movie-of-the-week with Donald Sutherland and Anne Bancroft and Diane Lane and got this pretty major part. You don't know when you're twenty-two how awesome that is. I'd leave Heathrow and fly back to Atlanta and shoot and then fly back and fly back again. It wasn't a huge part but it was a huge break. I was Taft-Hartleyed for that job, but I didn't have to join SAG because the job was in a right-to-work state. Then, two years later, when I left England and moved to LA, I realized that I should pay the money and get my SAG card.

What made you choose Los Angeles?

I still think about that: "Should I have gone to New York?" To me, New York is like when you backpack the summer after you graduate high school in Europe. You buy a *Let's Go* and you go with your friends and you get a Eurail pass and it's awesome. I would *never* do that now. Never. I would have it all planned out; we'd stay at really nice hotels—making sure that every one of them had a gym. I remember being in Egypt and running past men with guns and jumping over animal carcasses. I would never do that now!

Well, I feel that way about New York. That's what you do either early on when you're totally ready to be a poor, starving artist and you think it's cool or you do it when you've made it and have a nice view of Central Park. But I do have friends there and I go back and forth—in fact, I'm going next week to pitch a show. It's fun. It's nice to do the back and forth.

But to answer the question, when I left England, it had not been sunny for four months and it was truly depressing. I had been studying for my exams and I needed the sun. Plus my college boyfriend was from Beverly Hills so I was familiar with the palm trees and the sun. I went to a college where tons of people went into the business and a lot of them were already out here. I moved out here already having a great network of friends.

How did you get your first LA agent?

I went to Kirk Cameron's mom, Barbara Cameron, who was in Woodland Hills. She had an agency and mostly represented child actors and worked out of her home. She was representing Christine Lakin who was a little girl I used to baby-sit from the Atlanta Workshop Players. So, she was the only person I knew. I drove out there. She was very upfront: "I only represent kids, but sure, I'll send you out." She did, but the first audition that I got—and I got a guest star on a series—was because a friend from college was writing on the TV show. Actually, I had an audition before that because a friend was a writer for *Beverly Hills, 90210*, which I didn't get.

In the beginning it was all about friends and now, again, it's all about friends. Those friends from back then are now running shows. I have the most creative, amazing, brilliant people in my life with whom I would be friends whether or not we were in the same industry. It's gotten to a point in my mind—because now I'm producing a show—that if you have two people to choose from and they're equally talented and one of them is your buddy, that's not nepotism. Why else do this if you can't work with your friends?

You never know when you're planting seeds. When I was a sophomore at Harvard and I was doing *Lysistrata* with Mary Dixie Carter, and Lindsay Jewett (now Sturman) was the producer bringing in Entenmann's donuts, I wasn't thinking, "This is going to serve me in the future." I had no idea what anybody was going to be doing. But I was having an amazing time and I admired my friends. So you keep in touch. It's having faith that your friends will use you when the time is right. You should never have to ask your friends, "Hey can I audition for this?" That creates an awkward relationship. If your friends are looking out for you and vice-versa, they're going to call you in when it's right. They save their bullets until it's time to tell a network that this is your show.

I feel very lucky to be at a point in my career—and it's only just beginning—now that I'm producing this show. I feel very lucky to be able to bring people in who I know will do me proud. And when I've met with people who aren't right for it, it just means their creative juices would be better served elsewhere. It's not weird or awkward. As long as I'm honest and not making promises I can't keep, it works.

Did you know that you would end up wanting to produce?

No. I was so reluctant. I love acting first and foremost. Not to sound like an *artiste*, but I think that when you are an artist and that is your identity, there's a lot more ways to express yourself than just acting. Frankly, if I could be hired right now and be as busy as Meryl Streep and have ten movies lined up and two plays, then I wouldn't give a thought to producing. Acting is always my priority. My acting plate isn't so full that nothing else can fit on it.

I have the blessing in my life of having a manager who encourages me all the time to do more: "Oh, you're an actor? But look at how good you are at stand-up comedy. If you can write a joke, you can write this. If you can write this, you can produce this."

What do you consider your first break?

Being born to my parents was my first big break. After that, I would say *Significant Others*. I was recurring on a sitcom in '98 for one season and that was cool to drive to a set and have a parking space and a regular check, but I was still just in for eight weeks and didn't know everybody on the set. *Significant Others* is definitely my break, but it's not just because it is the first time I am a series regular. It is a break in my mentality. For better or for worse, it is outside legitimacy. You can walk around all day long knowing you're a professional, but to have a secret gun in the back of your pocket is huge. When I go into an audition and I don't get it, I walk out saying, "Oh, man, I wish I'd gotten that. But I'm still a lead on a show." I honestly wish I didn't get that extra sense of confidence from it, because that's fleeting, and it only came because I got cast on this show and it could go away. But there it is. You're like, "Here's my resumé. I'm the lead on a show." It's an important thing for me to recognize about myself, that I gain confidence from being cast. I need to try to transcend that, so that I feel confident and secure in my talent whether or not I get a part, whether or not I have a job.

The big lesson I've learned is that there's never just one shot. This show may be cancelled, I could be recast, but I'm producing a show. Guess what. I'll put myself on it! I'm not grasping at things anymore. The funny thing about having any sort of success is it just means you've climbed a mountain and then you have a view of all the mountains around you. If you had told me two years ago, "You're going to be a lead on a TV series," I would've thought, "Oh, my life's going to be amazing! I'm going to have a house in the Palisades and I'm going to be on *The Tonight Show with Jay Leno* every night." But all it means is I go to the set every week.

How do you prepare for a role?

Working in improv demands such a different kind of preparation—a different mindset—for a role than working in conventional drama or comedy. I think back to when I was doing *The Laramie Project*, which was just insane emotional preparation. Specifically for *Significant Others*, it's keeping myself in a really open mindset. You almost can't prepare or you do yourself in, with improv. On the other hand, you have to get yourself like a player before a game. That's a good analogy. A baseball player knows he's going out to play a game. He knows the rules of the game. He doesn't know how it's going to go, right? He doesn't know what kind of pitch he's going to get. I have to be in a very confident state of mind and also let myself off the hook: "They're going to edit the funny. Half of what you say may not be funny. Half of what your scene partner says may not be funny." I can't worry about what I say being funny. You can't worry about that in improv. You can't go for the joke, really. Very specifically though, for my character, any time I come across a word that I like, I write it down so I can use it. Who else is reading *The New Republic* on the treadmill before going to the set?

Who are *your* favorite actors?

It's so hackneyed, but Meryl Streep. Emma Thompson. The best actors to me are the ones who can seamlessly move between drama and comedy. They're just acting machines. They bring that same commitment, it doesn't matter what the genre is. I would throw Kate Winslet in there, too. The thing I admire about all three of those women is that I think their work is really marked by a lack of vanity, which I think is absolutely necessary to be convincingly dramatic or comedic. As far as comic genius: Megan Mullally. I bow to her. The thing she does so amazingly well is that she creates this really out-there character who never comes off as stagy. It doesn't feel like she's overacting. You really believe that this crazy person named Karen exists. You wish you knew her a little bit—but not a lot. Another thing all of these actors share is that they will surprise you.

Do you ever feel like giving up?

Not anymore. There were a few times that I really did. I sort of conflate that with the depression over losing my mom. It was just a very dark time. Certainly career issues didn't help. I remember thinking, "This is stupid. Why am I not getting my PhD? I could've spent one more year at Oxford, gotten my PhD, and be teaching." But that's just not as creative as I need.

What do you wish someone had told you at the beginning of your career?

I used to—and I still do, sometimes—think, "Oh my gosh, this is it. This is my big shot. This is *such* an important audition. This is such an important project." Especially when I pulled favors to get an audition, because I knew someone who knew someone, I'd get all wrapped up about it. I'd feel like the weight of the world is on my shoulders; like I have to make this person proud, I have to get the job. I don't have that mindset anymore. I hope it's healthy; I'm just like, "Fuck 'em. They didn't want me? Okay." That sounds way too belligerent. Usually I feel that way when I go in and read with a casting director who doesn't choose to look up from the script and I don't get a callback. I know they didn't really pay attention. I'm not going to lose sleep over that one. There was a time before I got my "big break" where I would go on five auditions, maybe get a couple callbacks, not get cast, and think, "Oh my gosh, should I not be doing this?"

When I moved out here, I was twenty-four. Again, like when I was fourteen and felt like I'd started late, I thought, "I'm so old!" There are so many people who don't go to college and they come out when they're eighteen and they get that running start. It makes all the difference. They get to play high-schoolers when they're in their twenties. I remember, when I was twenty-five, people would say, "Oh, you should do Groundlings classes." And I would think, "I'm too old to start that." But twenty-five is so young! I wish I hadn't thought I was so old. I don't know what a difference that makes, though, frankly. I didn't realize that then, but I don't think I was the type of person who was meant to *hit* in her twenties. I would hear that there are no roles for women over thirty so I felt this desperate need to make it before I turned thirty. And now I realize that's just not true. I have a lot more to say now. Had I known, when I moved out here, that there is this great demand for girls who can do comedy, I would've focused on that more. Now, it's sort of my niche. I wanted to do it all, then. Having said that, the first big part I got was a very dramatic part on *Star Trek: Deep Space Nine.* So, it didn't hurt that I wasn't focused on comedy. I just wish I could've done stand-up earlier and I wish maybe I had done more improv earlier. But what would I have said? "Oh, I'm twenty-five. My life is good. My mom's alive and I have no wrinkles." There are no jokes there!

I've finally sort of realized who I am and what my marketable persona is, which is actually the same thing as who I am. *Significant Others* is all improvised. I'm literally scripting a character. It's a phenomenal honor. It's the biggest compliment ever. The go-to place, if I'm improvising off the top of my head, is me. The character I play in the show is certainly a hyperbolic version of me and I'm put in situations where *Faith* would walk out the door and yell at somebody, but I obviously can't do that as Eleanor. It is a comedy, so I always go to the more comic choice, the more "patient wife" choice. I don't want to be a bitch all the time. Having said that though, part of it is me. I think that I get to play an exaggerated version of myself. I have a feeling that one of the reasons I was cast is that I used this crazy word in the audition. I'm a *wordophile*—I just made that up—I love language, I got my Master's in English Literature, and think that I have a great reverence for words and therefore scripts. It's kind of ironic that I'm on a show where I improvise because I am the one person in a play who gets mad if someone misses an article. I'm like, "A playwright wrote this! You can't *change* it! You can't even add a semicolon!"

On the show, I'm a very intellectual character. Instead of making that off-putting, I try to make her unknowingly pretentious. I think the show handles it well because we'll be in therapy and I'm spouting multi-syllabic words that nobody knows—including myself, because I looked them up the day before—and the guy who plays my husband gets us all to the point of laughter because he says, "I'd probably agree with her if I knew what the fuck she just said." I tried to do that on the VH-1 stuff where I was a pop-culture commentator and I got to be myself. I don't think there are enough funny, smart women on TV. I don't really think we've seen a good one since Diane on *Cheers*. If she's smart, she's a DA on *Law & Order* or she's humorless. Or she's like Lilith, who is an amazing, hilarious character, but she is a secondary character. She's not someone you can grab hold of and love. I very much run the risk of being self-aggrandizing here. I don't want to say: "I'm so smart." But I do have this very academic background and I feel like I'm at a point in my career where it's appreciated and utilized. To me, the appeal of academics was that you work really hard and you get this grade that is a stamp of approval. I kind of conquered that, so now it's like, "Let's try something harder!" There is nothing objective about acting. Getting to be a series regular is almost harder than being chosen as a Rhodes Scholar.

Tom Everett Scott

*Tom Everett Scott graduated with a Bachelor of Arts degree from Syracuse University. His career started in New York, where he did commercials (McDonald's, Coke, Diet Coke, Crest), an after-school special (*Love in the Dark Ages, *in which his character gives his girlfriend Chlamydia), and a recurring role as Grace's son on* Grace Under Fire.

Tom's feature films include That Thing You Do!, An American Werewolf in Paris, Dead Man on Campus, One True Thing, The Love Letter, *and* Boiler Room. *Television shows include* The $treet, Philly, ER, *and* ABC's love life. *His TV movies include* Karrol's Christmas *and* Surrender Dorothy.

Tom's theatre credits include The Country Club *by Douglas Carter Beane at the Drama Department,* Touch *by Toni Press-Coffman at the Women's Project Theatre, and* Turnaround *by Roger Kumble at the Coast Playhouse in West Hollywood. More information is available at http://us.imdb.com/name/nm0779866.*

photo courtesy ABC by Andrew Eccles
http://andreweccles.com

When did you know you wanted to become an actor?

I think freshman year of college was when I realized I was going to major in acting. I knew I was going to college because that was my parents' plan, and I was cool with that. I wanted to do it too. I have three sisters—two older and one younger. My two older sisters were already on their way to college so it was my turn to pick a college and at the same time kind of figure out what I wanted to do.

But even before that, I remember seeing my sister in *South Pacific*. She's four years older than me and I remember thinking, seeing her in this play, that she blew her moment. She was fine, but I was like, "*I* would've done that differently." They did three performances and I went to all of them. I memorized the moments on stage and couldn't wait to get up on the stage and show what *I* could do. At that point I started doing whatever plays were available to me in the fifth grade.

The AV club in high school—the guys who pushed around the VCRs and TVs into the rooms—had a studio in some room at the high school. They had three cameras set up and you could switch from camera to camera and record stuff. We would go in there and just sort of mess around. There was a kid who was into 8mm film, making his own films and showing them. Then the cable company came along and put a public access cable station where we used to have our little crappy camera set up at the school. They brought in all new equipment and a guy! Ralph Wadman was the program director of our local public access channel. He would come to our high school and sit in this little room with all this equipment. He was doing an evening show with guests—it was boring—but the rest of the time it was 24/7 character generator screens of, "East Bridgewater Current Events." So, at eight o'clock there'd be a person actually talking on this channel. I started hanging around and Ralph said, "Why don't you announce basketball games?" I said, "Sure!" So, I went down, took a camera, filmed the game, and I'd interview everybody.

Eventually, I said, "Y'know, what I really want to do is get my friends down here and we'll do, like, a show." We started putting together little sketches and stuff. Ralph was like, "You can do this as long as you come in with a script first." So, he gave me an assignment and I'd come in with a script for him and we started doing shows. This is when it really dawned on me that there was a future in this. I saw Ralph was getting paid to sit there and do something fun, so I asked him what he majored in. He said, "Communications." That was the first I had ever heard of that word used to describe something you could major in and do for a living. And it was like a five-dollar word, so I knew I could go repeat that to my parents and have them go, "Ooh! Wow! Yeah, that sounds good!"

So, I went to the college expo in Boston and we went on a school bus—me and all the juniors that wanted to go to college—and I just went from table to table going, "What kind of Communications department do you have?" Syracuse had this great Communications School. I didn't want to be a news guy. Bob Costas and Ted Koppel didn't excite me. It was just that this school had this top program, so I thought, "I'd better go to this top school." So, I applied and got into

Syracuse. When I interviewed with this woman at Syracuse—before I got accepted—she looked at my resumé of stuff that I liked doing and my essay that I wrote about performing and being in band and all the kinds of things that got me going. She said, "You seem more like an actor, not a journalist." I said, "Uh, no. I'm going to stick with Communications." I thought it was more realistic. I didn't really know that I wanted to be an actor. I was pretty sure that I didn't. In my mind, you were only an actor if you had nepotism going for you. It didn't seem possible that anybody from my hometown would be an actor.

Meanwhile, I'm doing summer theatre. I'm going down to this renaissance faire every summer in Rhode Island and doing these wild things, smoking pot for the first time, and doing wild performance stuff. So, I go to Syracuse and I'm majoring in Communications. Everyone was nice and I was learning a little something, but obviously the class that I loved the most was my public speaking class. I got to get up in front of everybody and perform. I knew I liked it. This really cute girl lived on my floor in my dorm. She was in the Drama department. She was going to be in a play called *The Member of the Wedding* and she said, "Wanna come down and see me in the play?" I didn't even know where the theatre was. Syracuse is this beautiful campus—great school, really fun—and the theatre is way off campus. I had to take a bus and I got off the bus, walked into the lobby, and saw kids my age—obviously Theatre and Musical Theatre majors—literally flitting. Goofy people! I thought, "This might be my crowd. I think this is where I want to be." I sat down in the theatre, the lights went down, lights came up on stage, and that's when it all came crashing down. I thought, "This is her major. She's not putting up with boring stuff with maybe one good class. This *is* her class! Ah!" That was it. It was a done deal. I went to my advisor and said, "How do I switch? Is it easy?" She said, "Yep! You can do it. Turn your Communications classes into electives. You have to audition for the department. That's it."

I wanted to make sure that I had answered all the questions that my parents would ask so that, when I told them about it, I had all the answers. My mom said, "Just do me a favor, before you do this. I want you to go to the renaissance faire guys and ask them if they think this is a good idea." They were the only professional actors we knew. They were like, "Yeah! Of course! Sure!" Little did they know, they sealed my fate as an actor. They then helped me actually prepare my monologue for my audition and stuff. I did a monologue from *The Glass Menagerie*. I auditioned, went the whole summer without knowing if I made it, signed up for all of my sophomore year Communications classes, kept getting the runaround from Syracuse College of Performing Arts, and then when I got there I bought all of my books for my Communications classes. I was so depressed. I couldn't believe I was on a waiting list or something like that. I just took matters in my own hands and went down to the office of the woman who was holding all of the information for the College of Visual and Performing Arts. I said, "My mom's been calling you all summer to find out if I'm in the Drama department. Am I on a list? Am I waiting?" She literally looked at a list and said, "Oh? Tom Scott? Oh, yeah! No, you're *in* Theatre. You've missed your first three days of class." I was so excited but I was also like, "Oh, no!" I realized I had money sitting on my desk in the form of useless books and returned all of them, ran down to the theatre, met with my new advisor—Donna Inglima, who was one of my most trusted adults in the Drama department—and she said, "You didn't miss a thing. Go on in! Meet everybody." And I was happy as a clam.

What was your first paid gig?

A McDonald's commercial, after college. While I was a sophomore, taking freshman core classes, there was this other kid, Jay Harrington, who is a working actor these days. He had done a McDonald's commercial and he was the most popular kid in the Drama department. I didn't know how people became actors and here I was pursuing it. I was thinking, "How did Jay Harrington get that audition? How did this happen?" There was so much to focus on, just majoring in Theatre, that was more about getting the acting down. We weren't really thinking about where we were going until senior year, when people started talking about where they'd go after college. Three cities always came up: LA, New York, and Chicago. My friends and I thought, "Chicago! That sounds cool. The Windy City! Let's go." But that never happened.

Syracuse does a scene night kind of like the Leagues. It's where all the seniors that got picked to go—you had to audition—would go into New York for this showcase. I got paired up with Sam Brown and we did the only comic scene out of anybody. We did Christopher Durang's *Beyond Therapy*—the blind date scene—and they're both crazy characters. This was my trip to New York. New York seemed like *forget it*! I went there once in high school with my band—a band field trip or whatever—and it seemed like this concrete place. I grew up in a small town in rural Massachusetts with three stoplights in the whole town. New York scared the hell out of all of us on this trip. We all sort of huddled close as we went around the City. So, when we went down there for this senior showcase, it was the same place—it gave me the same anxiety—but now kids that had graduated ahead of me that I knew were living there. They came to visit us when we did our scene night. They took us around after, and you know how New Yorkers walk around, crossing against the light, and I'm like, "Go? Really? Oh, now? Oh! Okay." That's when I realized that I could move to New York. If they could do it, I could do it.

This scene night, I got ten responses out of fifteen industry people there. We were awesome. I was so excited. I had casting directors and agents wanting to see me. They wanted me to call them. They had little boxes to check: "Send a headshot," "Please call," "No thanks," and I got all these "Please call" checkboxes. So I go back to Syracuse and call them the next day and they all say, "When do you graduate?" "When do you move to the City?" "When you're living in the City, give us another call. Come in. We'll meetcha." That was my foot-in-the-door, in terms of starting out. I had really crappy headshots that some guy at Syracuse had done for me, so they all told me to get new headshots. I was like, "No way! I just spent fifty-five dollars on headshots!" It was so funny.

I graduated. I went home to Massachusetts. I slept in my bed probably that first night back and I was in my bed going, "I've got to get out of here. What am I doing?" I packed my Dodge Shadow up, my sister drove me down there—I didn't need the car, so I handed it off to my sister—and there I was, in New York, living with a friend of a friend. It's so weird how we'll just live with somebody we've never met because we have a friend in common, but that's what you do when you're young and moving to New York, I guess. My buddy Craig Walker got me a job at the Firehouse at 85th and Columbus, waiting tables. I started looking up all these agents and casting directors.

Mitchell Riggs—my roommate—said the smartest thing to me that anybody had ever said to me at that point. He said, "Ask the casting directors if those agents on your list are any good." The first person I met with then was CBS' Maria Gillen—I don't know where she is now—and she looked at the list and said, "I only know one of these people." I said, "What does that mean?" She said, "Well, they submit actors to me in these manila envelopes," and she showed me like a pile of them, and then she said, "I'm only going to open the ones from agents that I trust to have good people. If you're with one of these people that I don't even know, I'm never going to see your headshot." There were a couple agencies I went to. They kind of gave me the whole, "Well, we'll freelance," thing. Some of them wanted to sign me right away. I held off, based on Maria's advice. She said, "Don't sign with anybody. Just freelance." And most agents were like, "Well, if you freelance, we're not really going to keep you at the top of our priority list." There was that moment of, "Am I doing the right thing?" Meanwhile, all these agents are telling me, "Why don't you change your hair? Wear this. Wear that." They really start dressing you down. They really start working on your confidence. Luckily, I just had this good feeling that I was getting good advice from both Mitchell and Maria. I just kind of hung in there and kept waiting tables and went on a couple of auditions from people I was freelancing with.

Jeff Bell—a competitive friend—and I, were jockeying for jobs. One day he said, "Did you meet with Tracy's agent friend?" Tracy was a bartender at the Firehouse. She was this cool girl. She wasn't an actress. She went to Law School and was just really cool. I didn't think I'd been talking with Tracy enough to go up to her and ask about her agent friend. He was like, "Well, Tracy's friend is an agent at J. Michael Bloom and I'm goin' in." So, Jeff went in, and they were like, "Sorry." My buddy Craig Walker went in and met the guy and they were like, "Sorry." Tracy came up to me and said, "My friend Rob is an agent at J. Michael Bloom and I think he'd like you." I was like, "Hold on, Tracy. Did you save this guy's life in *Nam* or something? How does he owe you something so much that you can keep sending him these guys that he keeps rejecting? He's not going to be your friend for long if you keep sending these waiters and bartenders that he keeps sending away!" She said, "I think you're a really great guy and he'd want to meet you." She gave me his number and I didn't call. Honestly, I thought it was a waste of time.

A week later we were working together, another shift, and she said, "I told my friend Rob all about you and you haven't called him yet!" So, I called up and met with Rob Claus and Mark Upchurch of the youth legit department for the East Coast office of J. Michael Bloom. They said, "We'd like to send you out on after-school specials, youth stuff. You're at the top of our age range, really, but you're too baby-faced for our adult division. So they had me go away and prepare two monologues. It was nerve-wracking, but I did it. I did a Howard Korder monologue from *Boy's Life* and my other monologue was one a friend from Syracuse wrote about a guy who was a high school football star who broke his leg. It was good! I did those two monologues and they told me they would think about everything and that I should give them a call the next day.

So they wanted to sign me, but I checked with Mitchell. He and Maria had been advising me through these three months. Mitchell said, "God bless, man. Sign. You're way ahead of the curve. This is a real agency. Unbelievable, Tom. I've been here four years and I hate my crappy agent. Sign." When I went to sign, I said, "What about commercials?" They said, "Oh, yeah! Meet so-and-so." We walked down the hall; they gave me some commercial copy. I read it and they said, "Great! We'll start sending you out." I didn't have any headshots that were worth anything, so they would take Polaroids of me each week—like ten or twelve Polaroids—and it was the most ridiculous thing to walk into an audition and have the casting director hold up a Polaroid and go, "What is this? This is ridiculous!" Literally, I was being made fun of each time I'd go in for an audition: "Seriously, man. Get a headshot." So, I did. Eventually.

So, after six months in New York, I booked that McDonald's commercial, quit my job at the Firehouse, and man did I quit too soon. I know people who've never quit their day job. I've always admired people who keep a day job just to keep their sanity. I wish I had because I lost my sanity in a way, living by the mailbox and harassing the payment person at Bloom: "Any residuals yet?"

What do you consider your first break?

The biggest break was *That Thing You Do!* I was with Bloom still and I was in a theatre company with Craig Walker—he and I started this theatre company—and I was down there in the basement on Twenty-sixth Street (we were renting this four-thousand square-foot basement to put shows up). I was down there in that office—that was kind of my alternate phone there—and my agent, Mark Schlegel, called there and said, "I've got this script. Tom Hanks has written it. It's a feature film for Fox and you're perfect for the lead. We just don't have a headshot." Now, I had already done the headshot! Here's the horrible truth. I got my headshots done, right when I got that McDonald's commercial. Andrew Brucker had taken these great headshots and Bloom had just run out of them at the time this was happening. I had a headshot at the theatre, so I grabbed it and I ran down to Bloom, gave it to Mark, and he gave me the script to read. Howard Feuer was casting it. They said, "You'll do a few scenes, but know the whole script." For no other audition had they ever said that to me.

Tom's not a hardcore, make-it-difficult kind of guy. He's a let's-make-it-easy kind of guy. Looking back, it was kind of odd that they were having me know this whole script for an audition. I went in on a Thursday right around my birthday—September 7th—and it was in '95. I'd been living in the City about three years. I went into Jonathan Demme's offices—he was producing and he had directed Tom in *Philadelphia*—and read for Howard Feuer and he said, "That was really great. I'm going to have you come back on Saturday and read for the director." And I'm like, "And the director is Tom Hanks?" And he said, "Yes. That'd be Tom Hanks." Again, he told me to be familiar with the whole script.

Basically, I knew that this was a role that I was perfect for. I had been auditioning for films since I'd signed with Bloom but not yet really booking anything. I was auditioning daily, like two, three auditions a day. That's really the best way to have a shot at it, is being out there all the time. There's no formula for getting an agent, but the agent is the one who can get you all of those auditions. Anyway, the role was perfect for me because it was about a guy who loved music and got an opportunity to be in a band and the band got a big break. I was like, "I'm an actor who is passionate about acting and if I got this film, this would be *my* big break." Literally, I was thinking I could go in and be this guy. This guy is me. I worked my ass off on the script and I went in and was sitting there. Josh Hamilton, who I knew from the movie *Alive*, was there, auditioning. I thought, "Well, I'll come close on this, but he's a guy with credits."

While I was waiting, I went into the bathroom and I heard Tom Hanks' voice. I heard him yelling at somebody, kidding around, in that really recognizable voice. I got really nervous. I went in and he kicked everybody out of the casting room—Howard and two readers—and it was just the two of us. He took my headshot and resumé and said, "Okay. Let's see here. It says here you play trumpet and bass guitar." I did *not* play bass guitar. I had *bought* a bass guitar in high school in the hopes of *playing* bass guitar someday and being in a band, but never really learned how to play bass guitar. Trumpet, I'd played from fourth grade, on. He said, "Because I'm an actor and I know that this could be a complete lie." I said, "Yeah, yeah! It's true!" He goes, "So you have some sense of rhythm?" I said, "Yeah." He said, "Okay." And that was it. That was the only, "Can you play the drums," line of questioning there was. The rest of it was, "Oh, you're in a theatre company?" and "If you become a film star, they'll all hate you," joking around. He asked, "What did you think of the script?" I said, "Well, I think this character is me." I gave him my point-of-view.

We read a couple of scenes—he had brought everybody back in, they taped it—and he said, "Great." That was it. I left. I said a little prayer on the corner of the block before I crossed the street, like, "I really want this job." I remember there was a music store on the corner with a vintage drum set sitting in the front window. I was like, "What a weird little omen to all that is happening!"

Monday at 10am, my agent called me and said, "Okay, you've got to go back in and read with Tom. He's flying back to LA tonight and you've got to go back in and read with an actress. Know the whole script." Same thing. I went in and I was sitting next to Liv Tyler in the waiting room. There were other boys there, but she was the only girl there. I knew who she was because the Aerosmith video was out. Basically, I went in, sat with her, and Tom gave her some notes—I can't remember what he told her to do—and he told me, "Don't do anything. Just read. Don't worry about doing a thing." We read the stuff and he said, "Okay, stand up next to each other." We stood up next to each other and she's tall. I'm tall. He was like, "Oh! Okay!" Like we weren't an obvious mismatch or something. He said, "Put these sunglasses on," and he took a Polaroid. I was just like, "Is this really happening?" What happened after that is, basically, I went into freak-out mode in my mind. I repressed all thought of this ever happening. I couldn't think about it, although I knew it went well.

Then they had me meet Jonathan Demme. We bullshitted about acting and theatre in New York and that was it. I had been on *Grace Under Fire*—I played Brett Butler's son and was recurring on that—and that was the only thing they had to look at, from the current season. So, Thursday, a week from my first audition with Howard, I got a call. My agent had said, at six, "We didn't get any calls today. I'm going to the theatre and I'll have my pager on me." I got a call from a guy like around eight o'clock, nine o'clock. He was like, "Is this Tom Everett Scott?" That's not typical. Everyone calls me "Tom Scott." So, I knew it was related to acting. I said, "Yeah, yeah. This is Tom." He said, "Okay. Just wanted to make sure this was your number." I said, "Wait, wait—who's this?" He said, "This is Ed Saxon from *That Thing You Do!* I'm a producer on the movie and I'm really just calling to make sure this is your number." So, I got off the phone and I grabbed my laundry bag. My girlfriend Jenny—now my wife—and my roommate Andrew Sgroi were like, "What was that?" I said, "I gotta get outta here. I'm gonna go get my laundry. Then let's go out and get a drink." I go down and then come back up with my laundry and ask, "Anything?" "Nothing." "Phone hasn't rung?" "Nope."

Phone rings. Scoop it up. Say, "Hello?" And this voice says, "Hi. Is this Tom?" I say, "Yep." "Tom Hanks." I was like, "All right." And that was it. I'm sitting in the kitchen of my railroad apartment and talking to Tom Hanks. He's saying all of these great things and, asks, "Do you wanna be in my movie?" That was my big break, that movie. Sure enough, it really did parallel what I was going through. What I was going through and what the character was going through was the exact same situation, really. There's things that started happening that didn't happen before: getting meetings with heads of studios; general meetings with all these people that just wanted to see my face, talk to me in person; and getting straight offers, not having to audition for some stuff. That's nice.

What made you choose Los Angeles?

Eventually, it was this series called *Philly*. It was on ABC with Kim Delaney for Steven Bochco. That's what brought us out here. We wound up coming out here in July 2001. September 11th happened that September and we got really serious about limiting the number of flights we took and also realized that LA was where we needed to be for work.

Do you ever feel like giving up?

I always say this—it's kind of my joke-y answer to that, but it's also really true—I don't think I can do anything else. Honestly, I don't think I'm *good* at anything else. The real answer might be that I'm so competitive that I have tried other things but realized that I wasn't as good at them as I am at this. I found the thing that I love and I'm also good at and can compete well at. That's really why I do it.

Who are *your* favorite actors?

I think Robert Duvall always jumps into my mind as somebody I've always believed everything he's ever done. Tom Hanks is obviously one of my idols—was always, even before. *Bosom Buddies* was such a great show. I honestly believe that the latest, greatest performance I've seen is what tends to qualify as my favorite, as favorite actors go. I just watched *Ray* and *Collateral* in the last month and Jamie Foxx now blows me away. I just watched *City of God* and I think everyone in that cast was brilliant.

What advice would you give to an actor starting out?

I've had a really lucky go of it. I have friends that still want to be actors at my age and they hit the pavement. I think that the biggest disservice you can do yourself, if you want to be an actor, is to wait for that break and not do anything until then. I think at any point, you should be doing plays, staying sharp. The only way to stay sharp is to do a play. I have never taken a class since college and I'm sure class is great—I know there are people who believe in it and love it and get a lot out of it, I probably would too—but I'd much rather spend my time rehearsing for a play that's actually going to go up in front of an audience and we're going to do the whole thing, get that adrenalin rush, and play that character more than once. That, to me, is the best way to stay sharp. I mean, look at what I was doing when I got the call for the audition for *That Thing You Do!*—basement theatre.

Craig and I had auditioned for a one-act play festival and wound up getting in but the guy didn't like our play. So, he had us do the scene from *Goodfellas* where Joe Pesci says, "You think I'm funny?" It was so embarrassing. We did it. But it was so embarrassing to do this as a part of a one-act play festival with people who were doing one-acts that were terrible. We were laughing. We were drinking before the performance. We thought, "If *this guy*—the guy that put this together—can put a one-act play festival together in this space and charge money for tickets, why can't we?" So, we did. We mounted a play and found a space and rented it out and did all of that, sold it out, made our money back. So, that's my advice: Go out and do that. Go out with your friends, rent a space, pick a play, pay the copyright, make posters, go out at midnight and put your posters up where you're not supposed to put 'em, and then put on your show. Feel great! Talk to your friends afterward in the lobby and do all of the fun theatre things that come with it and then see what comes from there. We took our profit and wound up renting that space in the basement and ended up working with writers. We did a couple of established plays, but they were obscure. We didn't want to do anything standard. We didn't want to be a "cover band," we always said. They weren't always great plays, but we felt they were great because they were ours. We were supporting each other and this was our clubhouse.

Jonna Tamases

Jonna Tamases grew up in Northern California where she honed her comedic skills with several improv and sketch groups before a two-year stint as a clown with the Ringling Bros. Circus. Since moving to LA, she has been in some television shows and movies, including 7th Heaven *and* Coming Clean. *Jonna writes and performs with ACME Comedy Theatre's Main Company and she is currently working on the movie version of her one-woman show* Jonna's Body, Please Hold. *Her one-woman show debuted at the Odyssey Theatre in 2003 and was nominated for two Ovations Awards: Best World Premiere Play and Best Lead Actress in a Play. There is more information about Jonna and her compelling story at http://lovejonna.com.*

photo by Rosemary Ryan

When did you know you wanted to become an actor?

I always did acting as long as I can remember. I put shows together in grade school, talent shows, and I was in children's theatre in grade school, junior high, and high school. I went to a traditional college because it didn't occur to me that I could be one of the people who does acting for a living. It just wasn't in there. I kept doing acting part-time through college. When I got out and started working in the field that I had prepared for—film editing—I was also doing acting. There came a point where I had to decide between the two because the schedules are mutually exclusive. If you are a film editor, you work ten to fourteen hours a day straight for a month or three months and then you're out of a job. So, you can't take on any acting projects or even audition because you're in the editing room the whole time. I decided to do acting full-time.

What was your first paid gig?

My first paid acting gig was a live gig, like a convention, playing a pirate I think. "Ahoy! Have another spring roll. *Arr!*" It was that type of thing. I was living in San Francisco after college and I fell in with a bad improv crowd there. I was doing improv every Saturday night in a little café. I was part of a class and a lot of people were doing convention work: character work at conventions. So, I just took pictures of myself in a lot of different costumes and put it all together in a little brochure and sent it around to the companies that do that kind of thing.

What do you consider your first break?

For me, there has not been one. It's been incremental and very purposeful. I have not had any sort of divine, miraculous thing happen to me. My journey has been things resulting from my actions and my efforts, not really a lot of surprises. Very slow, steady, incremental progress based on a tremendous amount of effort on my part. I really can see how the whole picture is a result of my effort.

I was doing character work in San Francisco and I was also marketing myself as a roaster at parties. You would hire me to come in character and roast the birthday boy. I was doing all of these different characters that I'd market. As I was doing that, I noticed that my friends who were making the big money were the ones who could walk stilts and juggle. So I thought, "I've got to go to clown college so I can make more money as a party character." I applied to clown college and I made a card that had my picture in the middle of a daisy that I drew and inside it said, "Pick me!" I flew to Nashville to be able to audition live, which was optional, but I wanted them to see me. I got in and then went to clown college for eight weeks and learned all these skills in Baraboo, Wisconsin, at the Circus World Museum, the Ringling Bros. and Barnum & Bailey Clown College. I had so much fun that when they offered me a contract to the circus at the end of those eight weeks, I threw everything else out the window and said, "I'm joining the circus!"

I knew being offered a contract at the end of clown college was a possibility, but I also knew I was under no obligation to accept it. I didn't plan to. I was just going to come home with those skills. But, golly, I had so much fun that I joined the circus. I felt like I had really only touched the surface of the whole world of physical comedy—and that's why I went to clown college, to study physical comedy. I like being able to convey something to an audience without words. I think that's really special and I like the theatrical challenge that it presents. That was the first time that I sort of did something unplanned. And two years later I married another clown who I'd met and we moved to LA. We had a straight wedding, although we did take one picture with clown noses on.

What do you wish someone had told you at the beginning of your career?

I can't say there's anything I wish I knew. I feel like, had I known then what I know now—or what I *feel* I know now—it would've dampened my enthusiasm. I'm actually glad I had all of those years of unbridled naïveté where I was sure that everything I submitted my picture for I would get called in for! "You have my picture. Why wouldn't you call me in? I gave you my picture! Now you call me. It's rude not to!" I'm glad I didn't know then what I know now: that here, in LA, it's an industry, not an art. It's a business here. The art is complete second or third fiddle. First it's an industry, then it's a club or a clique, and then maybe a little bit of artwork squeaks through. You just have to prepare yourself for being a product and not taking it personally when no one cares to purchase your product at this time. It doesn't mean it's bad product!

You know, maybe *that's* something I wish I could have been able to wrap my brain around when I started, the not taking it personally, because it hurts. There's a whole lot of hurt when you don't get responses. But I don't know if it's possible to *get* that. The enthusiasm sort of blocks out the possibility of hurt. You just have to be the real you all the time and your work is to find the person who wants to buy that product. People think their work is to change the product to fit whoever is buying. That's the worst thing you can do. You stick with your one product—your real self—and find the right customer.

When I first got to town and I was told I had to sort of put an age range out to describe myself, you know, "mid-thirties noodle type," I would say, "But I can play eight to eighty! That's what I've been doing in my sketch comedy in San Francisco and my improv. I can play any age. I'm not mid-thirties; I'm whatever you want me to be!" It took a year or so to clue in that you get booked for what you look like, not for what you can do. It makes sense: That's this business. It's making entertainment that roughly reflects their vision of reality. It's not theatrical. It's different.

What is your favorite thing about being an actor?

The chance to try on a lot of different people, personalities, emotions, life situations, without having to actually experience them. It's like a life buffet and you can take a little spoonful of "fat, angry librarian" and you can take a little spoonful of "jilted, haggard sea wife" and you can take a little spoonful of "male five-year-old"—whatever you want!

What is your least favorite thing about being an actor?

The begging. The begging for work. It's supply and demand. If I were more in demand than the supply of me, then I'd have the upper hand. But right now, the roles I want, I have a greater demand for work than there is interest in me. So they have the upper hand. Casting directors, producers, all of those have the upper hand over me. It's very difficult and I don't think I've learned how to cope with that well. I think, when I come in the room, I come in with an attitude of desperation, which I'm trying to combat.

I went in for Meg Liberman and I could feel the stink of desperation coming off me. It's so ugly and she doesn't want to see that. It's unpleasant for everyone involved. I should've just poked my head in the room and said, "Meg, I'm not going to burden you with my panic and anxiety and desperation. So, let's do this another time when I feel a little better about myself." I should've done that! Instead, I went in and tried to do these dramatic scenes. Meanwhile, she's drinking her coffee so I'm looking at the bottom of her coffee mug, trying to emote. I'm doing my heartfelt little lines and nothing. That made me feel *real* good!

I think it takes practice and I'm practicing not being desperate. I think it takes non-attachment to the outcome. And that is very much easier said than done. It takes practice. That's practice through meditation, religion—whatever—where you simply practice *being* and celebrating your being rather than focusing on what's going to happen or what it's going to mean or what's going to come of it. I think that's the important thing.

Any on-set mishaps, missteps, or funny stories you'd like to share?

The first time I performed my one-woman show in a big workshop performance with a big audience, at intermission I came backstage and realized that my fly was down and had been down the entire first act. It turned out to be a beautiful moment because, when the lights came up for the start of the second act, I walked out, center stage, and just reached down and went, "*Zzzzip!*" and zipped up right in front of the audience. They burst into hysterics because they'd seen, they knew. So I was laughing and they were laughing and I said, "Why didn't any of you *tell* me?" They laughed and laughed and we shared a nice bonding moment.

Do you ever feel like giving up?

Yes and no. It's hard to talk about. I was in therapy about ten years ago or so and the therapist at one point asked me, "What would you do if you weren't an actress?" I just went, "What?!? What does that mean? That has no meaning to me. These words... I don't know... I can't... What?" I do get very depressed sometimes that my career is not where I wish it was right now, but I can't fathom what else I would do with my life. There's nothing else I want to do every day except write and perform. I feel that I'm good at it and when I perform, people respond so strongly that I feel like there's nothing else I have to offer the world that's as cool as this! This is it. There really isn't anything else. But it does get deeply frustrating, putting out energy and putting out energy and putting out energy and not getting the response that you want. I wonder: Am I just beating my head against the wall? How long can I continue to do this? I want to be earning an ongoing living forever and ever as an actress in movies and on the stage. That's what I want!

How do you choose the material you work on?

Most of the material I work on, I create. That's just an absolute joy because I'm saying things that I want to say about life and the world, not big things but just things. I love just twisting it to make it funny. I love being absurd and playing in an absurd way. Comedy is rich and textured and nuanced to me. I'm drawn toward comedy and I like to play games. My characters tend to do that too.

How do you prepare for a role?

I learn my lines cold! It helps me so much. I absolutely learn my lines. I repeat them over and over and over again. I mostly do it in my head although it's smarter to do it with someone else if you can. Another way I do it is to transcribe them. I kind of tend toward the David Mamet school of acting—which is not a school, it's emphatically non-school—but it's to just say the lines audibly and don't try and add stuff. The less I add, the better. I'm learning that. You don't have to do a lot. Since I came from a children's theatre background, I'd be playful and fun and silly and over-the-top. I had to learn how to channel that energy. Playing big is fun! But simple sells.

What do you do when nothing is happening in your career?

That's the one cool thing about living in LA. There is always something to pursue. There is always a new path. There is always a new piece of marketing material you can create. There's a new group you can get involved with. There's a new casting director you can stalk—I don't mean stalk, I mean send postcards to on a regular basis in the hopes of being called in for a co-star—for a year. I belong to The Actor's Network and I love that organization so much. I'm in a power group where a group of us get together monthly and share our successes and what we're working on. Often times, someone will have a success and they'll say, "Such-and-such casting director called me in for a co-star role on *NYPD Blue* and that's because I've been sending them postcards every three weeks for a year and a half!" On the one hand, I'm really happy for them, but on the other hand I'm going, "A year and a half of postcards?" Just the heartache of when you put that stamp on—again—and you go, "Please call me in." It's just tough. But you have to detach from that. The point is, there's always something to be done. There's a play to audition for, there's a play to self-produce, there's agents to attempt to meet, there's the voiceover world to get into, there's improv, there's classes, there's recitals, there's open mic nights, anything! There's tons of things here in LA.

What made you choose Los Angeles?

It was the numbers. I thought: "This is where—by far—the largest percentage of the work is, so I will be here too." I think a key to keeping ahold of yourself and your sanity and your happiness while pursuing something that can be very discouraging is to have something creative that you control, that comes from you, that is your artwork that you love doing for no other reason than you love doing it. That's what's enabled me to keep going because I have that. I have my one-woman show, which I created and produced and have built up from the ground since I started writing it in '94. I started workshopping it in '98 and had the official world premiere run at the Odyssey in 2003. That show has been really great and I feel so wonderful about what I've created. I also love my work at ACME Comedy Theatre with the sketch comedy company. I simply love performing and writing sketch comedy.

Who are *your* favorite actors?

I love Jeff Goldblum. He's so cracked. He's off-kilter and he's himself. Meryl Streep blows me away. I know everyone says that but, my God, she reinvents herself. She's always fresh. No matter how many times you see her, she's fresh and real. She's just astonishing. I work with Ed Marques at ACME and he is free and fearless—a genius one-in-a-million clown. Alex Alexander is an inventive actress that I also work with at ACME. She's a brilliant comedienne with great timing. Charlotte Rampling has quiet depth and vigor. And William H. Macy has amazing range. Everything he does is organic and believable, whether he's playing a wimp or a tyrant.

Deborah Theaker

Deborah Theaker was born in Moose Jaw, Saskatchewan, but spent her formative years in Esterhazy, Saskatchewan (the potash capital of the world), where her dad served as mayor and local mortician. She received her Theatre degree from the University of Saskatchewan in Saskatoon. She joined the cast of Toronto's famous Second City in the mid-1980s and worked alongside Ryan Stiles, Mike Myers, and Linda Kash, creating original characters and material for the Second City stage, winning a Dora Award (Canada's equivalent to the Tony) along the way.

Deborah emigrated to the United States in the mid-1990s, earning her green card, and has gone on to appear in countless television shows and feature films, most notably the films of Christopher Guest and Eugene Levy, a fellow Second City alumni. The improvisational skills acquired from those years on stage at Second City have served her well, and Deborah continues to improvise weekly with other alumni in LA just for the pure joy of it. Great improvisers are like jazz musicians. They only get better with age. More information is at http://us.imdb.com/name/nm0857275.

photo by Dana Patrick

What was it like coming from Canada to work in LA?

I had different circumstances than most because George Lucas sponsored me. I was starring in the series that he produced. He and Eugene Levy together helped me get my green card. It's almost like you have to be big and you have to have big enough allies to really be able to do it. I know so many people who have tried and have been in touch with the right lawyers and stuff and it's still so hard. You come across the border and you lose all of your credit history. The fact that I owned a house in Canada but couldn't even get credit cards here for five years is just ridiculous. I was a star in my own country, if there is such a thing. And I came down here and I couldn't even rent an apartment because my credit history was wiped out. It's like coming from behind the iron curtain. At the time I came down here the dollar was fifty cents, so the money that I came down with was immediately cut in half.

Our unions aren't reciprocal—ACTRA and SAG—so I came down with no health coverage suddenly. I was on a wing and a prayer! But it's the same for everybody that does that. I don't like to see Canadians who come down without their work papers because, if they get found out, they get deported and they can't come back. I got offered a play in Oregon and I couldn't do it because American Equity said, "We want to go through all of our American Equity members before you and the Canadian Equity members join our union." All my health insurance—everything that I worked for in Canada—did not count here.

Here's a horror story. I could not get arrested. I had no health coverage, nothing. Tried to get an agent, nothing. I was catering the opening of *The Nutty Professor* and they said, "We have a really special job for you, Deb." I'm going, "Oh, no." They gave me a tray of foaming beakers filled with cocktails. Klump Cocktails, it turns out! And they gave me black, plastic glasses and a lab coat and I was supposed to stand at the door and greet all the people coming to the premiere party. Almost everybody who came, I had worked with or I knew. They never made eye contact with me or smiled at me. The only one who did was Richard L. Brooks from *Law & Order*. Any time I would wait on Canadians—when I tried to waitress—they would be like, "Oh, my God! What happened?!? You've fallen so far!" It was a great lesson in humility.

How did you know it was time to make the big move?

I was working for Second City. At one point, in 1990, they had a Second City in LA. It was Ryan Stiles and Robin Duke. They brought me in as a ringer from Canada to help them write a good show. There was an ACTRA Reciprocal Agreement there, so I could come down then. I didn't drive, because you don't need to in Toronto. It's much like New York. I had a driver's license when I was sixteen but I'd never been behind the wheel of a car. What was I going to do in LA? So I was doing things like taking cabs places.

The first day I was down here, I did a show—we were doing a benefit—and I looked out into the audience and there was Christopher Guest, Billy Crystal, Arnold Schwarzenegger, Danny DeVito, Steve Martin, everybody! I got a message the next day that Christopher Guest wanted to meet me and have me meet Norman Lear about a show he was working on. I was like, "Yeah, right, Ryan. Good one." But it was clear he didn't know anything about it so I said, "Wow, okay!" And I took buses, which meant it took me three hours to get there. I told them that and they were just killing themselves, laughing. I had running shoes and socks on with a dress, so I could change my shoes. Everybody just thought I was a freak. Oh, and that show never went anywhere. That was a show about Mary Hartman's daughter grown up. Norman Lear was creating it and Christopher Guest wrote it. Mary Kay Place was directing it. The pilots that don't go freak me out. All these people are doing this brilliant stuff that never sees the light of day. There's no rhyme or reason to what gets on the air.

How did you get involved with Second City?

I have a degree in Theatre from the University of Saskatchewan, believe it or not. I got out early and I moved to Toronto with my boyfriend. He wanted to take a Second City class. He paid his money, he got into class, and then he got some other gig, so I went and filled in for him at the class and ended up getting hired. It happened so fast. I started working immediately out of college for Second City in Toronto. My touring company was me and the Kids in the Hall. My boyfriend at the time was Mike Myers. Mike and I got into Second City and they fired all of the Kids in the Hall. They said they had no future and no talent. They were doing a show where they were taking suggestions from the audience. Somebody said, "Nudist colony!" So, they took off all their clothes on the spot and started doing the improv. Fair enough. It was a weird time. But six months later, once I went to the main stage cast, it was Ryan Stiles, Mike Myers, Linda Kash, and me. Comedy is a really small world. It's so interconnected and incestuous on so many levels. My best friend remains, to this day,

Scott Thompson from the Kids in the Hall. We still write together, we still hang out, although, he went back to Canada to try and develop our industry there, produce shows there.

What is the difference between the industry in LA and Canada?

There are economic differences—and of course it's nice to have socialized medicine and not have to worry about "making your insurance" every year through your union—but I don't want to get started on a whole "what's wrong with America" thing. So, here's what's different about show business in Canada. Say we're doing a movie in Canada. I'll get a call, "Hey, Deb? Can you pick up Joe and those guys? They're up the street from you grabbin' two-fours and sandwiches." That's a shoot in Canada. Here, it's like, "Whoa. That limo is for *me*?" I was talking with Timothy Spall on the set of *Lemony Snicket's A Series of Unfortunate Events* and he said, "The craft service budget on that movie alone would've made ten or fifteen British films." I was on set going, "I can't believe this!" Because in Canada, you're lucky if you have a folding chair. It's just not the same thing. Of course, things are changing. At one point, there were hundreds of things filming in Vancouver. At the time I was there last year, there were six. All these technicians, the whole film industry, my career at one time was based on working on American shows that came to Toronto. It's really changed. People who have worked for a decade full-time—like my sister who works as a film editor or my brother who is a great sound guy—are now looking into getting other jobs.

Is your whole family in the industry?

No. My dad is a retired mortician. He was the mayor and local mortician of the village I grew up in in Saskatchewan. I think, though, because we only had one channel, growing up, and they always gave us books and really encouraged our creativity, they ended up with a bunch of art tarts as kids. "Well, there's nothin' to do. It's snowin' outside. Let's make up a story!" We had such a creative upbringing that we all went into the arts.

What was your first paid gig?

It was doing a play by Allan Stratton at the Persephone Theatre in Saskatoon called *Nurse Jane Goes to Hawaii*. I was the ingénue. It's a really funny play. I wonder why it's never been done in the States! Hm.

What do you wish someone had told you at the beginning of your career?

I wish I had known how cyclical the business was and how there would be more twists than a bag of pretzels. You never know how many ups and downs there are going to be. If I'd known, then I would've been prepared for it psychologically. I also wish I had understood how casting is never personal. I bore grudges for people for years 'cause I started out so young. Then I finally got, "People all have their rightful part." Thinking casting was personal was like a weight around my neck—like an albatross! I didn't learn it wasn't personal until I came to LA, really. I saw, by the sheer volume of actors—a hundred and thirty thousand or however many members of SAG there are—that it can't be personal. I would see the show, after I had auditioned for it and gotten nasty, discouraging remarks from the casting director, and I'd see who they cast and go, "Oh. They're perfect." We don't have that sheer volume of actors in Canada, so I never quite understood casting. I would be playing every character. I'd do it all. By virtue of the fact that there's only a few thousand in the country that do acting, you really *do* do it all. You do everything! Same thing with England.

I wish I had had something to fall back on. Anything! Any kind of marketable skill—which I don't have—would've helped me. I wish I had had a solid something to fall back on during the lean periods—and there were lean periods. I cleaned Scott Thompson's house. I had never had a non-acting job before. I didn't know what to do when things were lean here!

I also wish I knew that everybody here has ambitions and is upwardly mobile. You have to be authentic and honest and have integrity in every dealing with everyone on every set that you get to. Every PA I sneered at became a director the next time out. There's no consistent thing in this business and that's why you have to be centered in yourself and have a life outside of your business. How many people go out and get rejected so much a week? People might face that kind of rejection in other jobs once every ten years or even every five years. We do it every day all day long. That kind of rejection can be psychologically very wearing. You have to learn to take nothing personally. I have the hide of a rhinoceros now, but I was such a bruised peach when I first came out here.

How do you handle rejection?

I've had to practice detachment. It took me until the last two years—and I'm not a young person—to develop that. I don't know how younger people do it. I'm an artist too, so I have that as an outlet. You have to empower yourself in whatever way that you do it. I write. I've pitched shows. I've sold options on so many shows. I continue to write and sell stuff all the time, although that's almost as difficult as acting—writing—because you know how little actually gets made.

What advice would you give to an actor starting out?

You need to have a body of work. The only way you can have a body of work is if you have the financial means to propel yourself forward to amass that body of work. Be willing to invest ten years or five years or three years or whatever you say—set a limit—and find a means to have some other income. This place is so big! And if the roles aren't there for you, find the means to create them for yourself. Get out there and write them for yourself, if that's all you can do.

How did you get your first manager?

The weird thing was, I had been nominated for an ACE Award—Best Actress in a Series—down here, for a show that never aired in California. When I came down for that award show, nobody knew who I was. I had a Canadian friend who was in an agency and they were aware, through her, of my body of work. She's still my manager. For twenty years, I've been with her. She was one of our producers of the Second City, years ago, and then emigrated down here. I trusted her judgment because she saw everybody's development all the way through. Our relationship was always based on the fact that I was never looking for the next best thing. I just wanted to be a working actor. I never wanted to be a star. I'm a character actor, so it's never going to be about the size of my ass—although, somehow it *is* about the size of my ass these days. People feel they can tell you anything about what you look like. I once did a pilot and I was playing the mother to this fat kid who is compulsively eating all the time. The first day, I walked in to wardrobe and met the woman for the first time. She looked me up and down and went, "Well, I guess the mom likes cinnamon buns too." I went off on her!

I've been told, "Oh, you're a big girl," "Oh, my God," and, "There's a real size to you," all the time. I'm five-foot ten! I'm a milk-fed farm gal from Southeastern Saskatchewan, I'm not going to be a zero or a two or a four! I see all these young girls with terrible body images. *I* get it all the time and *I'm* a character actor! So, maybe if I gained fifty pounds, then I'd be "funny fat" or something? I get this every day of my life and it really makes me crazy because it has no bearing. I know my peers don't get it. Nobody ever says to Eugene Levy, "Maybe you should cut your hair and lose the glasses. If you had contacts you'd work more." I had a time back there a few years ago when I would get really upset about the aging thing and about my size. And then I went, "Fuck this shit. Screw this shit." I have to really work at it to get beyond the age and get beyond the size. I'm not a number in either case. In Canada, I'm considered pretty. Here, I'm just fat and old. That's an American thing. Why doesn't Judi Dench live in Hollywood? Because she would've jumped off the big *D* in the Hollywood sign because they would've told her she had mud clumps for an ass. That's the nature of LA! Oh, if I had a nickel for every time I lost a show to a model—and I'm a comedian! I know so many anorectics and bulimics that are like forty years old! I'm the first one of my group not to have any face-lifts or anything. It should be against the law to have Botox in your face and go on screen. How can you reflect any emotion when you can't move your face? I understand the impulse that drives you to that because, even as a comedian and a character actress, every single job I've been on, I've been insulted to my face by the people I'm working with. It's always the people behind the scene—not my co-stars—who feel that they have to work on my image. My thing is: "I'm five-foot ten. I'm forty years old. This is who I am." Only the people that develop that kind of attitude are resilient enough to survive. It's like a war of attrition. The wily farm stock—the prairie type of people who can take adversity—will make it. This is the new frontier. If you can take all the shit being slung at you and spend six hours in your car, then you'll be okay in LA.

How do you choose the material you work on?

When I'm writing on my own, I choose the material and the people that I work with, obviously, but in acting, I'm not given the opportunity to make those choices very much. Coming from comedy—and factor in the Canadian thing—everybody I know is really nice. By nature of the work of sketch comedy, I've learned that you're always part of an ensemble. You only succeed if you make everyone else look good and serve the scene.

What is your favorite thing about being an actor?

Getting to do so much character work. That's the best part about being a character actor, for me. I get to do fantastic stuff. I get to work with my idols. I was in a movie with John Cleese and Rowan Atkinson. I used to love *SCTV* to such a degree that I would rush home to see it, and then I ended up being friends with all of those people. I was obsessed with *This Is Spinal Tap* and I'm friends with Harry Shearer and Chris Guest. It just happened that all the things I really loved or that I was obsessed with, work-wise, I ended up working with all those people later on. How many people can say that? I get to live a fantasy life in a way. For all the shit that goes on, I still get to work with and meet all of these people. It's great. The rest of it all falls by the wayside.

Al Thompson

Urged by his buddies to try acting, Al Thompson auditioned for and was cast in a student film for NYU. Al's world changed when the director yelled, "Action!" and the thrill of being on a movie set took hold of his soul, changing his life's direction. His first TV job was a guest spot on 100 Centre Street *for famed director/producer Sidney Lumet.*

He was cast as Danny Glover's son in the Academy Award-nominated film The Royal Tenenbaums. *He soon found himself flying from New York to North Carolina to shoot that film and* A Walk To Remember *simultaneously. Al followed those movies with the critically-acclaimed telepicture* A Season on the Brink: The Bobby Knight Story, *ESPN's first original movie. Al recently starred opposite Nick Cannon and Steve Harvey in the film* Love Don't Cost a Thing.

Al started writing three years ago. He and his writing partner are shopping around three projects for possible development. Al starts production on his untitled documentary project—marking his directorial debut—in 2006. While in LA, Al keeps his basketball skills tuned by playing in the NBA Entertainment League—a celebrity charity league comprised of players like Justin Timberlake, Ethan Hawke, and Ice Cube. Al is addicted to video games and has lost countless hours to PlayStation 2.

The members of Al's family are his role models. He enjoys spending time with them, knowing they will tell it like it is no matter what. Al's long-term career goal is to become the best "supporting actor" in the business. No need for superstardom, he wants people to say—when they see his face in a trailer for an upcoming film—"Oh, that guy is in that movie. I love that guy!"

Al resides in Harlem. More information is available at http:// althompson.net.

photo by Michael Anthony Hermogeno
http://8x10proofs.com

When did you know you wanted to become an actor?

Actors are never going to be truly honest about how things started for them, once they hit that celebrity status. It's always like the cutout design for what you're supposed to say about how it happened for you. Extra work is looked down upon so much. It's kind of sad, in a sense. I've been in meetings with producers for projects and I haven't wanted to say stuff like that. You want to tell these producers you've got things going and not really talk about doing extra work, when you're sitting in the room with producers with nominations for Academy Awards looking to put three TV shows on the air. You shape and mold your story to fit what you're going in for.

When I started acting, I was in school. A couple of buddies of mine were into the theatre and said, "You should try it. It's fun. There's girls in the play." I was like, "I don't know how you memorize all that stuff. I'm okay, man." They encouraged me to do anything with the play: "You could do the production class." This was two credits in high school and it was a pass or fail production class. I definitely needed some credits so I went to the stage production meeting. I volunteered to do lights: "I don't want to be seen." They said, "Yeah! You can work the lights." So, through that I got a chance to see how the rehearsals went down, how the director directed the actors, how wardrobe and costumes were designed. It was pretty amazing to me. I was like a fly on the wall watching this whole process go down and I was getting an automatic A for just working a spotlight, knowing when somebody was going to come out stage left.

Acting seemed to be a lot of work so I thought I'd try modeling, do some print work. When you live in New York, everything is pretty much here. I picked up *Back Stage* (somebody had told me about it). You know, you find somebody in there and you get ripped off for your pictures and you think these are like the hottest thing on the planet since Wonderbread. You're like, "Yo, I got comp cards! Look!" And they're pretty bad. But you go through the whole thing of sending them out all over the world thinking it's the best thing. Then you get a couple of calls for music videos and you say, "It's working!" At the time, I was still living at home, so I wasn't spending any real money. Everybody kept telling me I was more like commercial than fashion. I tried a little commercial print. I did the Kmart where you're holding a football: "Footballs—on sale!" All that stuff.

Then I thought maybe I would try the acting thing out. So, I got the calls for things like extra work. I never really go into this part of my life because it's kind of looked down upon, but the first time I was called to be an extra, I was in the shower and my mom was like, "The phone is for you! It's some casting director!" And I'm all, "Give me the phone! Give me the phone!" It was this guy, Ricardo Bertoni, who would do a lot of extras casting. He said, "We want you to come and be an extra in this movie with spaceships and aliens. You're going to be running down the street!" He's giving me this whole animated speech and I'm all excited. He says, "It's a hundred dollars." And I said, "A hundred dollars! All right!" Then he asked if I had a car and I said, "My dad has a car." "Well, you get an extra fifty dollars for the car." I'm like, "I'm there! This is great!"

So, this was my first time doing extra work and this was *Independence Day*. So, I go down there and there's thousands of people there on this Sunday. They said, "Are you SAG or non-SAG?" And I'm like, "I don't even know what SAG is!" And they said, "Okay, you're not SAG then." I said, "Fine." I checked in and they put me in this room with all these people and I was just chilling. Then they came to get us to the set and I couldn't even tell where the cameras were. Then they said, "That's lunch. Go over there and eat." And I saw this table of food. I said, "Oh my God!" They had such great food and it seemed like they never ran out. I couldn't believe it! I said, "If this is what acting is about, I'm in! I didn't even do anything. It's Sunday. I'm getting a hundred and fifty dollars. I can't believe this! It's beautiful here!"

Later on in life I learned that that was an eighty million dollar budget movie and all that stuff. But I was so overwhelmed I was like, "I could do this every day!" Later, once I did it a couple of other times, I met a lot of people. Everybody's trying to do the same thing and as time goes on people are going to be weeded out that really want to be actors and the quote-unquote career extras. It was such a cool New York type of family where everybody was willing to help other people. "*Law & Order* is looking for people for Tuesday. You should call right now. Do you have a police uniform? You can get more money." Everybody was like a real community of extras helping people.

Eventually everybody ends up getting into the union. Then you learn so much more about SAG. SAG isn't just about eating first. People think that! People think, "They eat first. They get more money." Once you read the handbooks that your union gives you, you understand being eligible to get pension and health benefits and dental and eye care. You learn your rights so that producers can't take advantage of you on set. It's pretty amazing. You're in a real union. But a lot of actors coming up don't know that.

Why did you choose to focus on learning the SAG rules?

The number one thing was just the respect of my peers. Other people I met that I respected were in the union, I wanted them to look at me as a guy who is really serious about being in this union, not just eating first and getting paid more. The biggest thing in this business overall is educating yourself, reading as many books as you can. The unfortunate thing in this business is that there are so many rumors and so much hearsay. Especially in the stupid magazines, you see, "This person was working at Pink's Hot Dogs on La Brea and he got discovered and he's in the new Denzel movie." But people who really know this dude know that he had a couple of lines on *Moesha* in '94 and that he did not just get picked up by doing this. This is something that the publicity department at Warner Bros. creates to put press behind this kid in his first movie, being in this project that they create. But people don't know to look into that. They read that and think it's that easy and they could do the same thing.

Dave Chappelle is an "up-and-coming actor" and he says, "Yeah, I've been 'up-and-coming' for fifteen years." People don't really understand that. So, there are so many false things people hear about, "All I got to do is this or that and I can be union." They don't know what a waiver is or what a must-join is. So many rumors float around about how to get into the union that are incorrect. One of the major things for me was educating myself overall, knowing what I'm talking about, and not looking like a fool talking about something that's not true.

What was your first paid gig?

One of the first things I did as far as *acting* on camera was a film at the New York Film Academy. Somebody called me and said, "They're filming some stuff downstairs. You should come down." So, I came downstairs and brought my comp card that I thought was hot like Wonderbread. That was one of my first experiences actually being on camera and acting. But the filmmaker never really finished the project. Then there was a film at NYU called *In Transit* that an undergrad student was doing. That was the first thing I ever did acting wise that got finished and I actually got the tape of it. It took them like two years to finish it but it was a great experience to finally be able to act and have a role.

Since I was in the position of still living at home and not really having bills and stuff like that, I was able to look at NYU and the films they do there. I looked at the fact that Spike Lee graduated from NYU, Scorsese, Oliver Stone, all of these great directors went there and I started to think that maybe the people who are at NYU right now are the future of directing, writing, and producing, just like I'm the future of acting. NYU is the top program here in New York and of course Columbia only has the grad program. Then there's USC and UCLA. But I was in New York.

What ended up happening was I did a film at Columbia which was a graduate film called *Muse 6*. This girl named Sarah Rogacki directed it. And I did another film at NYU, an undergrad film directed by Pete Chatmon called *3D*. We shot both these things. In *3D* I played this character whose girlfriend in the movie was Kerry Washington. She's a really good up-and-coming actress. Come December, the girl who directed the Columbia film called me. She's like, "Are you ready to go to Utah?" I'm like, "What the hell is in Utah?" Our film got into Sundance 2001. This is pretty cool. Then the NYU director calls me up and goes, "Al, you ready to go to Utah?" All of a sudden, out of nowhere, I have two short films that I'm the lead in at the Sundance Film Festival.

A buddy of mine had just moved out to LA and he said, "Come out to LA, we'll drive to Utah!" We don't even know where we're staying. "We can sleep in the car if it gets that bad," we're saying. I had been to film festivals that lasted four or five days before but Sundance is like a two-week film festival. Since I was there for two weeks, these student filmmakers had to go back to New York and they started asking me to get up and introduce their films before their screenings in that second week when they were back at school. Everybody wants to know why you're there when you're at Sundance.

I can't imagine going when you don't have anything going on because it would get so annoying with everybody asking what you're there for. It was really cool. The film screens and I go up to the front there at the Egyptian and I'm talking about *Muse 6* being a period piece and then the film starts. Well, after that, people knew who I was so they were coming up to me and I was getting bombarded. It was so crazy! With *3D*, Kerry Washington also had two films in Sundance. So we were both in the thick of the craziness from all the buzz.

How did you get your first manager?

I had an agent before Sundance, but no manager or anything. But after that, managers were calling like crazy. I went back to LA and had all these meetings with managers. I liked this one company and a week after signing with them they got me a meeting with Adam Shankman, who was casting his film with Mandy Moore, *A Walk to Remember*. They flew me out to North Carolina to meet with him. I met with him and they offered me the role. I went from Sundance to co-starring in this film with Shane West and Mandy Moore. Literally a week later, I went in and met with Wes Anderson for *The Royal Tenenbaums*. They said, "We'd love for you to be a part of the film." This was all like in two weeks after Sundance. Everything just kind of started happening so fast. I was still on point and on the right page to understand what was going on. It wasn't like I was so overwhelmed that I couldn't control anything. Everything happened at the right time—and it wasn't the first year I was working—so that was good.

What do you consider your first break?

Even before all of the studio films started happening, I was really involved at NYU. I got cool with a lot of the students at NYU and I sat in on classes. People started to think I went to NYU. It was hilarious. People would call me the "Mayor of NYU," "Governor of NYU," "Denzel of NYU." These were my nicknames. It was really cool. Everybody there has to finish a film to graduate so all these people would start asking me to be in their films. I would try to do something different in each of these films. I would do something different than what I might normally be cast as. That helped me a lot. There are times, when you're a Black actor, that you play the stereotypes of playing this role, that role, sticking this store up or whatever. Just because I grew up around that and I know what that is to play a role like that, it doesn't mean that I have to perceive myself that way or go on an audition grabbing my crotch. There will be casting directors who will say, "Well, we don't know if Al can play this role. He's such a nice guy and he speaks English so well. We don't know if this will work." I know these characters. I've seen these characters. I can do this, but I might have a hard time.

Sidney Lumet did so many great movies. He gave me an opportunity when he did *100 Centre Street*. I got to play this crazy character robbing a store. It was a great opportunity for me to play extreme. Usually, Black guys don't want to do that. They don't want to play basketball in a movie or stick a store up. I needed to do that once or twice because I wasn't getting cast like that. In ninety percent of the work I was doing, I was the only Black guy. It's fine, but you like to do different things. I didn't want to get stereotyped as the token Black guy in the teen movies. The tape from *100 Centre Street* opened up a lot of doors for me because they wouldn't see me for *Oz* before that or a lot of things where there were extreme characters like that.

When you start to do things and you're really in the public eye for having work all over the place, you never really know who is going to see your work or who is going to be interested in you. That's what happened with *Grand Theft Auto*: They sought me out a little bit. They knew I had worked on a video game prior to that—a football game for Acclaim. So they wanted to bring me in for this cop character. I played this motorcycle cop that was on steroids, real crazy. It was wild. I was excited about that. Everything evolves into something else. The video games are becoming big with the voiceovers now and they're making so much more money off of it now. It's another outlet. I remember when nobody was doing animation. Back in the day, there were no celebrities in music videos. Now they're doing them like they're movies and they have actual scenes in them.

So you never know where it's going to go. You create those relationships and people want to work with you. Whether you're a student filmmaker or a professional in the industry, people always want to work with people that, number one, they're going to be comfortable with; number two, that are going to show up on time; and number three, that aren't going to complain or get on their nerves. Just being prepared, knowing your lines, knowing what's going on—whether it's a student film that you're doing for free or the project is something you're getting paid for or it's a commercial for McDonald's—those are the three things that you have to do. And the biggest thing is to just be a cool person and not get on the director's nerves. Knowing the chain of command on the set is important. If you have a problem or something, you go to the producer. The director doesn't have time for that. The producer can help you if you didn't get your per diem, whatever. A lot of that I learned on the job during the NYU films. NYU was my training ground and my base for many things, just being on the set. I learned a lot actually doing stuff, especially the terminology. From "checking the gate" to "turning around" to "last looks," all the terminology you will probably not learn in an acting class, you know, when they're screaming this out, what it means.

What made you choose New York?

What I love about New York is that it's such a small community. You think it's big, but really it's not. Everybody knows each other through someone here. I'm an independent actor. I respect the independent film filmmaker and I respect independent film. I was pretty much raised where there is no trailer and there is no holding area. I think those things totally prepare you for the bigger things. When you and the other star actor are in a situation where it's cold and you've just got to wait because there's a hair in the gate and that person's complaining, you're just chilling. When I began to work with other actors who did TV shows, I would see the difference. These younger actors—thirty and younger—would complain, complain, complain. That stuff will catch up with them later. There are actors people won't work with again because the producer knows, "Hey, that kid was a pain in the ass. He will have nothing to do with the sequel."

Anyway, I'm such a New Yorker at heart. I've done movies in LA and been there for three months to do stuff, but it's such a major difference. Everybody always complains all day about LA. You can talk about LA for hours, whether it's the driving and the traffic or whatever. LA is the type of place where it's hard to establish a network of supportive friends. People are really out for *self*. It's hard to establish a network of friends who aren't in the business because you're surrounded by the business in LA. I can't deal with it twenty-four hours a day. It gets really ridiculous out there. But, people go to weather and they think they can make it. If you go out to LA with credits and a reel and an agent and a manager, you can make it. If you have all that, by all means, go out there. But bottom line, you have to work twice as hard when you're in LA. You can't just do a couple of rounds and drop headshots off and all the little things that we can do in New York. You can't get on the studio lots in LA like you can get into casting offices here in New York. You really have to prove yourself a lot more in LA and separate yourself out a bit more.

Who are *your* favorite actors?

I don't really have any particular favorite actors. All the Black guys go, "Denzel! Denzel!" I like to kind of be different. For me, overall, I don't want to be a movie star or a mega-star. I just want to work on quality projects and have some consistency with that. If Tom Cruise is doing a movie, if he's wondering, "Who's going to make me look good in this movie—not outshine me but do good work—so maybe we can get nominated for an award? Al Thompson!" I want to be that top co-star guy where people in the street might not know my name. They can't figure out where they know me from and then two blocks later it hits them, "That's that guy from such-and-such." People like John C. Reilly or Philip Seymour Hoffman, those guys are top actors that top directors want to have in their movies. They know they're going to ace the role and be a great contribution to the film. That's where I want to roll. Once you're a lead in movies, it becomes a whole other ballgame. Fun is usually not included in that. It's more of a numbers game about what the movie did at the box office. It can break you as an actor. A lot of people are in this business for the wrong reason. If you want to be a movie star, that's a tough one. You say it, but when it happens, is it what you wanted? I would rather just have my sanity and have my privacy, be able to eat chicken and waffles with nobody bothering me. I think that is more sacred to me than anything.

Suzanne Whang

Suzanne Whang is an actor, television host, and stand-up comedian. As an actor, Suzanne has appeared in The Practice, NYPD Blue, Strong Medicine, Robbery Homicide Division, Still Standing, Two and a Half Men, Norm, *and* VIP. *She most recently appeared in the feature film* Constantine *with Keanu Reeves. Suzanne also starred in the short film* Seoul Mates *which won Best Acting Award and Audience Award at the Los Angeles 48 Hour Film Festival.*

Suzanne is currently hosting her fourth season of House Hunters *on HGTV. Previous hosting experience includes* Bloopers with Dick Clark, Fox After Breakfast, New Attitudes, Breakfast Time, The Pet Department, *and* Personal FX. *Suzanne was also a red carpet host for* An Evening at the Academy Awards *and she emceed the Korean Concert Society Anniversary Gala at the Kennedy Center in Washington DC. She recently served as a celebrity judge at Kollaboration, a Korean-American talent showcase in LA.*

As a stand-up comedian, Suzanne recently won the Andy Kaufman Award at the first annual New York Comedy Festival and Best Up-and-Coming Comedian at the Las Vegas Comedy Festival, playing her controversial alter ego, Sung Hee Park. She will be appearing on Comedy Central's Premium Blend *in late 2005.*

Suzanne has worked at both the Las Vegas and Lake Tahoe Improv. In LA, she has performed at the Comedy Store, the Laugh Factory, the Improv, the Ice House, the Friars Club, Ha-ha Café, House of Blues, and the Comedy Union. Her act's slogan is, "Don't judge a gook by her cover."

Suzanne studies at the Beverly Hills Playhouse's advanced class with Milton Katselas, Richard Lawson, and Gary Imhoff. Suzanne has a BA in Psychology from Yale University and an MS in Cognitive Psychology from Brown University. More information is available at http://suzannewhang.com.

photo by Michael Pasco

How did your character "Sung Hee Park" come about?

I study at the Beverly Hills Playhouse—the place that Milton Katselas created. Richard Lawson is one of my teachers there. They encourage you to risk and challenge yourself and dare and write your own stuff and anything you want. It's an incredibly magical place, if you take advantage of what they're offering. I thought, "I'm going to try stand-up comedy." I'm known for my really big, big balls. I've been skydiving, hang gliding, bungee jumping. Why not stand-up comedy? I'm an adrenaline junkie. I decided to try stand-up just so I could say I did it once in the safety of my acting class. They're all my friends, they're supportive. My initial stand-up bit came from when I was a field host for *Fox After Breakfast*. That was a New York-based national morning show. I used to be one of the Road Warriors who would travel around the United States interviewing people, doing live, human-interest segments for the show. It was a phenomenal experience. It was the best job ever. I went to almost every state in the US, met interesting people doing wild things, and got to have adventures. I got to go SCUBA diving to an underwater hotel. I got to sit on top of a cable car thirteen-hundred feet aboveground with the guy who inspects the cables for safety. And I got paid to do things that nobody gets to do. It was so much fun.

However, I decided after my travels around the US that I wanted to write a book called *Stupid Shit People Say to Asian Women*. I know I look like this, but I was born in Virginia. The ignorance in people and the things they would say to me, I was like, "Fuck you." That was how my act came about, dealing with people in Alabama going, "Do you speak Oriental?" or in North Dakota: "How does that dry-cleaning process actually work? I've always wanted to know," or, "Can you teach me that karate?" or assuming that my vagina is on sideways—this is a myth about Asian women that I didn't know. Basically, I'd go around the country and people would say these things to me and I'd go, "Are you joking?" That was what my material was about: playing all the different characters who would say stupid things. It went great. My teacher said, "Fantastic. Go out and do that in comedy clubs. It's smart. You have a voice. You have a responsibility. Get it out there. You have a point of view. You have courage. You have humor. But I still would love for you to try to embrace the stereotype of Asian women that you hate so much." I wanted to kill him: "I spent my whole life proving to everyone that I'm *not* this." He said, "Exactly. You're spending so much energy resisting it that you're still at the effect of it. Why not embrace that as part of your artistic palette and just see what happens?" It was Earth-shattering advice. It changed my whole life.

I hated him at that moment. I thought he was wrong. I was contorting in the critique chair in the class. I wanted to kill him. I didn't say anything but I was like, "Oh my God, what are you asking of me?" They call that an "organ rejecting class." Somebody says something to you and you basically have an organ reject. "No. I'm sorry. That will not be accepted into my body. That's foreign matter. Forget it." I figure, I'm paying for the class, he's a very wise man, I've always taken his suggestions in the past, why pay for a class and then not do what the teacher recommends and at least see if it's worth something?

The only way that I could think of to approach this assignment was to work from the outside-in. I went to Koreatown the next day and I went to one of those little shops and I bought a full-length, pink *hanbok*—it's a full-length, Korean, traditional dress. I bought the dress, I bought the little Korean fan, I bought the little Korean shoes. I went to my house, put it all on, and I'm standing there. I have no idea what I'm doing. I'm just standing there in my house going, "Now what? What am I doing? I hate my teacher. This is stupid. I'm going to get hives. I'm going to projectile vomit." But I was patient enough—which has never been one of my best qualities—to wait for some sort of divine inspiration. Finally, I thought, "What if *she* were a stand-up comedian? What if she just got here from Korea? What if she has a really thick accent? What if she's terrible? What if she does it all wrong? What if she actually says racist, vulgar, horrific, inappropriate, offensive things, but she doesn't realize it because she's naïve and she just wants to do well, and she wants to come to Hollywood and make it and make people laugh and bring joy to people?" It made me realize sometimes people say things because they *don't* know, and it doesn't have to be out of malice. I don't have to get so angry about it. It was such a healing thing for me as an artist and as a human being. Unbelievable.

And now I have turned it into my ticket to the party. I won the Andy Kaufman Award at the New York Comedy Festival. I won the Las Vegas Comedy Festival. I'm going to be on Comedy Central's *Premium Blend*. Basically, I've had meetings at NBC and SpikeTV and Comedy Central in their talent development departments because of this character. Richard Lawson basically wants every actor to mine the gold within them. Sometimes the gold is the one thing that you are the most violently opposed to and resist. One thing he said was, "Whatever you criticize, you cannot have." That is so true. I had such a critic in me! Now it's become a satire of racism in America. Laughter levels the playing field. It breaks down people's defenses and you can get your message in. You sort of sneak it in instead of bashing them over the head with it, up on a pulpit. People sometimes just shut down to that. But people don't tend to shut down to laughter.

That's not to say that it's not controversial. Some people love it or they hate it, but I embrace the controversy. Some people don't get it. Some people are convinced that I'm trying to perpetuate racism in America. Why would an Asian woman born in America who has experienced racism have the goal to perpetuate racism? Some Asian-born Asians especially don't really understand American satire and all they know is they heard the word "gook" and that's it. Frankly, I think we give words power by not saying them or by whispering them sometimes. The way that Black people use the word—not nigger—niggah as a term of endearment sort of turns the power around. It desensitizes it for them. I'm America's favorite gook. I sign my emails, "In gooks we trust" or "In a gooka-da-vida" or "Yours gookly." My younger friends who look to me for advice call me their "gookru." And now that word sounds funny to me. There's no power in it. I don't go "Oh, ouch!" I'm not going to remain a victim about words. What's even funnier is that when I was a kid, people used to call me "chink" and "jap" and I'm thinking, "Hey, I'm a gook! At least get it right! I'm Korean! If you're going to slur me, do it right!" But we don't even get our own slur because the Vietnamese have the same one. I'm like, "Fuck! We don't even get our own? We get a *shared* racial slur? That's not right!"

What happened when you brought this character to class?

They gave me a standing ovation. They were falling off their chairs. They were hyperventilating. They were crying. I could tell, that night, from that response, that I was on to something that was going to be revolutionary and that was going to set me apart from every other stand-up comedian. It's more like performance art. It's a theatre piece more than strictly stand-up comedy. It still works in comedy clubs. The premise is, I have the emcee say, "Ladies and gentlemen, this next comic is brand new to the United States. It's her first time ever doing stand-up comedy. Please be nice to her. All the way from Seoul, Korea, please give a warm, United States welcome to Sung Hee Park." You can tell people want to sneak out the back door. They're so uncomfortable, going, "Oh, look. Poor thing. She's shaking. Oh, no." There was one time I was at the Comedy Store and there was a row full of Black women in the front and they kept going, "She did *not* say that!" They were laughing their asses off. I didn't know if the Black people were going to beat me up in the parking lot afterwards or the Hispanics or the Asians. I didn't know if people would get it. For the most part, it's the minorities who are the first people to run up to me and say, "Thank God! Thank you!" Political correctness can be very damaging, for us to all put a happy face on it. Mine is no different from Archie Bunker's character in *All in the Family*. Norman Lear's goal was not to increase racism in America. It was to shine a light on it, disturb people, have them laugh, have them uncomfortable, rattle them up enough to think. That excites me, about what art can do.

When did you know you wanted to become an actor?

I was always the outgoing, wild energy kid. I always sang and danced in musicals in junior high and high school and one in college. When I was seventeen, I acted in a short film that ended up on PBS and was nominated for a Daytime Emmy. It was about racism. It was one of those educational films where it was me and my Caucasian female best friend in high school. We wanted to go to the prom and I had an Asian boyfriend and she had a White boyfriend and her White boyfriend wanted to take her to the exclusive, all-White country club. There's conflict between the two friends and it ends unresolved. It's supposed to be shown in schools across the country and people discuss it. I think my mother's friend in the Korean church—the church organist or something—found out about this audition and so I went and I got it. That's basically been the story of my entire career. I just audition for it and I get it. I end up thinking, "Isn't that what happens? You just audition and you get it."

When you grow up with somewhat traditional Korean parents, they don't teach you, "Why don't you pretend for a living?" You're raised to be very practical. Normally, it's: Be a doctor, a lawyer, an engineer, or a professor and leave that other stuff to other people. When I left graduate school to become an actor—no, wait, I left graduate school because I hated graduate school—I got a job at a healthcare consulting firm in Boston. I ended up doing extra work on *Spenser: For Hire*. This is a guardian angel story. I was at my nine-to-five job, doing healthcare consulting in Boston. It was the only nine-to-five job I could ever have because, after two years, I was ready to kill somebody. I was listening to the radio and they were having a cattle call for extras on that show *Spenser: For Hire* with Robert Urich. I thought, "Oh, that'll be fun. I want to do extra work!" I had had a little experience, doing that film when I was seventeen. So I took a long lunch and I stood in line with everyone and their grandmother and their dog in Boston, getting their Polaroid taken and filling out a little size card. And then a month later, Ann Baker of Ann Baker Casting called and said, "We'd like you to come and do extra work next Thursday." I said, "Sure!" It was forty bucks I think for as many hours as they wanted. It was nonunion; bring your own lunch, that kind of thing. I didn't care.

Well, I'm not a morning person and the calltime was, I think, 7am. I called in sick to work. I used my acting skills! And then the power went out in my apartment building the night before. My alarm clock was plugged into the wall. And I probably went to sleep at like two or three in the morning. At like seven-thirty in the morning, when the calltime was seven, the phone rings. I wake up, the woman says, "Suzanne, this is Ann Baker calling. I'm wondering if you're planning to *show up* on the set this morning." I looked at my clock radio flashing and said, "Oh, Anne, I'm so sorry. The power must've gone out." The set was walking distance from where I lived so I said, "Please, please, please let me still go there. I can run there." She said, "You'd better get here *so* fast!" and she hung up on me. I didn't have time to shower. I don't know if I was wearing underwear or shoes. I was throwing shit together and running down to the location. And of course, nothing was happening! It was hurry up and wait. There were still four hours before we shot anything. I think I probably gave her flowers the next day to apologize. I'm sure they cost more than I made that day. But while I was on the set, I was soaking everything up like a sponge: "What is all this stuff? What is everybody doing?" Taking it all in. This character actor named Arnie Cox came over to me and said, "Who are you? How come I don't know you?" Everyone in Boston knew each other. There were like a hundred actors in Boston and they all knew each other. It was a big family. He said, "How come I haven't seen you around?" I said, "Oh, I have a real job," as if what he does for a living isn't legitimate. I totally insulted him, but he didn't care. He said, "Here's what you should do," and he wrote on a piece of paper and said, "You do these ten things tomorrow and you'll be working all the time as an actor in Boston." There were things like: Get your headshots taken, set up your resumé so it looks like this, send all these things to these five casting directors in Boston, start taking acting classes, take an on-camera class. Nothing crazy or magical, but stuff that I didn't know to do. I did those ten things and literally within a month I had quit my job, I was in SAG, I booked the first commercial I auditioned for, which was the *Boston Herald*, I was acting all the time. I was making my living as an actor! I don't believe in accidents. I believe that I was manifesting that my entire life to get to that moment. So, Boston was mainly an industrial market. I did a lot of industrials. I did a lot of commercials. I did a movie called *HouseSitter* with Steve Martin. That was quite an experience! I became big fish in a small pond there and then I moved to New York City.

What made you choose New York and then Los Angeles?

I moved to New York City because a friend of mine, Jesse Moore, kept saying, "You have to send your headshot to Carrie Morgan in New York City. She's at Cunningham-Escott-Dipene. And send to Carol Nadell, this casting director in New York City. You have to send your stuff." I was on top of the world in Boston. Why would I want to do that? New York City is disgusting and it's scary and it's dirty and it's crazy. He kept bugging me. So, finally, just to shut him up, I sent my pictures to both of them. Literally, I sent the pictures on a Monday and the next day, Carol Nadell called and said, "Suzanne, can you come to New York? I have a callback for an industrial. I would love for you to come in." So, I took the Amtrak—a five-hour train ride—to New York, went to the audition, wasn't even going to stay, and as I'm leaving the audition, she's running after me going, "Suzanne, you booked the part. They're not going to see anybody else. You booked it. Can you stay in New York and meet with my friend Carrie Morgan?" Of course, that's the other person I'd sent my picture to. She called her and said, "Carrie, you have to see this Asian woman who lives in Boston!" I said, "Oh, all right." Totally the opposite of the whole, "Please, please like me," thing. I go and meet with Carrie Morgan and she says, "So, when are you moving to New York City?" I said, "I'm not moving to New York City!" And I thought it was normal that she walked me around and introduced me to all of the seven other agents. Apparently, that never happens. I think it was my whole attitude of, "I don't need this. I don't need you. I'm confident. I love my life," that did it. So, as I'm leaving the building, she calls me on my cell phone and says, "Pack your bags. You're moving to New York. It's unanimous. We're signing you. You have to move to New York City." I ended up absolutely loving New York and having the time of my life. When I first moved to New York City, my agent told me, "If you get one out of twenty things, we would be ecstatic." I booked eighteen of the first twenty things she sent me on. She was like, "Who *are* you?" My nickname was "Booker" while I lived in New York City.

New York is where I became a television host. My first one was for FX for a show called *Breakfast Time*. It was a two and a half hour cable morning show with Tom Bergeron and Laurie Hibberd in a big apartment. It was a ball! That led to a job on *The Pet Department* on FX which is all about people who have everything from hissing cockroaches to ferrets to goats as pets. They made me hold a hissing cockroach—I have a bug phobia—and I left my body. I floated up to the ceiling. It was too traumatizing, and yes, I jump out of planes.

Then I did a show called *Personal FX: The Collectibles Show* which was about collectors. I got to travel the country interviewing people who collect things. It was so great because they're nuts. They're passionate and they're nuts, which makes for great television. Then *Breakfast Time* turned into *Fox After Breakfast*. So, Fox picked up the cable show and made it a network show. Then I got a job offer in LA to host *New Attitudes* on Lifetime. It was a half-hour, nightly show, magazine format, good stuff for women, informative. I co-hosted that with Leanza Cornett. So then I moved to LA. I grew so attached to New York; I did *not* want to live in LA. I especially didn't want to live in LA because it was so *yuck*! I'm an East Coast girl! Born in Virginia, went to Yale undergrad, went to Brown for my Master's, and moved to Massachusetts, and then New York: I am an East Coast girl! Instead of having a going-away party when I moved to LA, I had a wake. Everyone had to wear black.

I've made a great life here, now. My career is great, my personal life is great, I have such a fantastic life here, I like the weather, I bought a house. I still don't *prefer* LA. I'd rather somebody say "fuck you" to my face than act like they like me and then say "fuck you" after I've left the room. I really prefer not to have my time wasted. I like direct people much better. I like people who do what they say they're going to do. I was raised that you do what you say you're going to do, so I really appreciate that.

How does *House Hunters* handle your controversial alter-ego?

I always make sure that there is no morality clause in my contract so that no gig is allowed to tell me that I can't do or say something. But the truth is, with any contract, they could fire me for whatever reason they want and not say that it's because of my stand-up act. I've been doing *House Hunters* for five seasons. It's the number one show on the network. It's a whole different side of me, but it is part of me. It's the girl-next-door, very friendly.

What advice would you give to a performer starting out?

I think that you have to be persistent. You have to work on your self-esteem and not be looking to anybody in this industry to give you self-esteem. Don't take things personally. Sometimes you don't get a job because you're not the right height or you have the wrong haircolor or you remind the director of his ex-girlfriend who he hates. You can't control that. Always give people help when they want help. Karma is a big-ass boomerang. Any inkling that anyone has to be an actor or any sort of artist, embrace it and do it. I really do believe we were put on the planet to be creative. I think one of the reasons that people get miserable and we have war is because people are not nurturing the artist and creativity within them. They feel suffocated and miserable and act out in whatever way. Drinking, whatever—everybody has their pathology. I really think there'd be a lot less pathology if people were just nurturing whatever artistic thing is in them.

If your family members or close friends think you're stupid for doing it, then you really don't have to communicate with them. You can set very clear boundaries and say, "That's not okay! I'm going to get new friends that think this rocks!" Most of those people are just failed artists themselves that want to spew their bile onto you. They don't want you to have what they are too frightened to go for. I used to call them "My 911 Friends." They'd call me at four in the morning and go, "I'm in the emergency room! I need you to come help me! Everything's so bad!" I used to always just jump in there and fix it for them. So, when I say, "help people," I mean help them to do good stuff. I don't mean enable them. Go to an Al-Anon meeting if you're spending your life making everyone else's problems more important than your own.

One huge thing that is changing my life is this book by Lynn Grabhorn called *Excuse Me, Your Life Is Waiting*. I've bought it for everyone I know. If anyone who reads *this book* reads that book and has an open valve, we will change the world! I want to go out and leave copies on random people's doorsteps. I want to say, "You don't know me, but *read this*!" Also, get *The Artist's Way* by Julia Cameron. Every creative person needs those two books—and *this* one, of course!

Victor Williams

Victor Williams has played the role of Deacon Palmer on the CBS sitcom The King of Queens *for seven seasons. His many television appearances span such hit series as* The Practice, Homicide: Life on the Street, Law & Order, The Jamie Foxx Show, *as well as a recurring role on the NBC drama* ER.

Victor has also been seen in such feature films as Cop Land, Penny Marshall's The Preacher's Wife, *and* A Brooklyn State of Mind. *His stage credits include* Troilus and Cressida *at the New York Shakespeare Festival,* Ohio Tip-Off *at the Dallas Theatre Center, and numerous productions in New York University's graduate acting program, including* Summer and Smoke, Dancing at Lughnasa, King Lear, *and* Othello.

Victor graduated with a Master's of Fine Arts in Acting from NYU's Tisch School of the Arts and with a Bachelor of Arts in Theatre from Binghamton University. He is the founder and artistic director of the New American Theatre Company in LA. More information is at http://us.imdb.com/name/nm0931879.

photo by Mike Soccio

When did you know you wanted to become an actor?

Probably my junior year in college. I went to Binghamton University in upstate New York. I was supposed to do the whole Political Science into Law School thing. The seed was planted my senior year in high school. I'd pretty much taken all of the required classes and there was this woman I knew who was the high school actress queen. She was really cool. She said, "Hey, there is this English class you should take. It's like you read plays and at the end of the semester you do scenes from plays." I didn't have a crush on her or anything, but she had something. I thought, "Yeah. I'll take this class." It was fun. It was a great English class. At the end of the year, we did this scene. I didn't think anything of it but the response in class was amazing. She was a great actress, and I guess I hung in there well enough with her. The reaction was so great. It was such a great feeling that when I started college, as I was rounding out my schedule, I started taking acting classes. By my junior year, I realized I was taking just as many Political Science classes as I was Theatre classes. But more importantly, I was like a 2.3 in my major. I said, "There's something wrong here." I was like a 3.7 or 4.0 in Theatre classes. I knew there was something wrong. More importantly, I dreaded looking for the classes in Political Science. I was having a hard time finding a class that I liked. I was taking a lot of classes I didn't like. It was always easy to find a Theatre class I wanted to take. It was in my junior year I realized that clearly this is something I enjoy doing much more. I wound up getting my degree in Theatre.

Was your family supportive?

It's great now because my father is my number one fan. But it *was* tough. He was a History professor and he had his eyes on my going to Law School. He had this standard of education that he wanted both me and my brother to maintain. We stopped talking for a couple of years. He picked me up from school and Binghamton is a three-hour drive from New York and my parents had just moved out to Long Island so it was now like a four-and-a-half-hour drive. I decided that was when I was going to tell him. That was the longest ride of my life. After that, I went into my senior year.

I knew I wasn't ready to go out into the acting world with just the undergrad, so I applied to a bunch of graduate acting programs. My father was making it clear that he wouldn't provide me any financial support. "If you go to Law School, wherever you get in, I'll support you. If you go to actor school, you're not going to get anything." So I had to proceed to get financial aid. There's a point where you need your parents' information and he was sabotaging that. I remember I applied to Yale, and Yale was like, "We never received the information." I asked my father and it got nasty. "Are you calling me a liar?" Eventually he had to find himself compromising.

There's this thing called URTA where a whole bunch of colleges across the country do one big audition for all of the member schools. I did the two two-minute monologues: one modern, one classical. I was really interested in the University of Minnesota and the University of Washington and my father said, "At least go to school a little bit closer to home." So, I auditioned for Yale and, thankfully, I got accepted. With that, I overcame all my father's obstacles. He started accepting the fact that it was a possibility. In his mind he was trying to find compromises: "I feel comfortable telling my colleagues and family members that my son is going to Yale."

At the beginning of the auditioning process, I didn't know anything about any of the schools. One of my teachers was like, "Where are you applying?" I said, "Oh, I'm applying to Rutgers, University of Minnesota, Florida State, Penn State..." and he said, "You need to be more specific." He had taught at New York University. He felt strongly and he was someone whose opinion I valued highly. At the last minute, I was able to audition for New York University, which wasn't a part of this URTA thing. Thankfully I got in. And thankfully they gave me money. Actually, I got the money because the professor at Binghamton told me, "Hey, this is really competitive. You need to sort of negotiate and haggle." I had gotten accepted to Yale but the problem was, because my dad screwed up my financial aid, I got no money, so I couldn't even consider Yale because I couldn't afford it. Well, NYU wasn't giving me any money either then, but NYU was in competition with Yale. So my professor said, "Even though you know you're not going to Yale, tell them that you've been accepted." So the head of the NYU program, Ron Van Lieu—an amazing acting instructor who is now at Yale—was like, "We don't have any money." I said, "Well, I was accepted to Yale." Can you believe it? I got a full scholarship to NYU. I was like, "Wow! *This* is how this business works, even on a collegiate level."

What was your first paid gig?

My first paid gig was definitely Shakespeare in the Park, New York Shakespeare Festival. I was the understudy for Ajax and Achilles in *Troilus and Cressida*. I got paid three-hundred dollars a week. How better to start your career off than in New York in Central Park in the summer, outdoors, getting high after every show? I graduated in May and got the show in June. It was a great cast. The biggest name at the time was Stephen Spinella. Also Tim Blake Nelson, Steven Skybell, and Paul Calderon, these great theatre actors in New York. It was a great ensemble, but the reviews weren't that great.

My first movie gig was *Cop Land.* What was great about that and what was great about *Troilus and Cressida* was being around these actors who people in the know—whether they were casting directors or directors—knew these guys were phenomenal. To me, coming in, "phenomenal" meant, "Oh, you must be Meryl Streep. You must've made it." But these were actors who were working consistently who get so much respect throughout the business—but you don't necessarily know them by name. The lesson right away with those two projects was, "Yes, you can have a very successful, solid, well-respected career reputation and not necessarily have your name up in lights." It was great to start out that way, with those particular projects.

What do you consider your first break?

It had to be *Homicide: Life on the Street.* To me it was a break simply because it was a critically-acclaimed show. It felt like it helped a lot to have that on the notorious reel. To me, a break also has a lot to do with what is a confidence builder. Kathy Bates directed that episode of *Homicide.* Kathy Bates chose me. My thing all along has been—even when I was in undergrad, when I first started acting—that you have to take with you your successes because there's always going to be some rough times. So, "Crystal from high school put me in this class. She was the best actress in high school and she thought I was worthy of doing a scene with her." I even took that with me. And then one of my professors who taught at Juilliard, Yale, Carnegie Mellon, and NYU thought I was worthy of going to NYU. So I remembered that. And then Ron Van Lieu accepting me. And then Kathy Bates casting me in what I think was her directorial debut. There's tons and tons of rejection so I always draw from that. When times are rough or I don't work for six to eight months, I say, "Kathy Bates wanted me to play this particular role." So, the big breaks are to be able to say that I worked with these people who I respect and I can say that I was deemed worthy of working with them.

What do you wish someone had told you at the beginning of your career?

There's a casting director named Rosemarie Tichler who was the head of casting at the Public Theatre. She taught an audition class at NYU. At the end of our three years, she would bring us into her office and say, "These are things you need to work on. This is how I see you." This was just to give us an idea—going into the business—how we're seen, how we're viewed, what she thinks our strengths and weaknesses are. She told me something that I didn't apply.

I'm six-five and I was six-five when I graduated when I was twenty-four years old. And I've always had a deep voice. She said, "Victor, you're twenty-four years old. When you get out, you're automatically going to be going for roles that are like thirty, thirty-two just because of how you are, physically. You need to fight against that because there's an energy, there's an excitement, there's a joy in playing roles when you're in your twenties that you'll never get again. Once you get older, you're going to be playing fathers. You're going to be playing police officers. You have to allow yourself the opportunity to be that young, energetic, somewhat naïve young man. You have to fight against people, whether it's your agents or casting directors, putting you in that box."

I took that information, but for me, I was like, "Well, I want to work! I don't care about that!" So, of course, I went down the path of going for these older roles. The catch is that I never quite got the roles. I would compete for the roles and at a certain point, they'd realize, "He's young." So that sort of locked me out of certain roles. Now that I'm thirty-four, I'm going after roles that are more like forty. It's always going to be a thing for me now. In hindsight, I do wish that I fought against it a little more because now that opportunity is gone. Whether the character is a kid fresh out of college or in law school or the young love interest, how possible would it have been?

I don't know. It's bad enough that the business will sort of put you in a box, but I put myself in a box a little bit as well. I regret that. I understand it a little better now.

There's a kid that I'm mentoring now who's twenty-four. There's an energy and excitement that you have, coming fresh out of school. You don't get that back. I got *The King of Queens* when I was twenty-seven. Clearly, the role is of a guy with a wife and kids and they've been married for a while. They thought I was thirty-three all along. It's fine, but I think that I should've fought a little bit, at least to say that I tried to buck the trend, whether I'd succeeded or not.

What is your favorite thing about being an actor?

I'm sort of in a transition now. We all have our insecurities and with actors it's definitely magnified. Maybe it goes back to the physical obstacles I faced, growing up. There are so many obstacles to being too big for your age. I always had a problem fitting in in certain ways. I was *supposed* to play basketball. I was *supposed* to be really great at it. And I wasn't. People thought I was older and I really wasn't. I grew so quickly that I was a little uncomfortable in my body. All those things sort of made me feel awkward and socially inept. I think that there was something about being able to play other people and represent other people outside myself; I felt that these people had much more interesting lives and things to say. These characters who had social difficulties or inability to be heard: I was like, "I'll speak up for you." It was always that what I enjoyed was representing a writer's vision or representing a character's voice. It was never about me. And I think I still feel that way. I think that's what I like.

I think the obstacle I have now, in Hollywood, with the audition process and all, is that in a lot of ways, that goes against what this city is about. It has been difficult to say, "This is ME. There's nothing put on. There's no voice, there's no character creation. There's no voice I'm putting on. It's just me." You're allowed more flexibility and leeway with theatre to sort of create these characters; whereas more often than not, what you're bringing to the table and who you are is vital to success in TV and film. I'm trying to sort of embrace that more and be more comfortable and confident. But it's an ongoing struggle. I think I've always been drawn more so to theatre than film and television. I'm definitely more passionate about theatre. I can sort of engulf myself in it. The process of rehearsal, I adore. It's very tough to just get a script and say, "You just have to know your lines by this day." I definitely enjoy theatre much more.

What made you choose Los Angeles?

That goes back to another lesson. The one thing maybe that I should've learned sooner was patience. I graduated in '95 and I did Shakespeare in the Park in June and in September I did a play at the Dallas Theatre Center. And then for the next year and a half, I got no theatre. As much as I loved it, I was so frustrated I wasn't getting theatre work. I was impatient. In hindsight, it was just a year and a half. But at the same time, I was getting these TV roles and these movie roles and these commercial roles. I was getting *Homicide* and *Cop Land* and Stouffer's Lean Cuisine and Downy commercials. My whole thing was, "Well, fine. If theatre doesn't love me, I'll go where I'm respected." It was a business decision but also sort of an emotional decision. I wanted to work. I wanted to feel wanted. And when I looked at the resumé, I was getting some TV, film, and commercial work. So, I needed to move to LA then. I was with an agent that saw it was time too. Ambrosio Mortimer was a very good, small, bicoastal agency at the time that was very supportive of me moving out to LA. Meg Mortimer, who was my agent, was phenomenal. I think she's a manager in New York now.

How did you get your first agent?

What's great about a program like NYU is, they come to shows all the time. When we did our showcase, I think we had about six-hundred agents, casting directors, and managers show up. You can't ask for better than that. That's a tough thing. When people ask me how I got an agent, well, the people who really went through it and got an agent the really, really hard way, those are the people you need to talk to. Me? I was smart enough, lucky enough, whatever you want to call it. The best decision I probably made was knowing I wasn't ready to go into the business and that I needed to go into a training program.

Do you ever feel like giving up?

No! No, no, no. No! Going back to Ron Van Lieu, he said something to our class. First: The reality is, the majority of great actors don't go to training programs. Robert De Niro, Denzel Washington, they didn't go to those programs, so it's not to say you have to go to a program. Some people just need it. You need to be able to know who you are and what you need. Okay, so there was this one thing Ron Van Lieu said in class. It was a bad day. The scenes were bad in class and he was frustrated. Someone said something about, "Oh, this is so hard," and he said, "Okay, look. How do you think I picked you guys? We get a thousand applicants and we accept twenty people each year. Do you really think you're the best twenty? You may have been the best one hundred but from there I consider the chemistry in combination with what the needs of the school are. Honestly, there are certain people who applied who don't need to be in this program so they weren't accepted because they're ready. When it came down to making the final decision, I have a vision. The question I ask is, 'Who is going to be doing this forty, fifty years from now?' I don't know. I make the best guess I can possibly make. So, I don't want to hear, 'This is hard.' Because if you tell me it's hard, I start to think I picked the wrong person."

It stood out to me. He's saying, "I see you as people who, through all the adversity and through all the obstacles, will still be doing this fifty, sixty years from now." And when he said that, I said, "Yeah, that's me. I'm going to be doing this. No matter how hard it gets, no matter what level it's at, I'm not going anywhere!" You have to sort of make that commitment. You're not a failure if you decide to walk away from it, but you have to start out truly believing that this is what you want to do for the rest of your life.

How do you choose the material you work on?

I don't know if I have much choice. I have yet to be in a position where I can get to really choose the type of stuff I can work on. What I tend to do, if I get a script that I don't like or I don't think I'm right for, is I go in and say, "What is the vision of the writer? What's the vision of the director? How can I fit into that?" If it's something I feel extremely uncomfortable about, if I don't believe in the material, I will then put my own vision on it. I will say, "This is what I think I bring to the table." I've blown a lot of auditions for that, but my feeling is I have to feel comfortable doing it. Specifically, as a Black actor I say that because there have been times you get the material—and I think every actor experiences this, not just Black actors—and it is extremely stereotypical and you don't feel comfortable doing it. My feeling is, "Well, okay, you wanted a thug from Brooklyn? Flatbush? Fine. I grew up in Flatbush. I grew up around it. I know what it is and it's not that. So, this is my vision of what I experienced and if it's not thuggish enough for you, it's not gangsta enough for you, then I'm not the guy."

And if I lose the job, that's fine. I'm at a point where I can't be too picky. You've got to stick to your guns but you also have to choose your battles. I'm still trying to establish a film career so anything goes. I just did two lines on *Bewitched*. They're like, "Are you sure you want to do that?" I'm like, "Look at my resumé. I only have two feature films on there. So, I'll do it." There's only a handful of actors that have the ability to do *anything* they want. And even those actors, they have an arc as to when they can choose whatever they want. Going along the lines of longevity and consistency, I have to be open to anything and everything. Obviously, at a certain point, you have to say, "This goes against my beliefs," or "I don't think this will advance my career right now." You make those judgment calls, but for the most part you have to be open for everything.

I'm not very good at identifying what a good script is. With *The King of Queens*, honestly, I thought, "There's no freakin' way *The King of Queens* is going to make it on air." I did think it was going to suck. We did the pilot and I thought, "Fine, it got made, but it's not going to get picked up," and then it got picked up and I thought, "Fine, it's not going to make it past a year." All along, I had friends who came to the pilot, friends who watched the entire year and said, "Hey, you know what? This show is really, really good." And I just couldn't see it. That was probably the biggest lesson I learned.

Now, when my agent or manager calls and says, "This doesn't look good. This really sucks." I'll say, "Hey, let's go on in anyway." You don't know. Based on that experience, I clearly had no idea. I'm always very, "Let's just go for it." I've done independent films for no pay which I've thought weren't going to do well and they've done well on the independent film circuit, so honestly, I have no idea what's good material and what's not, so I just go in and do it.

What's been great for me on *The King of Queens* is the fact that a lot of Black audience members say, "Wow, there's not a lot of Black characters like you on sitcoms. You're just *normal*. You're not like jive talking or whatever. It's nice to see." And it's a really simple thing. What they do is they don't write me as a Black character, they just write the words.

Had you done a pilot before *The King of Queens*?

I had done a pilot in '97. I got on *The King of Queens* in '98. But in '97 I did a pilot that had two working titles: *Bakershift* and *Seattle Emergency*. Basically, it was *Third Watch* set in Seattle for the WB. The process was great. The casting director was Lisa Miller Katz. It was cool, because even though I had some credits coming from New York, it is very difficult to come out here and get that far when people don't know you. I've always been grateful to Lisa because she had no idea who I was. She was very happy with the audition and I met producers and that went well. It came time to test and when you have the material that long it can be such an empowering thing. It doesn't have to be something that knocks you out; it's like it's great to get the opportunity to do it twice or three times. You really feel more and more comfortable no matter how many producers are in the room. When it came to test time, I don't think I've ever auditioned for that many people. There had to be twenty-five people in an office space. By the time you get there, it's empowering to accept that there are things out of your control in terms of physical attributes and age, how they match up with the other needs. Each of the guys I went up against was clearly different, physically. So, it was like, "We have no idea what they want." It's out of your control, so you just go in there and do your thing. All you control are the words on the page and taking the direction. There's nothing else you can do. It was a great experience.

The thing about *The King of Queens*—and why I always say you never know where your opportunities are going to come from—is because that year there were three pilots that every Black actor wanted to get in on. There was Sydney Pollack's *Bronx County*, John Wells' *The Advocate*, and there was a pilot for ABC called *Cupid*. All three had really good Black roles we were all trying to get in on. I couldn't get in on any of them. I was so upset. *The King of Queens* came along and it was a guest star for the pilot. It wasn't even a series regular. And I was like, "This really sucks. Fine, whatever." I was still longing to be on *The Advocate, Bronx County, Cupid*, but I did the pilot, whatever, and then *The King of Queens* got picked up and they were like, "Congratulations. We want you to be a regular." I was like, "That's cool." Next thing I know, *Cupid* made it one season and it was done. *Bronx County* and *The Advocate* didn't even make it on the air. You can't tell. You fit in where you can.

How do you prepare for a role?

It depends. I've been accused of overpreparing. It depends on the project. When I think of the first pilot I did, *Seattle Emergency*, I was playing a paramedic so I read these EMT books and stories and such. They put us through a crash course to know what it is to be an emergency medical technician. What I've learned is, you have to be flexible in what your method is depending on the project. I didn't need to go and work on how it was like to be a delivery guy for *The King of Queens*. Knowing that job doesn't make a difference, for that type of show. That preparing had more to do with getting well-versed in sitcoms. It came down to learning and understanding and studying the formula and the timing and just sort of boning up on my sitcom knowledge just by watching and then specifically understanding the producer who had written for *Family Ties* and who created a show called *Ned and Stacey*. Learning and understanding what his sensibilities were and what type of humor he likes allowed me to discover he's not an over-the-top guy. He's a very witty, very smart, very subtle-humor kind of guy. This sort of knowing and understanding the environment is very important. It's like being on stage and walking the space to understand the environment, the world of the sitcom. What's the tone of the writing? What's the energy? Sitcom isn't always over-the-top, and knowing specifically what the writer's vision and temperament is was the process with preparing for this particular project. At times you have to decide it's a character study and at times you focus on what the environment of the project is. And at times you focus on the past work of the playwright or the screenwriter.

What is your least favorite thing about being an actor?

Being out of work. Technically, we do twenty-five episodes a year. Even when you're a working actor, more often than not, you're not working. I work twenty-five weeks out of the year, but I still have twenty-seven weeks to try to find other work. I'm still out of work half the year! There are times when you need time to yourself. This is your instrument, so you have to go out there and experience life so you can bring that into your audition. Travel, take classes that have nothing to do with acting. History of China was a class that I took. Don't know why. I just picked it. You should, as an actor, at some level know a little about things outside of the realm to round you out, make you more versatile. There's a time to do that. Just don't get stale. There's an actor named Cedric Harris from Juilliard (I can't believe I'm quoting Juilliard actors—that's another story), who said,

"The cream always rises to the top. Just make sure it's not sour when it gets there." You have to be ready. Whatever form it takes, everyone will get an opportunity. You have to be ready when it's there because you have no idea when it's going to come. Be ready.

Who are *your* favorite actors?

My favorite actors tend to rotate. Every year I pick a new favorite actor. Lily Taylor was it in '97. Before that it was Emma Thompson. Last year it was Denzel Washington and Meryl Streep—I went old school a little bit. I'll see them in something and go, "Oh my God, you're so amazing." Right now I worship Zach Braff. I'm not even that familiar with his work. I saw *Garden State* and I'm crazy about him now. He's an actor who took control of his career. He put his heart out there. He clearly laid it out there. On top of that, based on that same film, Natalie Portman is a favorite simply because I wasn't really well-versed in her before. Those are my flavors of the year so far. I want to see what else they're doing based on those performances.

In Closing

Afterword

A few years back, I went into Susan Shopmaker's casting office in New York City to audition for a film or something. While waiting my turn to audition, I read an article posted on the wall. The gist of the article was that Jack Lemmon—while working with Kevin Spacey—had shared this thought (and I'm paraphrasing here):

As artists, we all experience ceilings in our careers. Whenever we are fortunate enough to "break through" one of these ceilings, it is our responsibility to go back down and bring another artist back up with us.

I've thought about that a lot, since the day I read it. If we are in this business for a while, we will eventually know many, many talented people. I think we have a responsibility to one another as people and as artists. We each know how tough and random this business can be.

It is my hope that these conversations provide some element of Jack's ideal. You've just heard from twenty-nine artists who have done it: paid their bills, succeeded. Through their very generous, personal, and thoughtful remarks, they have built a bridge for you.

It was my gut feeling that themes would occur as we talked to these artists; no matter how unique each person and how unique each journey. Here are some of the themes that jump out at me.

❖ Only pursue this business if you are absolutely sure this is the only thing you can and must do.

❖ Seek out an artistic community, a peer group, other people who do what you do and support you and your artistry. The role of mentorship is so valuable to this community. There is comfort in knowing you are not alone.

❖ Pursue work, not people. Don't waste time trying to get agents or managers. Instead, go get a job. Do a play. Take a class. Work, work, work. When the time is right, those people will come into your life.

❖ Find balance in your life. Do not put this business at the top of your priorities to the exclusion of your development, growth, and happiness as a human being. Find other joys and things to do.

❖ Audition for yourself. Too many variables determine who gets cast, so find the freedom to enjoy doing it for yourself. Be empowered by that freedom, in audition situations.

❖ If you can't do this job without being bitter and unhappy, don't do it. Get out. Be happy.

❖ If you're not humble coming into this business, this business will find a way to humble you.

❖ Get better all the time. Take classes, do readings, learn skills, read books, see plays and movies, discover more and more about yourself.

❖ Don't get used to the money, when you are "making it." Live on less than you have. Someday, you may have to.

❖ Figure out who you are and what you are selling. If you don't know who you are, the industry won't know either—and probably won't care.

❖ Every rule is made to be broken, but if you're breaking a rule, know it. Don't be an idiot about your choices. Own them and do things because they work for you—not because you've seen those choices work for someone else.

❖ Be authentic, be authentic, be authentic. That's a personal journey, so keep working on it.

❖ Unless you are a child star—and even then—*no one* is an overnight sensation. Careers take time to build. Don't believe the spin doctors, PR, and hype machines that would like to have you believe otherwise.

❖ Don't give yourself a time limit for being in this business. Though I have heard of it working in people's favor, I think doing that gives you a date by which you'll have to get out of the business. So, if you insist upon giving yourself an "out date," don't wait. Just get out now.

❖ Do for others, and not just for the karma of it (which is a good enough reason). Think about it: people that you've helped tend to help you back. If they don't, *so what*! Move on. Many will help. Give it time. It took me a long time to realize the value in asking for help. A few caveats: help yourself more than you ask for help (nobody wants to help people who aren't helping themselves), make sure you are someone who is always willing to help others (help can come in many forms and it should always be given without expecting anything in return), and be very specific when you ask for help (it improves your chances of getting a clear yes or no and helps the person you're asking to help you do so in a more powerful way).

Blake Robbins

* * *

There is no one recipe to success as a performer. There is no one way "in." The road you take is as unique as you are and the experiences you have will differ based on when you encounter each turn in the road. Enjoy the process. Share your toys. And live your dreams! If you don't, someone else will.

Bonnie Gillespie

About the Authors

Bonnie Gillespie is an author and casting director. Her books include *Casting Qs: A Collection of Casting Director Interviews* and *Self-Management for Actors: Getting Down to (Show) Business.* Bonnie specializes in casting SAG indie feature films and provides career consulting services to actors. She is co-founder and co-host of Hollywood Happy Hour and co-founder of the Flickering Image Short Film Festival. Her weekly column, *The Actors Voice*, is available at Showfax.com. Bonnie lives in Santa Monica with her fiancé and three cats.

* * *

Blake Robbins is a husband, a father of two beautiful daughters, and an actor. As an actor, he has appeared in Broadway, Off-Broadway, and regional theatrical productions. In addition to acting in many short films, dozens of television commercials, and a few feature films, Blake has worked on numerous episodic television programs (most notably, as Dave Brass on the critically-acclaimed HBO series *Oz*). This is Blake's first book.

Index of Names

Why have we included a comprehensive index of names? In assembling these interviews, we found it fascinating to see which actors credit certain people for their breaks and who has worked with whom. Perhaps you'd like to track the paths of working actors to observe where they cross. Can't recall who told us that a particular actor was his or her favorite? Start here in the index, then find the passage within the book. If you are trying to track down a casting director, agent, or manager mentioned in this book, please be sure to check the most-current publications from Breakdown Services for contact information, as many people in the entertainment industry move around quite frequently.